MARTIN LUTHER

Luther
for the busy man

Daily devotions
from Luther's sermons
on the Standard Gospels

Translated and compiled
by P.D. Pahl, BA, STM, DD,
Emeritus Lecturer in Church History,
Luther Seminary, North Adelaide, South Australia

Lutheran Publishing House, Adelaide

National Library of Australia
Cataloguing-in-Publication data

Luther, Martin, 1483-1546
    Luther for the busy man: daily devotions from the
    standard gospels.

    ISBN 0 85910 410 9.

    1. Lutheran Church — Prayer-books and devotions. 2.
    Bible. N.T. Gospels — Meditations. I. Pahl, Paul David,
    1910-   . II. Title.

242'.5

Printed and published by
Lutheran Publishing House,
205 Halifax Street, Adelaide, South Australia.   LPH 88-748

The Luther House in Wittenberg. Luther received the house as his property in 1526 from Elector John the Steadfast. This was Luther's home after he was called to Wittenberg in 1508.

The pulpit of the city church in Wittenberg. This pulpit from which Luther preached very frequently dates back to 1490 and is now in the Luther House.

Preface

The devotions in this book are taken from Luther's sermons on the Standard Gospels. They are, in the main, an exact translation of what Luther wrote. However, for the purposes of this book, certain minor modifications had to be made, usually at the commencement and end of each devotion.

For those who may wish to check the original, references have been included from the St. Louis Edition of Luther's Works.

We believe that it is very desirable in our day to gain a greater familiarity with the writings of Martin Luther. It is important, also, to provide material which will restore the fine custom of family devotions to its rightful place in the home.

The lessons, texts and short prayers which have been included make this a very valuable book for devotional use.

Lutheran Publishing House is to be commended for producing a volume whose Gospel-centered devotions so beautifully illustrate the fact that Christ was always at the heart of Luther's preaching.

We send this volume on its way with the prayer that through its pages the Gospel of Jesus Christ may again prove to be "**the power of God for salvation to every one who has faith**". **Romans 1.16.**

E.W. Wiebusch, Editor.

The door of the Castle Church in Wittenberg.

SUNDAY

LESSON: MATTHEW 21.1-9

Behold, your king is coming to you, humble, and mounted on an ass, and on a colt, the foal of an ass.
Matthew 21.5

This Gospel in a special manner arouses and demands faith. It portrays Christ in His coming grace. No one can really receive and accept Him unless he believes that He is the man in the sense portrayed in this Gospel. All that is set forth here in Christ is pure grace, gentleness and goodness. He who believes this regarding Christ is saved.

Look at Him! He rides no stallion, an animal mostly associated with war. He does not come in splendour and power, inspiring terror. He sits upon an ass, a peaceful animal, accustomed to burdens and toil in the service of men. In this way He shows that He comes not to tempt men, nor to come down upon them with force and suppress them, but to help them, to bear their burden and to take it upon Himself.

Although it was the time-honoured custom of the country to ride on asses and to use horses for war, as often recorded in Scripture, all that is narrated here is intended to make known how this King rides in gently, with nothing but good intent.

To demonstrate this point, a prophetic statement is introduced here (Zechariah 9.9) to draw us to faith and the acceptance of Christ in a very friendly manner. For the sake of this statement, the events of this Gospel took place and were set down in writing as the evangelist also declares. Let us pay careful attention to this statement and the chief point of this Gospel, for herein Christ is highlighted for us in regard to what we are to hold and believe concerning Him, what we are to expect from Him, what we are to seek in Him, and how we are to avail ourselves of His help and make use of Him.
SL.XI.1,2

PRAYER: Lord Jesus, fill us at all times with your saving grace. Lead us to true faith and preserve us therein, for your love's sake. Amen.

9

MONDAY

LESSON: LUKE 1.68-79

Faith apart from works is dead.   James 2.26

Faith is of two sorts. The first is that you believe that Christ is a man like the Christ described and proclaimed in the whole Gospel, but you do not actually believe that He is such a man for you. You have your doubts that all He achieved is for you. It may be for St. Peter, Paul and the holy saints, but you are not at all sure that it is for you.

Such a faith is really nothing. It never really receives Christ or tastes of the things that really count in Him. Even the devils have this faith.

The one faith which is entitled to be called real, true Christian faith is to believe without any wavering that Christ is not only such a man for St. Peter and the saints, but also for you, indeed, for you more than for all others.

Your salvation does not consist in believing that Christ is a Christ for the pious, but that He is a Christ for **you** and is **yours.**

This faith brings it to pass that He pleases you in a most delightful manner. Then love and good works follow without any compulsion.

If works do not follow, it is quite certain that faith is really absent. Where faith exists, the Holy Spirit is also present working love and what is good in us.

SL.XI.2,8-9

PRAYER: Bestow your Holy Spirit upon us, O Lord, to lead us into true faith, active in love and producing the works pleasing to you, for the welfare of your kingdom and our neighbour. Amen.

TUESDAY

LESSON: HEBREWS 10.19-25

Behold!   **Matthew 21.5**

"**Behold!**" Mark this word well. With this word the Holy Spirit wakens us from sleep and unbelief as one who wants to set forth something important, strange and noteworthy which one has long desired and should receive with joy. And we really need such an awakening, because our reason and nature despises all that concerns faith and finds it most unsuitable.

How can it possibly be that this man who rides along in such poverty and humility should be the King of Jerusalem and that He is riding only a strange, hired ass? How can nature and reason possibly grasp this? How can such an entrance be squared with that of a great King?

Faith is of such a kind that it does not judge and follow according to what it sees and feels but according to what it hears. It clings to the Word alone. Appearance and outward looks count for nothing at all. Therefore the only ones here who really accepted Christ as a King were those who followed the word of the prophet. They believed in Christ and His kingdom not with their eyes, but accepted Him with the spirit.

These are also the true "**daughter of Zion**". For the man who wants to follow Christ according to outward appearance and feeling cannot avoid becoming offended at Him. One must cling firmly to the pure Word alone.

SL.XI.4,14

PRAYER: Enable us at all times, O Lord, to cling with all our faith to your pure Word alone, so that we behold you as you really are and thus ever cling to you in love and obedience, for your truth's sake. Amen.

WEDNESDAY

LESSON: PSALM 24

Your king.   Matthew 21.5

Here this King is separated from all other kings. He is **"your king"**, the one promised to you and whose own you are. He is the one who rules you and no one else. But His rule is a spiritual, not a secular, rule.

This is a comforting word for the believing heart, for apart from Christ, man is subjected to many raging tyrants who are not kings but murderers. Under these he endures great misery and terror.

Such tyrants include the devil, the flesh, the world and sin, as well as the law, death and hell. At the hands of all these the wretched conscience is oppressed, suffers heavy imprisonment, and lives a bitter, uneasy life. For where sins are, there is no good conscience; where there is no good conscience, everything is quite uncertain and there is unending fear of death and hell before which there can be no firm joy or delight in the heart. As Moses declares, such a heart is terrified at the rustling of a leaf (Leviticus 26.36).

Wherever a heart receives this King in firm faith, it becomes established and does not fear sin, death, hell or any misfortune. It knows and does not doubt that this King is the Lord over life and death, sin and grace, hell and heaven and that all things are in His hands.

SL.XI.5,16

PRAYER: Lord Jesus Christ, my King, establish your rule in my heart in such a way that my heart becomes your throne, and peace and joy may reign therein for evermore. Amen.

THURSDAY

LESSON: PSALM 25.1-10

Your king is coming to you. Matthew 21.5

Learn from this Gospel what happens when God begins to make us godly, and what is the beginning of becoming godly. There is no other beginning but the fact that your King comes to you and begins to work in you.

This comes to pass as follows. The Gospel must be the very first thing in this context; it must be preached and heard. In this you hear and learn how your work is nothing before God and that all you do or attempt is sin. But your King must be in you beforehand and rule you. That is the beginning of your salvation. You then give up your own work, and despair of self, because you hear and see that your own work is nothing, as the Gospel tells you. You begin to receive your King through faith, you cling to Him, invoke His grace, and entrust yourself solely to His goodness.

That you hear and accept this is also not of your own strength but of God's grace, which has made the Gospel fruitful in you, so that you believe Him when He declares that your own work is nothing.

You see how few there are who accept His grace. Jesus also wept over Jerusalem. The papists not only reject this doctrine but actually condemn it. They do not want their own work to be sin and nothing. They want to lay the first stone and they rage and storm against the Gospel.

SL.XI.8,23

PRAYER: O Lord, take from our hearts all self-pride and trust in our own works and efforts, and grant us grace to trust solely and wholly in your mercy and grace, granted us through our Lord Jesus Christ. Amen.

FRIDAY

LESSON: 1 PETER 2.21-25

To you.   Matthew 21.5

"Your king is coming to you." You do not seek Him, you do not find Him, He finds you; for the preachers come from Him, not from you; their preaching comes from Him, not from you; your faith comes from Him, not from you; and all that faith works in you comes from Him, not from you. So you see quite well that if He did not come to you, you would remain on the outside where there is no Gospel and no God, only sin and corruption.

Therefore, do not ask for a beginning of a godly life. There is no beginning of such a life except where this King comes and is proclaimed.

He comes **"to you"**. **"To you"** — what is this? Is it not enough that He is **"your king"**? If He is yours, why does the text say, He comes **"to you"**?

All is set forth here by the prophet to depict Christ in the most loving manner and to urge us to faith. It is not enough for Christ to save us from the tyranny and dominion of sin, death and hell and to become our King. He must give Himself as our very own so that all that He is and has becomes ours. St. Paul speaks of this when he says, **"He who did not spare his own Son but gave him up for us all, will he not also give us all things with him?" Romans 8.32.**

SL.XI.9,25-26

PRAYER: Lord Jesus, our King, rule supreme and alone in our hearts and souls so that all the treasures of your truth and salvation may be ours personally now and for ever. Amen.

SATURDAY

LESSON: PSALM 25.11-22

Thanks be to God for his inexpressible gift!
2 Corinthians 9.15

The daughter of Zion receives twofold gifts from Christ. The first is faith and the Spirit in the heart, whereby she is cleansed and freed from sins. The second is Christ himself. And she can glory in the blessings received from Christ just as though all that Christ is and has is her very own, so that she may rely on Christ as her inheritance. Of this Paul speaks when he reminds us that Christ is our Mediator before God (Romans 8.34). If He is our Mediator, He accepts us as His own and we, for our part, accept Him as our own.

In Corinthians, Paul also states that Christ in us is made by God to be our righteousness, wisdom, holiness and redemption (1 Corinthians 1.30). Isaiah says concerning the two-fold gifts, **"Comfort, comfort my people, says your God. Speak tenderly to Jerusalem, and cry to her that her warfare is ended, that her iniquity is pardoned, that she has received from the Lord's hand double for all her sins." Isaiah 40.1,2.**

Here, **"He comes to you"** means, "for your good, as your very own". Inasmuch as He is your King, you receive grace from Him in your heart. He keeps you from sin and death, and also becomes your King with you as His subject. But inasmuch as He comes to you, He becomes your sin so that you gain command also of His blessings.

This is a delightful and comforting Word! Who is going to despair or become fearful of death and hell if he believes these words and wins Christ as His very own?

SL.XI.10,27

PRAYER: Thanks and praise be to you, loving heavenly Father, for the wonderful gifts of grace which you have so richly bestowed on us, through Jesus Christ our Lord. Amen.

SUNDAY

LESSON: LUKE 21.25-33

Then they will see the Son of man coming in a cloud with power and great glory.   Luke 21.27

Here you can interpret **"power"** as referring to the host of angels, saints, and all creatures who will accompany Christ on His coming to judgement. This I consider to be the correct interpretation. The evangelist does not just say, "He will come", but **"they will see the Son of man coming"**.

He also came into the world by bodily birth, but that coming was seen by no one. He also comes daily into the hearts of believers in a spiritual manner by means of the Gospel. This coming is also seen by no one.

But this second coming will take place in a public manner in which all men will see Him, as is declared in the book of Revelation: **"every eye will see him"** *[1.7]*. They will see that He is none other than the human being Jesus Christ in bodily form, as He was born of Mary and recognized here on earth. He could have merely said, "they will see Me", without any obvious reference to His human form. But He says here that they will see the Son of man. By this He clearly states that He is referring to a bodily seeing of Himself in human form.

This will take place in great power, with a great host of angels and in great glory. He will sit on a bright cloud and with Him He will bring all the saints. Of His coming, Scripture speaks quite often. It is something of very great importance.

SL.XI.60,36

PRAYER: Lord, keep us ever mindful of your second glorious coming to judgement so that we, with all your saints, may ever dwell with you in the blessed kingdom you have prepared for us, for your love's sake. Amen.

MONDAY

LESSON: 2 PETER 3.1-11

When these things begin to take place, look up and raise your heads, because your redemption is drawing near.

Luke 21.28

You might feel inclined to say in this context, "Who could possibly raise his head in the face of such wrath and judgement? Will not the whole world rather lower its head in terror and look downwards in fear and dismay? How are we in such a situation to look up and raise our heads?" The latter without a doubt signifies joy and eager longing.

The answer to this is: All this is spoken to Christians alone — to real Christians, not to the heathen or the Jews. Real Christians are involved in great temptations and persecutions from sins and all kinds of evil, so that this life often becomes distasteful and quite ugly for them. And so they wait with eager longing and pray to be delivered from sins and all evil, as is also said in the Lord's Prayer: "**Thy kingdom come**", and "**deliver us from evil**".

If we are real Christians, we will also pray this earnestly from the depths of our heart. If we do not pray this earnestly from our hearts, we are not yet real Christians. SL.XI.61,37

PRAYER: O Lord, you have so often promised in your Word to deliver us from all the trials and tribulations which we experience in a world of sin and sadness. Receive us into your heavenly kingdom, for your truth's sake. Amen.

TUESDAY

LESSON: LUKE 17.20-30

When these things begin to take place, look up and raise your heads.   Luke 21.28

If we are to pray fervently that God's kingdom may come, then it is certainly necessary that we should look forward to these signs, horrible as they may be, with joy and eager longing, as Christ admonishes us when He tells us to raise our heads. He means to say, "Do not be afraid or lower your heads, for the object of our earnest prayers is coming".

If, then, we are really in earnest about getting rid of our sins, death and hell, we must look forward to this coming with eager and loving longing. In anticipation of this day, St. Paul delcares: **"Henceforth there is laid up for me the crown of righteousness, which the Lord, the righteous judge, will award to me on that Day, and not only to me but also to all who have loved his appearing". 2 Timothy 4.8.**

If He gives the crown to all who have loved this appearing, what will He give to those who have hated it and been afraid of it? Without a doubt He must assign them to hell as His enemies!

Likewise, in the Epistle to Titus, Paul says that we await **"our blessed hope, the appearing of the glory of our great God and Saviour Jesus Christ". Titus 2.13.** In Luke's Gospel we read that we should **"be like men who are waiting for their master to come home from the marriage feast". Luke 12.36.**

SL.XI.61,38

PRAYER: Thanks be to you, dear Saviour, for the forgiveness of sins, life and salvation which you have procured for us by your suffering and death for us, and by which we also await your coming in joy and confidence, for your mercy's sake. Amen.

WEDNESDAY

LESSON: PSALM 80

You are not lacking in any spiritual gift, as you wait for the revealing of our Lord Jesus Christ.   1 Corinthians 1.7

No one is better prepared for the advent of the last day than the one who earnestly desires to be without sin. If you have such a longing, why are you afraid? Thereby you are in full accord with all that this day betokens. Jesus comes to save from sins all who long for His redemption, and this is also what you are longing for. Give thanks to God and remain in this frame of mind! Christ says that His coming means redemption.

But see to it that you are not deceiving yourself when you say that you would be very glad to be free from sin, and that you do not fear the advent of that day. Perhaps your heart is false and you are really afraid of that day. You do not really want to be free of sins but in His presence you cannot sin freely and securely.

See to it that your light is not darkness! For a heart that truly wants to be free of sin rejoices in confidence at the thought of that day which will fulfil all longings. If this joy is lacking, there is no real longing to be free of sin.

SL.XI.63,42

PRAYER: Lord Jesus Christ, fill our hearts with such joy and confidence in connection with your Day, that we really raise our heads as those who await you, knowing that your coming betokens our final entrance into the blessed abode which you have prepared for those who love you, for your name's sake. Amen.

THURSDAY

LESSON: PSALM 50.1-6

May our Lord Jesus Christ himself, and God our Father, who loved us and gave us eternal comfort and good hope through grace, comfort your hearts and establish them in every good work and word. 2 Thessalonians 2.16

How could our Lord Jesus Christ admonish, comfort and strengthen you more lovingly? First, He says: "You will hear of wars, but do not be afraid!" (Luke 21.9). When He tells you not to be afraid, what else is it but bidding you to be confident, and to recognize such signs with joy? Secondly, He tells you to look up joyfully. Thirdly, you are to raise your heads; and fourthly, He mentions your redemption.

What is going to comfort and strengthen you if these words fail to do so? Could you believe that He is lying to you and wants to deceive you with a false confidence? Do not be one to whom these words are addressed in vain! Thank God and confidently rely on these words!

There is no other help or comfort if these words are consigned to the winds. It is not a matter of condemnation but of your redemption, Christ says for your consolation and comfort. Will you turn these words about and say it is not your redemption but your damnation as you flee from your own salvation?

Will you not greet God when He meets you, and will you withhold your thanks to Him when He greets you? Without a doubt these words so well spoken are also especially intended to help those who are inclined to be somewhat despondent and even fearful in regard to the things Christ sets forth as heralds of His coming.

SL.XI.63,44-45

PRAYER: Lord Jesus Christ, fill our hearts with such confidence that we may recognize the signs which you have given us as heralds of your coming, and receive such signs with joy. Amen.

FRIDAY

LESSON: ISAIAH 11.1-10

Thy kingdom come.   Matthew 6.10

Even though the Lord's Prayer is prayed on all sides throughout the world by countless numbers of people, there are really only very few who pray it correctly. For all but a very few would much prefer that there should never be any day of the Lord's coming. What else is this but to wish that God's kingdom should never come? In this way their heart prays against their mouth, and God judges according to the heart whereas they judge by the mouth.

So men devise and engage in many prayers, babble all the churches full in all the world, and all this goes by the name of prayer. But basically all this amounts to saying, "May Thy kingdom not come!" or, "May it not come yet!" Tell me, is not such prayer real blasphemy, of which the psalmist declares, "**Let his prayer be counted as sin!**"? **Psalm 109.7.**

A tremendous amount of money and worldly goods is wasted in cramming every nook and corner with such blasphemy which men call the worship of God. Because there is such abuse in the use of prayer is no reason why the true children of God should not continue to pray earnestly to their heavenly Father for the coming of His kingdom and the full realization of all their hopes and joys.

SL.XI.65,48-49

PRAYER: Enlighten and guide us by your grace, O Lord, that we always look forward to your coming in confidence and with our heads raised in joy. Amen.

SATURDAY

LESSON: ROMANS 15.4-13

And he told them a parable: "Look at the fig tree, and all the trees; as soon as they come out in leaf, you see for yourselves and know that the summer is already near. So also, when you see these things taking place, you know that the kingdom of God is near." Luke 21.29-31

These are words of sheer joy! Jesus does not give a parable for autumn or winter when the trees are bare and it is a gloomy time of the year. He gives us a parable for spring and summer which is a joyful, happy time, when all creatures revive and are joyful. Hereby it is very clearly taught that we should look forward to the last day and console ourselves with the gladness and eager longing with which all creatures joyfully await the spring and the summer.

What else could this parable suggest to us if that is not what the Lord is teaching here? Here He is telling us, "It will not mean hell and condemnation for you, but the kingdom of God".

Therefore, look to your life and search your heart to determine how you are minded as far as the last day is concerned. Do not rely on your good life, for it can soon put you to shame! Strengthen your faith so that this day does not overtake you unawares with those who are damned and perverse. May you eagerly wait for it, and when you hear it mentioned, or think of it, may your heart leap for joy.

SL.XI.66,51-53

PRAYER: Lead us at all times by your grace, O Lord, that we eagerly await your coming as the consummation of all our hopes and joy. Amen.

SUNDAY

LESSON: MATTHEW 11.2-10

The Spirit of the Lord God is upon me, because the Lord has anointed me to bring good tidings to the afflicted.
Isaiah 61.1

Kings and priests are normally anointed to a kingdom and priesthood respectively. But this anointed King and Priest, Isaiah says here, is to be anointed by God Himself, not with any temporal oil but with the Holy Spirit who rests upon Him as He says: **"The Spirit of the Lord God is upon me"**.

And so He preaches the Gospel, restores sight to the blind, heals all manner of sickness and preaches the acceptable year, the time of grace. **"Behold, your God will come and save you. Then the eyes of the blind shall be opened, and the ears of the deaf unstopped; then shall the lame man leap like a hart, and the tongue of the dumb sing for joy."** Isaiah 35.4-6.

If we compare the Scripture with Christ's works and Christ's works with the Scripture, it becomes evident that in Christ we have the right man. Luke declares that at the time when the disciples of John the Baptist came to question Him, **"he cured many of diseases and plagues and evil spirits, and on many that were blind he bestowed sight"**. Luke 7.21.

Here we must take Christ's example to heart. He takes up His stand on His works and tells us to form our ideas about the tree from its fruits.
SL.XI.77,10

PRAYER: Thanks be to you, O King of grace and salvation, for the fullness of your works of grace and salvation encouraging us at all times to place our full faith and reliance in you alone. Amen.

MONDAY

LESSON: PSALM 85

The Spirit of the Lord God is upon me, because the Lord has anointed me to bring good tidings to the afflicted; he has sent me to bind up the broken-hearted, to proclaim liberty to the captives, and the opening of the prison to those who are bound; to proclaim the year of the Lord's favour.

Isaiah 61.1,2

What does Jesus mean when He says, "**The poor have good news preached to them**"? Is not the good news also proclaimed to the rich and the whole world? How can the Gospel be regarded as something so important and as a great blessing when there are so many who are hostile to it?

Here we must know what the Gospel is, or we cannot understand this passage. We must diligently observe that from the beginning God has sent two words or forms of proclamation to the world — the Law and the Gospel. These two forms of proclamation you must recognize and separate. I tell you that hitherto, with the exception of the Scriptures, no book has ever been written, not even by a saint, in which these two forms of proclamation have been correctly divided. And yet this is such a basic issue.

SL.XI.80,18

PRAYER: Grant us your Holy Spirit, O Lord, the Spirit of truth and understanding, that we may correctly understand your Word, correctly separating Law from Gospel, and never being confused in our faith. Amen.

TUESDAY

LESSON: 1 TIMOTHY 1.8-11

The law is holy, and the commandment is holy and just and good . . . but I am carnal, sold under sin.

Romans 7.12,14

The Law is the word by which God teaches us and instructs us in what we are to do and not to do, as He does in the Ten Commandments. Where nature stands alone, without God's grace, it is impossible to keep God's Law for the reason that man, after Adam's fall in Paradise, is corrupt and has nothing but evil lust leading him into sin. It is impossible for him to be well-disposed to the Law from the depths of his heart.

We all experience this. There is no one who would not prefer to be without any Law at all. Every one of us realizes and feels in himself that it is very hard to be pious and to do good, and very easy to be wicked and to do evil.

Such shortcomings and unwillingness to do what is good force us into transgressions of God's Law. What is done reluctantly, poorly and unwillingly is of no avail at all before God. God's Law overcomes us. We learn this from our own experience as we are by nature wicked, disobedient, lovers of sin and enemies of God's Law.

SL.XI.81,19

PRAYER: Lord God, our heavenly Father, guard against all spiritual pride and self-righteousness so that when we look into the mirror of your Law we may see ourselves as we really are, lost and condemned sinners, whose only hope rests in our Saviour and Redeemer, Jesus Christ. Amen.

WEDNESDAY

LESSON: ROMANS 1.16,17

The gospel of the grace of God.   Acts 20.24

The Gospel is neither Law nor command; it makes no demands on us. If wretched distress and misery in the heart have come about through the first word of the Law, the Gospel comes as a loving and living word; it promises and assures us, undertaking to give us grace and help so that we may get out of such distress. It not only forgives us our sins but actually destroys them and, in addition, gives us love and the desire to fulfil the Law. This divine assurance of God's grace and the forgiveness of sins is what the Gospel really is.

I say once more that one should not understand the Gospel as anything else but God's promise of grace and the forgiveness of sins.

The reason why Paul's epistles have for so long been misunderstood and, indeed, cannot be understood, is that men do not really know what is Law and what is Gospel. They regard Christ as a lawgiver and the Gospel as nothing but the proclamation of a new law. This is nothing else but locking up the Gospel and hiding everything.

SL.XI.83,24-25

PRAYER: Enlighten us, O Lord, in such a way by your Holy Spirit, that we really understand that your sole purpose and aim in the revelation of your Gospel is to lead us to salvation as a completely free gift of your wonderful grace in Christ. Amen.

THURSDAY

LESSON: PSALM 98

Christ Jesus our hope.   1 Timothy 1.1

The Greek word for Gospel [*euaggelion*] means "a joyful message" because in it there is proclaimed the salutary doctrine of life by God's assurance and grace, and the forgiveness of sins is offered us. So the Gospel is not a matter of works, for it is not Law. The Gospel is a matter of faith alone, because it is absolutely nothing but the promise and offer of divine grace.

He who believes the Gospel receives grace and the Holy Spirit. As a result of this, the heart becomes joyful and well-pleased with God, and a willing and free obedience to the Law ensues. There is no longer any fear of punishment and the pursuit of meritorious works. The heart is content and satisfied with the grace of God.

From the beginning of the world, however, such promises have all been based on Christ. God has not promised such grace to anyone but in Christ and through Christ. Christ is the messenger of divine promise to the whole world. For this purpose He also came into the world and has sent out this promise through the Gospel into all the world. Before His coming He made known this promise through the prophets. Everything points to Christ and is concluded in Christ. He who does not hear Christ does not hear God's promise. For just as there is no law outside of Moses and the prophetical Scriptures, so God gives no promise except through Christ alone.

SL.XI.84,26-27

PRAYER: Thanks be to you, O heavenly Father, that you have conferred your grace and salvation upon us on the certain and sure ground of faith in Christ alone, our one and only hope of eternal life. Amen.

FRIDAY

LESSON: MATTHEW 7.15-27

Jesus answered them, "Go and tell John what you hear and see: the blind receive their sight and the lame walk, lepers are cleansed and the deaf hear, and the dead are raised up, and the poor have the good news preached to them. And blessed is he who takes no offence at me."   Matthew 11.4-6

Our faith is strengthened and improved inasmuch as Christ is set before us in His own simple works. He is simply concerned with the blind, lame, lepers, deaf, the dead and the poor, and has nothing but pure love and well-doing for all who are poor and needy. In short, Christ is nothing else but a consolation and a refuge for all who have a troubled and weakened conscience.

Here there is need of faith that builds on His Gospel and relies on it without any doubt that Christ is just as His Gospel portrays Him. Such faith holds nothing else about Christ and will not suffer any other view to be upheld about Him. And such faith has the Christ in whom it believes and as His Gospel describes Him. For as you believe, you will receive. **"Blessed is he who takes no offence at me."**

In this way we recognize Christ aright and receive Him in true faith. This is what the Christian faith includes. Those who think that they can render satisfaction to God by their works and become righteous thereby, do not really know the Christ portrayed in this Gospel. If they persist in their mistaken views they will be lost.

SL.XI.93,52-53

PRAYER: Give us a simple faith, Lord Jesus, that we always believe with our whole hearts that you are our Lord and Saviour in the simple manner you have revealed yourself to us in your holy Word. Amen.

SATURDAY

LESSON: MATTHEW 18.1-9

Blessed is he who takes no offence at me.   Matthew 11.6

Be on your guard against all and every offence. Who are those who cause offence here? All those who tell you to concentrate on works instead of faith.

Such teachers turn Christ into a lawgiver and a judge and will not let Him remain a pure helper and comforter. They plague you with the idea of having dealings with God and for God on the basis of works. They say you must make atonement for your sins to obtain God's grace. Such people, of whom there are always many in this world, direct you to a different Christ from the one to whom you are pointed in this Gospel. If you want to have true faith and really attain to Christ, you must give up all hope in works as a basis for negotiating with God and before God. Works are all so many offences to keep you away from Christ and God.

Before God, no works at all avail except Christ's own works. These you must plead on your behalf before God, and perform no other work before God but to believe that Christ has performed these works for you and offers them before God on your behalf. Your faith must always remain pure faith, doing nothing and keeping silence, allowing itself to be benefited, accepting Christ's work and allowing Christ to exercise His love upon you.

You must be blind, lame, dead, leprous and poor or you will become offended in Christ. The Gospel does not lie. Christ permits Himself to be seen only by those who are really in need and bestows His blessings only upon them.

SL.XI.94,53

PRAYER: O Lord, grant us your grace in full measure, that we learn to entrust ourselves to you alone and are never offended at your humility. Amen.

SUNDAY

LESSON: JOHN 1.19-28

This is the testimony of John, when the Jews sent priests and Levites from Jerusalem to ask him, "Who are you?"
John 1.19

What were the Jews from Jerusalem seeking? Christ tells us when He says, **"You sent to John, and he has borne witness to the truth . . . He was a burning and shining lamp, and you were willing to rejoice for a while in his light."** **John 5.33, 35.**

From these words it is clear that they wanted to increase their own reputation by making use of John, and they wanted to avail themselves of his "lamp", that is, his high and famous name, to deck themselves out before the people. For, had John shown them favour and accepted the proffered honour, they would have enhanced their reputation before the whole people as those who were worthy of the friendship and respect of such a great and holy man.

What other result could have ensued except that their greed, tyranny and villainy would have been confirmed as pure holiness and something precious? These men tried to make out of John a Judas Iscariot who would be prepared to justify all their vice and immorality and gain them his approval and the people's support.

Are they not fine manipulators, offering John honour in order to bring his honour upon themselves? They offer him an apple for a kingdom, and try to exchange pennies for dollars. But he stood fast like a rock.   SL.XI.99,8-9

PRAYER: Give us constancy and steadfastness of faith, O Lord, that we may ever serve you in singleness of heart and stand fast whatever the cost. Amen.

MONDAY

LESSON: 1 JOHN 1.5-10

He confessed, he did not deny, but confessed, "I am not the Christ".   John 1.20

The confession of John contains two parts: first, that he confesses; secondly, that he does not deny. His confession is the confession of Christ when he says that he is not the Christ. He confessed: "I am not the Christ". His confession also includes the confession that he is not Elijah or a prophet. When John declares that **"he did not deny"**, it means that he confessed who he was in stating that he was the voice of one crying in the wilderness and preparing the way of the Lord.

His confession is a free confession, which confesses not only what he is not, but also what he is. For that part of a confession in which one confesses what he is not, is still dark and incomplete, and from which it is impossible to know what and how one should think of a man.

But here John openly states what one should think of him, as well as what one should not think of him. He leaves no grounds for uncertainty, inasmuch as he confesses that he is not the Christ, and does not deny that he is the voice preceding His coming. Inasmuch as he stands quite firm and confesses what he is, and what he is not, his action is a precious confession before God and no denial.

SL.XI.100,10

PRAYER: In your mercy and grace, O Lord, give us a clear and certain faith which knows what is right and good in your sight, and acts accordingly without any fear of consequences. Amen.

TUESDAY

LESSON: MALACHI 4.1-6

And they asked him, "What then? Are you Elijah?" He said, "I am not".   John 1.21

In the question whether John was Elijah, the Jews were evidently referring to the prophecy of Malachi. I am of the opinion that Malachi had in mind no other Elijah but John, and that there are no grounds for assuming that there would be a return of Elijah the Tishbite who ascended into heaven in a flaming chariot (2 Kings 2.11).

The words of the angel Gabriel spoken to Zechariah, John's father, also support this opinion: **"He will go before him in the spirit and power of Elijah, to turn the hearts of the fathers to the children, and the disobedient to the wisdom of the just". Luke 1.17.** In these words one sees that the angel Gabriel is referring to the prophecy of Malachi and quotes the same words of the prophet who also says that Elijah will **"turn the hearts of fathers to their children and the hearts of children to their fathers". Malachi 4.6.** Had Malachi prophesied a different Elijah, the angel would certainly not have applied his words to John.

He followed the same course with the Virgin Mary when he applied Isaiah's words to her: **"Behold, a young woman shall conceive and bear a son". Isaiah 7.14.** These words Gabriel applied to Mary when he said: **"Behold, you will conceive in your womb and bear a son". Luke 1.31.**

In his work as the forerunner of Christ, John the Baptist would be a real Elijah preaching repentance to prepare men for Christ.

SL.XI.101,14

PRAYER: Thanks and praise be to you, O God, for the great cloud of witnesses who have witnessed to your Son and the salvation you have prepared for us in Him. Amen.

WEDNESDAY

LESSON: ISAIAH 40.1-11

They said to him then, "Who are you? Let us have an answer for those who sent us. What do you say about yourself?" He said, "I am the voice of one crying in the wilderness, 'Make straight the way of the Lord', as the prophet Isaiah said".   John 1.22,23

This is the second part of John's confession in which he confesses who he is after denying any suggestion of being Christ, Elijah, or a prophet. What he means to say is: "Your salvation is much closer than the presence of any prophet might suggest; do not look so far back into another age that is past. The Lord of all the prophets is here Himself; there is no need of a prophet here. I am this Lord's forerunner. He is following in my footsteps. I am not prophesying about Him in the capacity of a prophet, but I am crying out as His forerunner, to make room for Him and a way for Him, so that He may enter in.

I do not say, "Behold, He is about to come", like the prophets, but I say, "Behold, He is coming and is here. I am not speaking words about Him, but am pointing to Him with my finger, just as Isaiah proclaimed long beforehand that such a cry would arise in the wilderness to prepare the way of the Lord (Isaiah 40.3). That is who I am, and not a prophet. Therefore, stand aside; make room and let the Lord Himself walk among you personally, and look for no more prophecies concerning Him."

SL.XI.106,24

PRAYER: We thank you, O Lord, for the full and complete testimony of your prophets concerning our Lord Jesus Christ and His salvation, a testimony for us to accept in full confidence and assurance. Amen.

THURSDAY

LESSON: LUKE 15.1-10

"**Make straight the way of the Lord**", **as the prophet Isaiah said.   John 1.23**

The special office of John was to make straight the way of the Lord, to humble the whole world and tell it that all men in general are sinners, lost, damned, poor, needy and wretched and that no life, no work, no estate is so holy, beautiful, or creditable that it does not deserve damnation.

The only way in which this wretched condition can be changed is by Christ the Lord's indwelling, activity, and life and where He becomes everything and is everything through faith. Men must be brought to realize that they need Christ and His grace, and they must partake of this grace with all eagerness.

Where preachers proclaim that the whole of our works and life are nothing, you have the true voice of John crying in the wilderness and the pure, unalloyed truth of Christian doctrine.

This is also what Paul means when he says, "**All have sinned and fall short of the glory of God**". **Romans 3.23**. This is what it really means to him, and to prune out and bring to naught all presumption. This is what it means truly to make straight the way of the Lord.

SL.XI.107,27

PRAYER: Lord God, heavenly Father, you have assured us that it is your will that all men should repent and accept your salvation in Christ. Humble us at all times in true repentance, and thus prepare us for your salvation in Christ our Saviour. Amen.

FRIDAY

LESSON: 2 CORINTHIANS 1.12-22

Among you stands one whom you do not know.   John 1.26

When John says here, **"Among you stands one whom you do not know"**, he means to say, "Do not direct your eyes too far into the future! He of whom the prophets have spoken has already been among the Jewish people for thirty years. Take heed and do not let Him go! You do not know Him, and I have come to you to show Him to you."

When John says, **"Among you stands one"**, he is following the manner of Scripture which says, "A prophet will arise" or "appear" (Deuteronomy 13.1). Similarly we are told in Matthew that false prophets **"will arise"** or "appear" or "come forth" (Matthew 24.24). God also says to Israel, **"The Lord your God will raise up for you a prophet from among you, from your brethren"**. Deuteronomy 18.15.

It is John's office to demonstrate that such establishment, appearance, arising and awaking has been fulfilled in Christ; He has already come forth in the midst of their brethren as God has promised, and they know it not.

It is also part of John's office as an evangelical preacher to comfort men by showing them how to get rid of their sins. This he does by pointing them to Christ, the coming Saviour.

SL.XI.112,41

PRAYER: Open our hearts by your Holy Spirit, O Lord, so that we are at all times fully awake to the completed work of our Saviour and find our full salvation therein. Amen.

SATURDAY

LESSON: 1 JOHN 3.1-10

I am the voice of one crying in the wilderness.   John 1.23

If you can now believe that the voice of John is true, fix your eyes in the way he is pointing and recognize the Lamb of God who is taking your sin upon Himself. You are victorious. You are a Christian, a lord over sin, death, hell and all things.

Your conscience must also be joyful and begin to love the tender Lamb of God, and to love, praise and thank our heavenly Father for such a boundless richness of mercy preached through John and given in Christ. Then, also, we will become most willing to carry out God's will as much as we can and with all our strength.

What is more comforting and pleasant to hear than the message that our sins are no longer ours or lying upon us but upon the Lamb of God? How can sin condemn such an innocent Lamb? It must be conquered and destroyed in Him. And so, together with sin, death and hell must also be conquered as the wages of sin. Behold, then, what God the Father has given us in Christ!

SL.XI.117,53

PRAYER: Gentle Jesus, Lamb of God, who takes away the sin of the world, fill us with your love so that we readily do the will of our heavenly Father in the power of your grace. Amen.

CHRISTMAS

LESSON: LUKE 2.1-14

In that region there were shepherds out in the field, keeping watch over their flock by night. And an angel of the Lord appeared to them, and the glory of the Lord shone around them and they were filled with fear. And the angel said to them, "Be not afraid; for behold, I bring you good news of a great joy which will come to all the people; for to you is born this day in the city of David a Saviour, who is Christ the Lord".   Luke 2.8-11

In a most clear manner the angel proclaims the Gospel besides which nothing else is to be preached in Christendom. He assumes the office of the Word in accordance with the Gospel and says, **"I bring you good news"**. He does not simply say, "I preach to you", but, "I bring you the Gospel; I am an evangelist; my word is a Gospel". Gospel means a good message of joy which shall constitute preaching in the New Testament.

Of what does the Gospel treat? Listen to what He says! "I am proclaiming a great joy to you; my Gospel tells you of a great joy." Where is it? Listen further! **"To you is born this day a Saviour, who is Christ the Lord, in the city of David."** See here what the Gospel is, namely, a joyful proclamation of Christ our Saviour.

He who proclaims Christ correctly, preaches the Gospel, and it is sheer joy. How can our heart hear a greater joy than that Christ has been given to it as its very own possession? He does not declare only that Christ is born, but he applies this birth to us and says, "Your Saviour".

SL.XI.132,42-43

PRAYER: We thank you, dear Saviour, for all the joy of Christmastide and especially for the glorious gospel that you are indeed our Saviour, Christ the Lord. Amen.

CHRISTMAS II

LESSON: LUKE 2.15-20

They made known the saying which had been told them concerning this child.   Luke 2.17

The faith of the shepherds produced action. St. Paul says, **"The kingdom of God does not consist in talk but in power"**. **1 Corinthians 4.20.** So also here. The shepherds do not only say, **"Let us go and see!"** but they actually went; indeed, they do more than they say. For the text says, **"They went with haste"**. This is more than just going as they had proposed to do. Faith and love always do more than they actually propose to do, and whatever they do is always something living, busy, active, and abundant.

A Christian must be a man of few words, rich in deeds. He proves himself such if he is a true Christian. If he does not prove his faith in deeds, he is not yet a true Christian.

The shepherds also confess and openly proclaim the word which was told them concerning this child. This is one of the most important duties in Christian life. One must risk body and life, property and honour. For the evil spirit does not launch such a heavy attack against correct belief and a good life in secret, but he will not abide it if we venture forth to spread the faith, confess, preach and praise it for the sake of others. So Luke says here that the shepherds not only came to see something, but they also made known what they had heard on the field, not only before Mary and Joseph, but before all men.

SL.XI.149,18-19

PRAYER: Grant us the joyful faith of the shepherds, O Lord, that we may go forth as witnesses, confessing you and your salvation to all our fellowmen. Amen.

CHRISTMAS III

LESSON: JOHN 1.1-14

In the beginning was the Word, and the Word was with God, and the Word was God.   John 1.1

"The Word was with God." Where else could the Word be? Outside of God there was nothing. Moses also says this when he writes, "**And God said, 'Let there be light'** ". **Genesis 1.3**. In order to speak, He had to have the Word with Him.

There is a clear distinction made here in the persons of the Godhead: the Word is a different person from the God with whom He was. This statement of John does not allow us to suppose that God was alone, because he states that something was with God, namely, His Word.

If there had been only a single person there, why would he say, "**The Word was with God**"? To have something "**with**" Him is not being alone or by Himself. We should note particularly that the evangelist places special stress on the "**with**". He repeats it (v.2) in order to give clear expression to the personal distinction in the Godhead and to counter the arguments of natural reason and future heretics.

Since natural reason more easily comprehends the fact that there is only one God and this doctrine is supported by many passages of Scripture and this doctrine is also true, natural reason still finds it very difficult to accept the fact that this same God is more than one person. The Son is a different person from the Father, but He is not a different God.

SL.XI.161,21

PRAYER: Great indeed, O God, is the mystery of our religion. Your Son, Jesus Christ our Lord, the Word who was with you at the beginning and who is truly God, was manifested in the flesh to be our Saviour and Redeemer. Thanks be to you, O God, for your inexpressible love! Amen.

CHRISTMAS IV

LESSON: 1 JOHN 1.1-4

He was in the beginning with God.   John 1.2

These are statements on which our faith is based and to which we must cling. That there are three persons in the Godhead and that each person is completely the whole of the one God absolutely transcends all the powers of our reason. Moreover, there are not three Gods, but one God.

Our schoolmasters, with all sorts of fine-spun subtleties, explained it this and that way in an effort to make it comprehensible. But if you do not want to fall into the net of the evil foe, have nothing to do with their foolish refinements, conceits and subtleties; take cover and remain in hiding like a hare in his stony crevice. If you go abroad and expose yourself to their human twaddle, the enemy will lead you on and finally trip you up so that you do not know where reason, faith, God, and you yourself eventually are.

Believe me, as one who has experienced this and struggled with it, I am not just talking by rote. Scripture has not been given to us to no purpose. If reason could have given us correct guidance we would have had no need for Scripture.

Let Arius and Sabellius* be warning examples. Had they been content to abide with the Scriptures and not sold out to reason they would not have been the cause of so much trouble. Our schoolmasters, too, would also have been Christian had they given up their tomfoolishness and subtleties and remained in the Scriptures.

SL.XI.164,26-27

*An ancient Unitarian.

PRAYER: Lord, keep us steadfast in Thy Word;
Curb those who fain by craft or sword
Would wrest the kingdom from Thy Son
And set at naught all He has done. Amen.

CHRISTMAS V

LESSON: ROMANS 5.6-11

In him was life, and the life was the light of men.   John 1.4

The evangelist says, "**In him was life**", as though he were speaking of something in the past, and not, "In him is life". But this must not be understood as a reference to the time before the world or the beginning. For the evangelist does not say here, "In the beginning there was life in him", as he says just prior to this, "**He was in the beginning with God**".

One must refer this to the time of Christ's life or sojourn on earth, when the Word of God manifested Himself to men and among men. It is the evangelist's intention to write about Christ and His life, during which He accomplished all that was needed for us to have life: "**In him was life**". Jesus Himself said:"**As long as I am in the world, I am the light of the world**". **John 9.5.**

We should understand the evangelist's statements to refer simply to the time of Christ here on earth. This Gospel is not as difficult as is sometimes supposed. Men have made it difficult with their lofty, deep and powerful researches. The evangelist wrote it for all Christians, however simple they may be, and he set forth his word in a manner that is quite comprehensible.

If someone simply disregarded Christ's life and sojourn here on earth and tried to find by his own resources that He is now sitting in heaven, he would be sadly mistaken. We must seek Him as He was and sojourned here on earth. Then we will find life, for He came to bring us life, light and salvation. During this life on earth, all was accomplished that we should believe concerning Him, so that John declares most emphatically, "**In him was life**", not that He is not now our life and that He does not now do what He did then.

SL.XI.169-170,40-41

PRAYER: Lord Jesus Christ, shine into our hearts with the light of your truth and be the true light of our life, for your truth's sake. Amen.

41

CHRISTMAS VI

LESSON: JOHN 12.35,36

The life was the light of men.   John 1.4

The thinking of human philosophy draws us away from Christ into ourselves. The evangelist wants to draw us away from ourselves to Christ. He refuses to deal with the divine, almighty, eternal Word of God and to speak about Him, except in the flesh and blood in which He walked here on earth.

He does not want to disperse us among the creatures created by Him, so that we should follow after Him, search for Him, and speculate about Him, as the Platonists do; he wants to gather us from the same wide-ranging and fleeting thoughts to Christ.

It is as though he said: Why do you step forth and search so widely? In Christ, the man, there is everything. He has accomplished all. In Him is life. He is the Word through which all things were made. Remain in Him and you will find everything. He is life and the light of all men. Anyone who tells you to look elsewhere for Him is misleading you. For He has given Himself to us in this flesh and blood, and He wants us to search for Him and find Him in this flesh and blood. Follow the witness of John the Baptist who points you to no other life or light than this man who is God Himself.

This light must, therefore, be understood as being the true light of grace — Christ — and not the natural light which sinners, Jews, heathen and the worst enemies of light, also have.

SL.XI.171,44

PRAYER: *Thou only art true life:*
To know Thee is to live
The more abundant life
That earth can never give.
O risen Lord, we live in Thee
And Thou in us eternally. Amen.

CHRISTMAS VII

LESSON: PSALM 43

He [John the Baptist] was not the light, but came to bear witness to the light.   John 1.8

The Gospel endures no other doctrine beside itself; it simply wants to be a witness to Christ and lead men to this light, namely Christ. Therefore these words, **"He was not the light"**, are worthy of being written in large letters and carefully noted against those men who push themselves forward and want to enlighten men with their own doctrines and self-made laws. Reject anyone who does not preach the Gospel and give him no kind of hearing.

He who teaches you to believe in Christ and to put your trust in the eternal Light, without building on any of your own works, is preaching the Gospel. Hence, be on your guard against everything you are told that is outside of the Gospel. Do not rely on it, and do not regard it as a light which enlightens and improves your soul, but regard it as something external, like eating and drinking for the needs of the body, that you can make use of according to your will or to please another, but not for your salvation. In regard to the latter, nothing is useful or necessary for you apart from this Light.

What a horrible thing is the doctrine of men, now rampant, which has actually banished this Light! Men themselves want to be this Light, and not witnesses of the Light! They are silent about it, or teach it in such a way that they are prominent, close beside it.

Being silent is even worse than denying, for from this procedure Samaritans are shown as serving God and idols at one and the same time (2 Kings 17.33).

SL.XI.184,81-84

PRAYER: Reign in our heart and reign there supreme, O Lord, so that we fully and completely believe your saving Gospel with all our heart, that Christ's light may at all times lead and direct us in the way of your choice. Amen.

43

NEW YEAR

LESSON: GALATIANS 3.23-29

In Christ Jesus you are all sons of God, through faith.
Galatians 3.26

The reason why St. Paul always stresses the need of faith in Christ is because he knew that men would have the presumption actually to suggest that man can have dealings with God outside of Christ, just as if God and our human nature were quite good friends, and as though righteousness were quite fond of sin and gave ear to the promptings of sin. Therefore, let us be wise and recognize Christ aright, namely, that before all else we should hear the Gospel and believe.

Christ is set forth in the Gospel not just for His sake, as an exalted character, but because He is the man who took the place of our sinful nature, loaded Himself with the whole wrath of God, that wrath which we merited despite all our works, and rendered it satisfaction. All who believe that they have this in and from Him will certainly be saved through Him from the same wrath of God, and obtain His grace.

From this we should learn what great need we have of Christ, and of what great use He is to us. Moreover, the idea that a man can do all this for himself, and that God's grace is given him by his natural powers, is a lie of the devil himself. For if nature can obtain grace there is no need of Christ as a substitute and a mediator.

SL.XII.265,50

PRAYER: Thanks be to you, Lord Jesus, for all that you took upon yourself as our substitute and mediator. We know only too well that without you we can do nothing. Amen.

CHRISTMAS IX

LESSON: ROMANS 6.1-4

Now before faith came, we were confined under the law, kept under restraint until faith should be revealed. So that the law was our custodian until Christ came, that we might be justified by faith. But now that faith has come, we are no longer under a custodian; for in Christ Jesus you are all sons of God, through faith. For as many of you as were baptized into Christ have put on Christ. **Galatians 3.23-27**

The Apostle Paul observes an excellent flow of thought in this context. He says, "Now that faith has come, we are no longer under a custodian". Why so? "In Christ Jesus you are all sons of God, through faith." How does it come to pass that we become God's children? "As many of you as were baptized into Christ have put on Christ."

Christ is God's child. Therefore, he who clothes himself in God's child, is also God's child, for he steps forth as God's adopted child, which certainly makes him God's child. If he is God's child, he is not under the subjection of the Law, in the position of an abject slave, but free. When we put on Christ in baptism His righteousness becomes our righteousness, and thus all the claims that the Law can make on us are fulfilled, and we are now God's free children in Christ.

SL.XII.265,51

PRAYER: In your mercy and peace, O Lord, you have freed us from the curse of the Law and made us your free children in Christ. For this we praise and thank you, and ask your grace so that we may always serve you in the freedom wherewith you have made us free. Amen.

CHRISTMAS X

LESSON: COLOSSIANS 3.12-17

Put on Christ.   Galatians 3.27

What is meant by "putting on Christ"? The unbelievers have a ready answer here. They say it means following Christ and measuring up to His example. But in this way I could also put on St. Peter, Paul and other saints, and putting on Christ would have no special significance at all. Therefore we let faith speak here, which Paul delightfully describes under the idea of "putting on".

It is obvious that those baptized have not previously followed Christ, but begin to follow Christ in baptism. Therefore Christ must be **"put on"** before one follows Him. "Putting on Christ" must be something quite different from following Him.

"Putting on Christ" is a spiritual matter. It comes to pass when the soul puts on Christ and all His righteousness, takes confidence in and relies upon that righteousness. This is just as though the soul itself had achieved all this and merited it. It is just like a man putting on his clothes. Such a putting on of Christ is a spiritual matter.

SL.XII.266,52

PRAYER: We thank you, Lord, for your wonderful means of grace, and especially that you accepted us as your dear children in baptism, in which we have put on Christ and all that He is and means to us as our Saviour. Amen.

CHRISTMAS XI

LESSON: EPHESIANS 1.11-14

He is the source of your life in Christ Jesus, whom God made our wisdom, our righteousness and sanctification and redemption. 1 Corinthians 1.30

It is quite certain that Christ has been given to us so that all His righteousness, and also all that He has and is, stands before us as though He is our very own possession. He who believes this will also experience, it, just as St. Paul said, **"He who did not spare his own Son but gave him up for us all, will he not also give us all things with him?" Romans 8.32.** Likewise, in the Epistle to the Corinthians, **"He is the source of your life in Christ Jesus, whom God made our wisdom, our righteousness and sanctification and redemption". 1 Corinthians 1.30.**

So, you see, he who believes in Christ in this way, puts Him on. Faith, therefore, is such an important matter that it saves such a man and justifies him; for faith brings him all the blessing of Christ on which the conscience can comfort itself and rely.

Such a man also becomes joyful in Christ, and happy to do all good and avoid what is evil. He fears neither death nor hell, nor any evil, and is richly clothed in Christ.

Hereby a full satisfaction is also rendered to the Law, and such a man is never under the subjection of the Law. For he has also received the Holy Spirit with the garment in his soul: he is clothed with God's adoption and so he is God's child.

SL.XII.266,53

PRAYER: Thanks and praise be to you, O God, for the fullness and riches of your mercy and grace in Christ, and not least for the earnest of your Spirit in my soul, assuring me that I am, indeed, your beloved child. Amen.

CHRISTMAS XII

LESSON: ROMANS 5.15-17

Thanks be to God for his inexpressible gift!
2 Corinthians 9.15

He who does not have the faith which believes that Christ
with His every blessing is his very own, does not have true
faith, and is not a Christian. His heart also cannot be truly
joyful and happy. For true faith will make Christians joyful
and happy, sure and blessed, as God's dear children in whom
the Holy Spirit also dwells. What a lovely, bright and
precious garment this is, to which is attached the most costly
adornment, jewels and gems, every kind of virtue, grace,
wisdom, truth, righteousness and whatever else there is in
Christ. Little wonder that Paul exclaims, **"Thanks be to God
for his inexpressible gift!"** 2 Corinthians 9.15.

St. Peter joins him when he speaks of **"his precious and
very great promises".** **2 Peter 1.4.** This is Joseph's
many-coloured robe which his father made for him in
preference to all his other children (Genesis 37.3), for Christ
alone is full of grace and truth. This is likewise the special
garment of the high priest Aaron in which he served God
and on which we could say a great deal.

Just as we put on Christ and receive Him as our own, so
He also puts us on and receives us to Himself with all that is
ours, as though we were His own possession. He finds nothing
good in us because we are full of sins. These He takes upon
Himself and drives them from us.

SL.XII.267,55

*PRAYER: O Lord, bless us richly in and through your
Word, that our hearts may be filled with real joy and
happiness and become the dwelling of your Holy Spirit, for
Christ our Saviour's sake. Amen.*

SUNDAY

LESSON: MATTHEW 2.1-12

Arise, shine; for your light has come, and the glory of the Lord has risen upon you.   Isaiah 60.1

The admonition to **"arise"** is without doubt spoken to one who has not arisen, that is, to one who is lying asleep, or is dead. I think St. Paul had this passage in mind when he said in Ephesians, **"It is said, 'Awake, O sleeper, and arise from the dead, and Christ shall give you light'"**. **Ephesians 5.14**.

Without doubt Christ is the **"light"** of which Isaiah speaks here, the light which through the Gospel shines forth throughout the whole world and gives light to all men who arise and desire Him.

But who are these sleepers and dead men? Without a doubt they are all those who are in subjection under the Law, for they are all dead through sin. They also include those who are dead, who disregard the Law and live a free life without the restraints of the Law.

The work-righteous are the sleepers who do not feel any shortcomings at all. Neither of these two groups pays much attention to the Gospel. They keep on in their sleep and a life which is nothing but death. The Spirit must awaken them so that they see and recognize the light.

There is a third group who feel the Law biting their conscience: they also long for grace and sigh for the Gospel; they also see to it that the Gospel comes and is given to men; they proclaim it, like Isaiah, to awake the sleepers and those who are dead so that they may accept the light.

SL.XII.288,4-5

PRAYER: Shine in our hearts, O Lord, with true Epiphany light, that we, through this light, may at all times be a true light in this world to all our fellowmen. Amen.

MONDAY

LESSON: 1 PETER 3.13-17

**Blessed are those who are persecuted for righteousness'
sake, for theirs is the kingdom of heaven.   Matthew 5.10**

It is a good thing for us that God so rules and orders
matters that the Sacrament should not be without
persecution. For He instituted it that it might be a password
and distinguishing mark of Christianity whereby we may be
recognized. For if we did not have it, we would not know
where Christians are to be found, who the Christians are,
and where the Gospel is bearing fruit. But, when men attend
the Sacrament, we can see who those are who have given ear
to the Gospel, and we can also observe whether they lead
Christian lives. The Sacrament is a distinguishing mark from
which it can be seen that we confess God's name and are not
ashamed of His Word. When I go to the Sacrament and
receive it under both the bread and the wine, I am bearing
witness to the fact that I am taking the Gospel quite
seriously.

If we want to confess Christ, we must receive the
Sacrament in both kinds, so that men may know that we are
Christians with a deep concern for the truth of God's Word.
If we lose our life in this confession, we must suffer this,
knowing that God will make a more than adequate
recompense to us as far as life is concerned. It is quite in
order for us to suffer persecution here. If we found nothing
but honour everywhere, we would never find ourselves in a
truly confessional situation. So we remain in our normal
sphere, incurring shame and disgrace. Sometimes we are
even threatened with death for the Lord's sake, as was the
case also in the early Church.

SL.XI.591,15

*PRAYER: We thank and praise you, Lord God, heavenly
Father, for the great honour and distinction you bestow upon
us in regarding us as worthy to suffer and even die for your
sake, in and through our Saviour Jesus Christ. Amen.*

TUESDAY

LESSON: 1 CORINTHIANS 11.23-25

The cup of blessing which we bless, is it not a participation in the blood of Christ? The bread which we break, is it not a participation in the body of Christ?   1 Corinthians 10.16

Christ's words of institution in the Lord's Supper cannot be denied by man or the devil. On these words we must take our stand. No matter what explanations are added to them, we have here a clear word of God which declares that the bread is Christ's body given for us, and the cup His blood shed for us. We are also told to celebrate the Sacrament in remembrance of Christ.

There was a time when the clergy forbade the laity to interpret the Word of God, and even denied them the right and ability to do so. But the laity have the same God and the same Word of God as the clergy. When it comes to the things that are to be believed, the layman has only one course to follow — to take his stand on the clear Word of God, to defend his faith with the clear Word of God, and to refute all doctrine that is contrary to God's Word with the clear Word of God. Every layman has the right to interpret the Word of God for himself, and to hold fast to the clear Word of God against all gainsayers.

In the words of institution, the evangelist says that Jesus took the cup, and when He had given thanks He gave it to His disciples saying, **"Drink of it, all of you; for this is my blood of the covenant, which is poured out for many for the forgiveness of sins"**. Matthew 26.27,28. So we say: Unless we can be taught that drinking here means something quite different from what it has meant everywhere else in the world, we stick to the opinion that all should drink of the cup in the Sacrament, just as all should eat of the bread.

SL.XI.592,17

PRAYER: We thank you, O God, for the clarity with which you have revealed your plan of salvation to us and also for the simple language in which you have taught us that the Holy Supper is one of your chief means of grace. Continue to bless us and strengthen our faith through your means of grace, for Christ's sake. Amen.

WEDNESDAY

LESSON: HEBREWS 10.19-25

The blood of Jesus his /God's/ Son cleanses us from all sin.
1 John 1.7

We must take hold of Christ's words in the Sacrament and be quite sure that we understand them. For the whole power and might of the Sacrament depends on these words. We must all know them, understand them, and cling to them in firm faith so that we may defend ourselves with them and, when the need arises, repulse our enemies with them. Hence, if you want to partake of the Sacrament, heed these words and be quite sure that they contain the treasure on which you are to take your stand and place your reliance for they are spoken to you individually.

Jesus speaks of His body which is given and His blood which is shed (Matthew 26.26,28). Why does He speak in this way? That you should do nothing but eat and drink here? No! Note very carefully how He adds: **"for the forgiveness of sins".** Matthew 26.28. This is the point which really concerns you. Everything else that is done and spoken in this connection is calculated to emphasize the central fact that your sins are forgiven you in this Sacrament.

If the Sacrament is to serve you in regard to the forgiveness of sins it must also help to conquer death. For where sin is wiped out, death is also wiped out, and hell as well. Where these three foes are vanquished, all our misfortunes are removed, and nothing but salvation and eternal blessedness remains for us.

SL.XI.594,19

PRAYER: O Lord, may your body and blood given and shed for us on the cross, and now offered to us in the holy Sacrament, always be a pledge and seal of the forgiveness of sins, for your name's sake. Amen.

THURSDAY

LESSON: HEBREWS 9.11-14

Come to me, all who labour and are heavy laden, and I will give you rest.   Matthew 11.28

Concentrate on the great treasure in the Sacrament, the forgiveness of sins, and have nothing to do with the tomfoolery of the schools of theology and their preoccupation with all kinds of curious questions in efforts to explain how Christ's body is in the Sacrament and how He hides Himself under such a restricted form.

You must prepare yourself so that the words of the Sacrament really have their intended effect upon you. This takes place when you feel the bite of sin and your conscience troubles you with temptation from your flesh, the world and the devil. You may be subject to bouts of anger and impatience; covetousness and the cares of this life may assail you. Offences continually cross your path and at times you even fall in a rather gross manner, doing harm to the welfare of your soul.

You also experience how you are nothing more than a poor, wretched, human being whom death terrifies; you become despondent and all joy disappears. On such occasions it is high time for you to come before God with an open confession of your needs saying, "Dear Lord, you have instituted the Sacrament of your body and blood and left it to us as a testament in which we may find the forgiveness of sins. I know full well that I need this Sacrament. I have fallen into sin, and I have my fears; there are even times when hopes are rather dim. I am not at all bold in the confession of your Word, and there are always so many besetting weaknesses. So I now approach your throne of grace in the Sacrament looking for healing, consolation and strengthening."

SL.XI.594,20

PRAYER: You have given us many invitations to come to you in all our needs, dear heavenly Father. Strengthen us especially when we turn to you in repentance, and seek forgiveness in the Sacrament of the body and blood of your Son our Saviour. Amen.

FRIDAY

LESSON: ROMANS 6.15-19

Where sin increased, grace abounded all the more, so that, as sin reigned in death, grace also might reign through righteousness to eternal life through Jesus Christ our Lord.   Romans 5.20,21

The Sacrament should be given only to those who have declared their need before God and are seeking strength and consolation through it as a means of grace. If a man does not really feel any great need for the Sacrament, he would be better advised to stay away from it. He should not follow the example of those who observe a special period of real ascetical martyrdom before they come to the Sacrament, and who nevertheless do not really know why they come.

When you have received the Sacrament, go forth and practise your faith. Participation in the Sacrament enables you to say, "I have publicly received the Word which assures me of the forgiveness of sins, and have taken the public sign of this in my mouth. This I am able to attest as I have publicly confessed it before the devil and the world." If death and a bad conscience assail you, you can take your stand on this with boldness against the devil and sin, and thus strengthen your faith and lighten your conscience over against God.

On this basis you can also look for improvement from day to day. Without the Sacrament, you become sluggish and cold, and the more you withdraw yourself from it the more sluggish you become. But if you feel that you are sluggish, weak, and lacking in faith, where else can you find strengthening than here? If you make a long delay until you become pure and strong enough, you will probably never come to the Sacrament, and it will be of no use to you.

SL.XI.595,21

PRAYER: Dear God, enable us at all times to recognize the open door which you have provided for us in the Sacrament, so that our faith is increased and we derive strength from it to follow in the footsteps of your Son, Jesus Christ our Saviour. Amen.

54

SATURDAY

LESSON: PSALM 97

Rejoice in the Lord always; again I will say, Rejoice.
Philippians 4.4

When the Sacrament is used properly, the conscience is not tormented, but comforted and lightened by the joy of faith. For God did not give us the Sacrament as a poison or an instrument of torture, so that one should be terrified by it. This is what happened to us when we were taught the very unskilled doctrine that in the mass we offered our own piety as a sacrifice to God, and lost the real meaning of the Sacrament, namely, that it contained for us words of comfort and salvation, to strengthen our conscience, to refresh us, to make us joyful and to free us from all misfortunes.

This is how one should regard the Sacrament, a source of the sweetest grace, consolation and life. It is poison and death for those who rush into it in a brazen manner, without feeling any kind of weakness, shortcoming, or need which should impel them to seek the Sacrament, and who act as though they were previously quite pure and pious. The Sacrament is for those who recognize their shortcomings and failings, who know in themselves that they are far from perfect piety, but who have the keen desire to improve.

So much depends here on the recognition of our real condition and our real needs, for we are all subject to weaknesses and are sinners, but we do not all confess this. This is enough about preparation for the Sacrament and strengthening our faith through the words of the Sacrament, that we here receive Christ's body and blood, given and shed for us for the forgiveness of sins. Through these words the benefit, fruit and practice of the Sacrament are adequately indicated and expressed, as far as we are to make use of it for ourselves.

SL.XI.595,22-23

PRAYER: Heavenly Father, refresh us, strengthen us in body and soul, and make us really joyful Christians in the use of your Holy Supper, for Christ's sake. Amen.

THE WEEK OF EPIPHANY I

SUNDAY

LESSON: LUKE 2.41-52

When they saw him they were astonished; and his mother said to him, "Son, why have you treated us so? Behold, your father and I have been looking for you anxiously."

Luke 2.48

Although the holy mother Mary who was blessed (Luke 1.42) and highly-favoured with all kinds of grace (Luke 1.28) without a doubt found the greatest of happiness and joy in her child, the Lord still governed her in such a way that she should not have her paradise in Him and reserved it for her future life, as He does also in the case of others. And so on earth she also had to suffer her share of misfortune, pain and sorrow.

The first distress that came upon her was that she had to give birth at Bethlehem, a strange place, in which there was no room for herself and her child except in a stable. Soon after this, when the time of her purification was past (Luke 2.22), she had to flee with her child into a foreign country, into Egypt, a small comfort for her under the circumstances. She probably experienced many blows of the same kind which have not been recorded.

Here, too, the Lord laid a similar misfortune upon her when her Son stole off into the temple and she had to search for Him for so long without finding Him. This gave her a terrible shock and grieved her so much that she exclaimed: **"Behold, your father and I have been looking for you anxiously"**. We can well imagine that her heart was ready to admit, "The child is mine alone, as I well know. God gave Him to me with instructions that I should look after Him. How has it come to pass that I have lost Him? It is my fault for failing to look after Him well enough."

SL.XI.430,2-3

PRAYER: O Lord, you have clearly told us in your Word that you chasten all whom you love for their betterment and well-being. You did not even spare your handmaiden, Mary. Let us not despair when your chastening comes upon us, but open the eyes of our faith so that we may also readily see "the way of escape" [1 Corinthians 10.13] that we may be able to bear it. Amen.

MONDAY

LESSON: JAMES 1.12-15

We are afflicted in every way, but not crushed; perplexed but not driven to despair.   2 Corinthians 4.8

When God has given us a fine, strong faith so that we go forth in firm confidence, and are quite sure and certain that we have a gracious God on whom we can fully rely, we are in paradise. But when God suffers our heart to slip away from us, so that we come to think that God wants to tear the Lord Jesus from our hearts, and our conscience feels that we have lost Him, and then flounders and loses courage, so that our confidence sinks, the result is wretched distress.

Even if our conscience cannot recall any particular sins it is still in such wretched condition that it thinks, "Who knows if God really wants me?" just as Mary begins to have her doubts (Luke 2.41-52), so that she no longer knows whether God still wants her as a mother.

When the heart receives such blows it is inclined to say, "It is true that hitherto God has given you a fine faith; but perhaps He wants to take your faith from you and no longer have you". It requires a strong faith to withstand such knocks, and there are not many whom God assails in this way. But we must prepare ourselves so that we do not despair if this should happen to us.

SL.XI.432,7

PRAYER: Heavenly Father, strengthen our faith through your Word and Sacraments, that we may successfully overcome all trials and temptations we may meet in life, and stand firm and steadfast in the confidence that we are always more than conquerors in and through Jesus Christ, our Saviour. Amen.

TUESDAY

LESSON: PSALM 94.12-15

My son, do not regard lightly the discipline of the Lord, nor lose courage when you are punished by him. For the Lord disciplines him whom he loves, and chastises every son whom he receives.   Hebrews 12.5,6

Trials, chastenings, and temptations come upon us so that our faith may be exercised and become stronger and stronger. God especially arranges matters in this way to preserve His children from the kinds of misfortune which might otherwise come upon us.

When men become boldly confident and very strong in spirit they could eventually have such confidence in themselves that they think they are capable of accomplishing everything in their own strength and power. God sometimes allows their faith to be found wanting, and to suffer an eclipse, so that they may realize who they are and say, "Even if I want to believe, I cannot". In this way God humbles His saints and holds them to their own knowledge.

Nature and reason are always keen on falling upon God's gifts and clinging to them as though they were attainable by man's own abilities. God must deal with us in such a way that we realize that He must put faith into our hearts. We have no way of influencing Him to do this.

Fear of God and confidence in God must always be closely related for us. Both of these relationships must remain decisive for our lives, so that a man does not become presumptuous and too secure, and eventually come to rely upon himself. This is one reason why God allows temptations to come upon His saints.

SL.XI.433,9

PRAYER: Lord God, our loving, heavenly Father, we know that all things, even trials and temptations, work together for our good. Bring us safely through all trials and temptations, thus strengthening our faith as your children in and through Jesus Christ, our Saviour. Amen.

WEDNESDAY

LESSON: PSALM 119.97-104

And he said to them, "How is it that you sought me? Did you not know that I must be in my Father's house?"
Luke 2.49

I have often said, and I say it again, that nothing should be preached in Christendom but the pure Word of God. This Gospel (Luke 2.41-52), in stating that they could not find Jesus **"among their kinsfolk and acquaintances"**, also reminds us of this.

It is no good saying that one must believe what the church councils have decided, or what Jerome, Augustine and other holy fathers have written. One must point to a definite place where Christ can be found and none other, namely, the place which He Himself indicates when He says, **"I must be in my Father's house"**. One will find Him nowhere else than in God's Word.

One should not receive what the holy fathers teach in such a way that one trusts it with one's whole conscience and seeks comfort in it. If someone therefore asks you, "Shall I not trust the holy fathers?", you can answer: Christ did not suffer Himself to be found among His kinsfolk and acquaintances.

It would be a good thing for us Christians to take good note of this example from this Gospel and make a kind of proverb out of it to be used against all doctrine which is not God's Word.

SL.XI.435,15

PRAYER: Your Word, O Lord, is the rock of our salvation because it points us to Christ our one and only Saviour. We thank you, Lord, for all the comfort and consolation in Jesus Christ, which you have so freely conferred upon us through your Word. Amen.

THURSDAY

LESSON: JOHN 8.31-33

Sanctify them in the truth; thy word is truth.   John 17.17

This Gospel (Luke 2.41-52) is a very telling blow against all doctrine and consolation and whatever else might be named that is not the Word of God and does not flow from the Word.

You can now say: I don't care what happens; exalt reason and the light of nature as high as you want to, I still reserve my right not to entrust myself to it. I grant that councils and pope have made decisions, and that the holy fathers have taught in accordance with their will, but I do not rely on such decisions. If they grant me this, we will soon be one. I will retain my freedom and they can decide and set up whatever they will, but let me say, "If it pleases me, I accept it; but I do not accept it as though I were doing something precious thereby".

They will not grant this, for it will never satisfy them that such procedure should be a matter of freedom. They always look for the addition that one should rest one's confidence on these decisions and derive consolation from them just as though one were trusting Christ and the Holy Spirit in this whole matter. We must never abide this false delusion and confidence which they try to inculcate, namely, that it is a good work to accept their decisions and a sin to reject them.

SL.XI.437,21

PRAYER: Thanks and praise be to you, dear Father in heaven, for giving us the precious gift of your holy Word, in which you have revealed all that a man should know for his salvation in and through Christ our Saviour. Amen.

FRIDAY

LESSON: ROMANS 3.21-26

He saved us, not because of deeds done by us in righteousness, but in virtue of his own mercy, by the washing of regeneration and renewal in the Holy Spirit, which he poured out upon us richly through Jesus Christ our Saviour, so that we might be justified by his grace and become heirs in hope of eternal life.   Titus 3.5-7

We should never place our confidence in the doctrine of men and the holy fathers. God has given us many examples to teach us not to build on men or to put our confidence in men.

Even the saints make mistakes. We read that, something like eighteen years after the ascension of Christ (Acts 15), the apostles and the group of those who were Christian came together in Jerusalem. The question to be decided was: Should one compel the Gentiles coming into the church to be circumcized? Some of the leaders of the party of the Pharisees who had become believers came forward and said that the Gentiles should be circumcized and ordered to keep the law of Moses. Much strife ensued and many were in danger of accepting this viewpoint.

Peter, Paul, Barnabas and James opposed this suggestion. Peter in particular said: God has given His Holy Spirit to the Gentiles, who received the Gospel by my mouth, just as He did to us, and made no difference between them and us but cleansed their hearts by faith. If, then, they received the Holy Spirit without being circumcized, why do you want to bind them in addition and impose a yoke on their necks which neither our fathers nor we have been able to bear? We believe that we shall be saved through the grace of the Lord Jesus Christ, just as they will. Acts 15.7-11.

SL.XI.439,23

PRAYER: We thank you, Lord, for the gift of full and free justification in Jesus Christ, our Saviour. Grant us at all times fully to understand and appreciate all that you have done for us in your Son. Keep us always fully reliant on your grace in Christ, for Christ's sake. Amen.

SATURDAY

LESSON: 2 THESSALONIANS 2.13-17

Whatever was written in former days was written for our instruction, that by steadfastness and by the encouragement of the scriptures we might have hope.   Romans 15.4

In this Gospel (Luke 2.41-52) we are given the consolation that, whenever suffering becomes our portion, we should realize that we will not be able to find any other consolation excepting in the Scriptures, the Word of God. God has set it down in writing that we should learn, as Paul says, **"Whatever was written in former days was written for our instruction, that by steadfastness and by the encouragement of the scriptures we might have hope".   Romans 15.4**

Here He states that the Scriptures are comforting and give patience and consolation. There is nothing else that comforts the soul more, even in the slightest temptations. For anything else whereby a man seeks consolation for himself, however great it may be, is quite uncertain. For the heart always has the nagging feeling: "Who knows whether it is right? O that I could be quite sure!" When the heart clings to God's Word, it can say without any wavering: "This is God's Word; it cannot lie to me or mislead me. Of that I am certain."

The greatest struggle in which we must engage is to keep the Word and remain steadfast in it. If this Word is torn from a man's heart, he is lost.

SL.XI.441,29

PRAYER: Grant us steadfastness of faith, O Lord, so that the precious Word of salvation which you have made known to us in Christ, our Saviour, may never be torn from our hearts, and that we may continue in it until all our hopes are fully realized in Christ. Amen.

SUNDAY

LESSON: JOHN 2.1-11

On the third day there was a marriage in Cana of Galilee, and the mother of Jesus was there; Jesus also was invited to the marriage, with his disciples.   John 2.1,2

It was a great honour for Jesus to make His gift of wine at this lowly marriage feast by means of a great miracle. Hereby Jesus became the bride's most important donor. In any case, He may not have had any money for precious gems to give her as a gift. Such an honour Jesus never accorded to any of the Pharisees. In this way He confirms marriage as a work and ordinance of God. No matter how despised it is, or regarded as insignificant by men in general, God nevertheless recognizes His work and is pleased with it.

Because the estate of holy matrimony can rest on the comforting fact that God has established it and is pleased with it, and because Christ Himself honours it for our consolation, all men should really be pleased with it. They should regard it as an honourable estate and be very favourably inclined to it, being sure that God is well pleased with it.

They should also be ready joyfully to endure everything that is difficult in this estate, even if matters sometimes seem worse than they actually are. It is an estate which practises and cultivates faith in God and love towards one's neighbour by means of trouble and toil, unpleasantness, the cross, and disagreeableness of all kinds. All these are not uncommon experiences where God's Word and work are taken seriously.

SL.XI.464,3-4

PRAYER: Lord God, heavenly Father, in many ways and places you have taught us that holy matrimony is an estate well-pleasing to you and to be honoured by all men. Thanks be to you, Lord Jesus, for the striking way you honoured this holy estate at the wedding in Cana, giving us strong encouragement to follow your holy example in this respect. Amen.

MONDAY

LESSON: COLOSSIANS 1.9-14

I will greatly rejoice in the Lord, my soul shall exult in my God.   Isaiah 61.10

In this Gospel (John 2.1-11) Christ makes it quite clear that He finds no fault with providing expenses for a wedding and all that is needed for a wedding, adornment and merry-making, eating and drinking, as the usage and custom of the land require.

It is true that this seems to be excess and wasted expenditure and a worldly matter. Suitable moderation must be observed here, without completely destroying the wedding celebrations. The bride and bridegroom must be suitably adorned, and the guests must eat and drink and be joyful. Provisions may be supplied and usual procedures followed with a good conscience.

Scripture often refers to these matters with approval. Mention is made in the Gospels of the bride's adornment, the marriage garment, the guests, and the good fare at the wedding. Even the Old Testament sets forth examples with approval. Abraham's servant gave Rebekah, Isaac's bride, jewellery of silver and of gold as well as raiment (Genesis 24.53).

We should never pay too much attention to the hypocrites and self-made saints with their sour looks who are pleased with nothing except what they themselves teach, and will not even suffer a bride to wear a garland or any other adornment.

SL.XI.466,7

PRAYER: O Lord, we thank and praise you for all the joys and pleasures which you have given us to make us happy here on earth. We pray for your grace to enable us to enjoy these things, following the example of our Lord and Saviour, Jesus Christ. Amen.

TUESDAY

LESSON: GALATIANS 5.22-25

Rejoice in the Lord always; again I will say, Rejoice.
Philippians 4.4

God is not concerned about external matters like a marriage, provided that faith and love remain and, as has been stated, moderation is practised, as is fitting for every estate. For the marriage at Cana, although it was a poor and lowly affair, still had three tables. This is clear from the mention of the "steward of the feast", who usually had charge of three tables. The bridegroom did not attend to these but had his servants. They also had wine to drink.

All this could well have been dispensed with on considerations of poverty, as happens also among us. The guests here at Cana, moreover, did not just allay their thirst with the wine, for the steward of the feast remarks that the good wine should be served first and afterwards **"when men have drunk freely, then the poor wine". John 2.10.**

Christ lets all this pass, and we should also let it pass and not cause men conscientious scruples on this score. They were not children of the devil, even if some of them exceeded the needs of quenching their thirst and became merry. Otherwise you will have to reckon it as a fault in Christ that He was the cause of this with His gift, and also His mother who requested it. Eventually we will reach the position that both Christ and His mother were sinners here if the saints who can only see what is sour are to judge the matter.

SL.XI.466,8

PRAYER: Preserve us from a judgemental spirit, O God, which sees nothing but sin in what our fellowmen are doing, and overlooks the fact that your children are not only permitted to rejoice, but commanded to rejoice in Christ their Saviour. Amen.

WEDNESDAY

LESSON: ROMANS 14.5-12

So, whether you eat or drink, or whatever you do, do all to the glory of God.   1 Corinthians 10.31

The reason why excess is so frequent among men is that they do not just eat and drink, but gorge themselves and guzzle, carouse and gormandize, and behave as though it were a mark of cleverness or strength to gorge and guzzle. Their objective is not to become joyful, but to become mad and to be full. These people are pigs, not human beings. Christ would not have given such people wine or accepted their invitation.

In their adornment, also, such people have no consideration for a wedding but to show themselves off, and to prance around as though the strongest are the best. They are loaded with gold, silver and pearls, and do their best to wear as much silk and fine clothes as possible. Donkeys and blockheads could easily do the same.

How, then, is moderation to be determined? Reason should be our pride here. We should follow the example of other lands and cities where such excess is not the order of the day. Each one according to his estate! So also with food and drink and other similar matters. Is it sin to have music and dancing at a wedding, seeing that it is claimed that there is much sin in connection with dancing? I do not know whether the Jews danced; but because it is customary among us, just as inviting guests, adornment, eating and being joyful is customary, I cannot condemn dancing if it does not involve any excess or become lewd. If it involves sin, it is not the fault of the dancing in itself. People can sin sitting at table or even in church! So also with eating and drinking. If dancing were sinful, it would have to be denied even to children.

SL.XI.467,9

PRAYER: As your children in Christ Jesus, O Lord, you have given us all things for our happiness and enjoyment. In this connection grant us the moderation and a sense of what is fitting and proper, so that our lives may always be happy and joyful in all good conscience. Amen.

THURSDAY

LESSON: HEBREWS 12.1-4

For in Christ Jesus neither circumcision nor uncircumcision is of any avail, but faith working through love. Galatians 5.6

There is a real conflict for faith in this Gospel (John 2.1-11). We should therefore pay close attention to what Christ's mother, Mary, does, and also to what she teaches us. How hard His words sound, and what an unfriendly attitude He seems to adopt! But she interprets everything in her heart in such a way that she does not even think of any wrath in Him, or anything that might conflict with His goodness, but remains firm in the conviction that He is good. She will not allow this opinion to be taken from her by the rebuff she has suffered, on the basis of which she might well have imputed disgraceful conduct to Him in her heart, and not regarded Him as good and gracious.

That is what those do who lack faith and fall away at the first blow and hold no more to God. They feel like horses and mules do, to whom the psalmist refers when he says, **"Be not like a horse or a mule, without understanding, which must be curbed with bit and bridle, else it will not keep with you". Psalm 32.9.**

If this mother had allowed herself to be scared off by these hard words, she would have gone away quietly in annoyance. In telling the servants to do whatever He commanded, she proves that she has overcome the rebuff and that she is awaiting nothing but sheer goodness from Him.

SL.XI.470,16

PRAYER: We thank you, God, for all the examples of triumphant faith which you have given us for our learning and instruction in your holy Word, like the example of Mary, Christ's mother. As her faith in you never wavered, so may we at all times trust in your goodness and mercy in and through our Saviour Jesus Christ. Amen.

FRIDAY

LESSON: ROMANS 8.31-39

We know that in everything God works for good with those who love him. Romans 8.28

The most important lesson in this Gospel (John 2.1-11), and what we should especially note here, is that we should accord God the honour of being good and gracious, even though He seems to have shown Himself in quite a different light. Sense and feeling must be disciplined in us, and the old Adam put down, so that true faith in God's goodness, and not feeling, remains in us.

Here you see how a pure faith remains in Christ's mother and is held up before us as an example. She is sure that He will be gracious, even though she does not feel it. She is also sure that she feels otherwise than she believes. So she leaves the whole matter completely to His goodness.

She does not set up any time or place, any method or measure, any person or name. He must do just as He pleases. If it is not done in the middle of the meal, let it be done at the end of the meal. She keeps the rebuff to herself. She does not reproach Him for His disdainful conduct before all the guests, for His ungracious attitude which made her blush. He appears to be sour, but He is sweet. Of this Mary is quite sure. And if we act in this way under such conditions we are true Christians.

SL.XI.471,18

PRAYER: Lord, you know that we sometimes experience conditions in which we see only as through a glass darkly, when we do not immediately recognize your guiding hand and goodwill toward us. Grant us your grace so that we always firmly believe that even in such situations all things must work together for our good. Amen.

SATURDAY

LESSON: MARK 8.31-35

Jesus said to her, "O woman, what have you to do with me?" John 2.4

We should note here that Jesus adopts a harsh attitude to His mother not only to give us an example of faith, but also to remind us that in the affairs of God and in His service we do not know father or mother.

Although there is no authority on earth greater than the authority of father and mother, it is of no avail, when it is a matter of God's Word and work. In the affairs of God neither father, mother, bishop, nor any other man is to lead and teach us. The Word of God alone must do this.

Where father and mother order, teach, or even request you to do something against God, or to observe something in worship that God has not clearly commanded and ordered, you should say to them, **"What have you to do with me? What is there for you and me to do in common?"**

Christ here simply refuses to do the work of God at the wishes of His own mother.

SL.XI.471,19

PRAYER: You have shown us in many clear passages of your Word, O Lord, that as your children we must always obey God rather than men [Acts 5.29]. Strengthen our faith at all times, O Lord, so that we always have the courage to do this in and through our Saviour Jesus Christ. Amen.

SUNDAY

LESSON: MATTHEW 8.1-13

A leper came to him and knelt before him, saying, "Lord, if you will, you can make me clean".   Matthew 8.2

See how the faith of the leper manifests itself. He is under no delusions at all. All that he desires and hopes to obtain is the pure goodness and grace of Christ, freely and without any merit at all on his part. We cannot claim here that the leper earned the privilege of drawing close to Christ and speaking to Him, begging His help. He comes to Christ because he is conscious of his impurity and unworthiness, and he places all his reliance on Christ's goodness.

This is true faith, living confidence in God's goodness. If this confidence is in a man's heart, his faith is right; if this confidence is not in a man's heart, his faith is wrong. All who do not keep the pure goodness of God in sight, and who always look first of all to their good works in the hope of meriting God's favour and goodness for themselves, have this wrong faith. Such people never have the boldness to invoke God with real earnestness or to approach Him.

This confidence or faith, or the knowledge of the goodness of Christ, would never have developed in the leper as the fruit of his own rational understanding. In all probability he had received a good report of Christ beforehand to the effect that Christ is good, gracious and merciful, ready to help all men and to supply comfort and consolation for all who come to Him.

SL.XI.478,2-3

PRAYER: Thanks be to you, O Lord, for the examples you have given us in your holy Gospel encouraging us to come to you at all times, in all our needs, with the assurance of your grace and help. Amen.

MONDAY

LESSON: GALATIANS 1.6-9

Continue in the faith, stable and steadfast, not shifting from the hope of the gospel which you heard.

Colossians 1.23

The Gospel is the beginning, middle, and end of all that is good, and our one source of salvation. We have stated repeatedly that first of all one must hear the Gospel, and then faith, love and good works follow. We mut not put good works first, turning the whole matter back to front, as the teachers of work-righteousness do.

The Gospel is a good report, discourse and proclamation of Christ, announcing that He is nothing else but pure goodness, love and grace. Such a report could not possibly be made concerning any other human being, or any of the saints. For, although the other saints were men of quite good repute, a report on them does not constitute the Gospel as such. It is Gospel only when the goodness and grace of Christ are proclaimed. Even though mention is made of famous saints and their doings, this does not make the report the Gospel. The Gospel bases Christian faith and confidence solely on the rock, Jesus Christ.

SL.XI.480,4

PRAYER: We praise and thank you, loving heavenly Father, for the clear revelation of the good news of salvation in the Gospel of your Son, and for the faith, trust and confidence which you have given us in connection with this Gospel, in and through Jesus Christ our Saviour. Amen.

TUESDAY

LESSON: GALATIANS 2.11-16

We hold that a man is justified by faith apart from works of law. Romans 3.28

You see how the example of the leper (Matthew 8.1-4) supports faith against works. For, just as Christ helped this leper out of pure grace through faith without any works or merits on his part, so He helps all men. He also wants men to regard Him as such a helper, and to expect help from Him on this basis.

Had the leper come to Christ with all sorts of claims declaring, "See here, Lord, I have prayed and fasted so and so much. Please take note of all this, and make me clean accordingly", Christ would never have cleansed him had he been so minded. Such a person does not rely on God's grace, but on his own merits. In such a case, God's grace is not praised, loved or desired, but personal works claim all the honour, and God is robbed of His due honour. As Isaiah declares, **"They bow down to the work of their hands, to what their own fingers have made", Isaiah 2.8**, that is, they put their confidence in their own works, and confer on their own works the honour belonging to God's grace alone.

SL.XI.480,5

PRAYER: Lord, preserve us from that presumption which urges us to trust in our own works to the rejection of the grace, help and salvation which you are always ready and willing to bestow on us freely in and through Jesus Christ our Saviour. Amen.

WEDNESDAY

LESSON: 1 JOHN 3.11-18

No man has ever seen God; if we love one another, God abides in us and his love is perfected in us.   1 John 4.12

I have often remarked how faith makes us free lords and love makes us slaves. Through faith we become gods and partakers of the nature and name of God as the psalmist declares, "I say, 'You are gods, sons of the Most High, all of you'". Psalm 82.6. Through love we become at the same time the poorest of men.

By faith we are in need of nothing and always have full supply; in love we are the servants of all men. By faith we receive good things from above, from God; in love we let them flow out below to our neighbour.

With us it is something like it was with Christ during His earthly ministry. According to His godhead He lacked nothing; but according to His humanity He was the servant of all who needed His help.

We have often said that we also through faith are born as God's children and gods, lords and kings, just as Christ in eternity was born true God from the Father. Nevertheless, through love we are to do good to our neighbour, just as Christ was born a man to help us all. Just as Christ became man only to serve us after being God in eternity, we also do good to our neighbour and show him our love only after we have become righteous, free from sin, living and blessed children of God.

SL.XI.481,7

PRAYER: By faith in Christ you have made us free lords and kings, O God, thus conferring upon us all the spiritual blessings we need for our salvation. Grant us your grace, that in the power and strength of all this we may prove our faith in love and service to our neighbour. Amen.

THURSDAY

LESSON: COLOSSIANS 3.12-17

Only say the word, and my servant will be healed.
Matthew 8.8

We learn from the example of the centurion at Capernaum that we must begin with the Gospel and put our whole faith and trust in it without looking to any merits or works. The centurion makes no appeal to any merit or work; he reposes his whole confidence in Christ's goodness alone. Here we see how all the works of Christ set forth examples of what the Gospel means in terms of faith and love.

We have here an example of Christ's love in bestowing His blessing freely without any requests and gifts. The centurion also gives us an example of love in the concern which he shows for his servant. He acted as Christ acts in receiving us: he does good to his servant freely and for the servant's good. Luke says that the servant **"was dear to him"**. Luke 7.2.

His love for his servant impelled him to concern himself for the servant's welfare and prompted his action. Let us follow this example and not deceive ourselves into thinking that in the possession of the Gospel we do not have to concern ourselves with the needs of our neighbour.

SL.XI.482,9-10

PRAYER: Give us, O Lord, the faith which is always active in love towards our neighbour, after the example of our Lord Jesus Christ in His work of salvation for us. Amen.

FRIDAY

LESSON: MATTHEW 6.5-15

Lord, if you will, you can make me clean. Matthew 8.2

This modest prayer of the leper must not be understood as an expression of doubt in Christ's goodness and grace. For such a faith would be quite worthless, even if he did believe that Christ was almighty and able to do all things in His omniscience. A living faith which does not doubt also believes that God is good and that He has the gracious will to perform what we pray for. Faith never doubts that God in His good will is always favourably inclined towards us, that His intentions and purposes for us are always good.

We do not always know, however, whether our welfare will really be promoted by what we ask in our prayers. God alone knows this. The prayer of faith leaves everything to God's gracious will, requesting that He grant our petition if it will serve His honour and our real need. The prayer of faith never doubts that God will hear our prayer. If God does not answer the prayer, faith believes that God did not answer because of His grace towards us, and because He deemed it better for us to leave the prayer unanswered.

In all this, our faith in God's good and gracious will remains sure and steadfast, whether He answers our prayer or not. Paul reminds us of this when he says that we know not what or how we should pray (Romans 8.26). Likewise, we pray in the Lord's Prayer for His will to be done.

SL.XI.482,11-12

PRAYER: Bestow your grace upon us, O Lord, that we always have the confidence to bring all our needs before you in prayer and supplication and, at the same time, have the assurance that you will hear and answer our prayer according to your will. Amen.

SATURDAY

LESSON: 1 THESSALONIANS 2.13-16

When Jesus heard him, he marvelled, and said to those who followed him, "Truly, I say to you, not even in Israel have I found such faith". Matthew 8.10

The words of Jesus to the centurion have caused no end of trouble to the commentators. They have raised the question whether Jesus really told the truth in these words. On the basis of these words, one would have to infer that the mother of Jesus and His apostles were inferior to this centurion.

I would like to point out here that Christ is speaking of the people of Israel to whom He had preached and to whom He had come, and that His mother and apostles are really excluded because they were normally a part of His company. Nevertheless I will still stick quite simply to the words of the Lord and take them just as they read.

It is not contrary to any article of the faith to believe that the faith of this centurion did not have any parallel among the apostles or even in the faith of God's mother. Where Christ's words do not conflict openly with an article of faith, we must allow them to stand just as they read, and not twist them or guide them by our expositions and interpretations, not even for the sake of a saint, or an angel, or even for God's own sake. For God's Word is the very truth above all saints and angels.

SL.XI.483,13

PRAYER: Your Word, O God, is the truth and the whole truth. Grant us, at all times, such a faith that we trust you fully in your Word and derive from it the full confidence of salvation in and through Jesus Christ our Lord. Amen.

THE WEEK OF EPIPHANY IV

SUNDAY

LESSON: MATTHEW 8.23-27

Why are you afraid, O men of little faith?   Matthew 8.26

In what does the unbelief of the disciples consist? It sees no more than it feels! Life and safety are no longer in their feelings — there is nothing here but the waves crashing over the ship, and the sea which threatens all kinds of danger and death. While they feel all this, and concern themselves with it unremittingly, the terror, the trembling and the faint-heartedness do not abate. The more they pay attention to all this and feel it, the harder does death and fear drive them on and threaten to engulf them at every moment.

Unbelief cannot rid itself of such feelings, and it cannot think otherwise even for a moment. It has nothing at all to which it can cling for comfort. Unbelief can have no peace and quiet even for a moment. This is how things will be also in hell where there is nothing but sheer trembling and terror without end.

Had there been real faith among the disciples, they would have put the wind and the waves of the sea out of their minds. Instead of allowing the wind and the storm to claim all their attention, they would have remembered God's might and grace pronounced in His Word. They would have put their trust in them as though they were on a firm rock in the midst of the moving waters, as though the sun was shining brightly and all was peace without any storm at all.

SL.XI.498,2-3

PRAYER: You know, O God, how often we are beset in this life by various trials and temptations. Strengthen our faith through your means of grace, that we may always emerge from these trials chastened and strengthened, for Christ's sake. Amen.

MONDAY

LESSON: JOHN 15.18-27

Whatever is born of God overcomes the world; and this is the victory that overcomes the world, our faith.   1 John 5.4

God so arranges matters that our faith is not called upon to concern itself with unimportant matters, but with matters which exceed the competence of all men, matters such as death, sin, the world and the devil.

There is no one in the whole world who can withstand death. All men flee from death and quake in terror before it. Nevertheless, they are overtaken by death. But faith remains firm and stands up against death which gobbles up the whole world. It conquers death and devours this ravenous glutton.

So also, the whole world cannot constrain or suppress the flesh. It is in control of the whole world and what it wills must happen, so that the whole world is fleshly. But faith takes hold of the flesh and subdues it. Faith bridles the flesh into obedience.

Similarly, no man can endure the raging, persecution, blasphemy, reproach, hatred and jealousy of the world. Every man gives way and becomes exhausted. The world gains the upper hand and carries off the victory. It makes a mockery of faith and treads it under foot, and even finds joy and pleasure in all this.

Faith alone is the victory that overcomes the world.

SL.XI.499,4

PRAYER: We know, O Christ, that by your glorious resurrection from the dead you have conquered and destroyed death as far as we are concerned. Keep us ever mindful of this truth, especially in the hour of death and amidst the ragings of the world. Amen.

THE WEEK OF EPIPHANY IV

TUESDAY

LESSON: 1 PETER 5.6-11

Put on the whole armour of God, that you may be able to stand against the wiles of the devil.   Ephesians 6.11

Who can withstand the ragings of the devil with his countless cunning suggestions and insinuations by which he hinders God's Word, faith and hope, and occasions so many errors and sects, and so much seduction, heresy, despair, and superstition — abominations without number? Over against the devil, the whole world is like a spark of fire in a spring of water. The world perforce is subject to the devil, as we also see, hear and comprehend.

But faith gives the devil something to think about. It not only withstands his temptations, but also exposes his villainy so that his treachery does not succeed at all. He becomes wearied and gives up. We see this also today from what is happening with indulgences.

Similarly, no one can appease and quieten the slightest sin; it keeps on biting and gnawing at one's conscience so that no help would come even if the whole world comfort and stand by such a person. He would have to be consigned to hell.

Here faith emerges as a real hero; it quietens all sins even if they were as many as the whole world has committed.

SL.XI.500,5

PRAYER: We know that your salvation, O Lord, is sufficient for the needs of all sinners. In this confidence grant us the strength of faith to withstand all the wiles of the devil when he tries to fill our hearts with unbelief and to rob us of the faith that saves us. Amen.

WEDNESDAY

LESSON: ROMANS 5.1-5

For whatever is born of God overcomes the world; and this is the victory that overcomes the world, our faith.

1 John 5.4

Must we not declare that faith which can withstand such mighty enemies as death and the devil, and carry off the victory, is something surpassingly great and wonderful? It is, indeed, as John says, "the victory that overcomes the world". 1 John 5.4.

Not that all this comes to pass in peace and quietness. This involves a battle which cannot be fought without bloody wounds. In this strife the heart also feels sin, death, the flesh, the devil and the world so strongly, that it cannot help thinking that all is lost, that sin and death have gained the victory and the devil is on top. It feels little of the power of faith.

This is also the state of affairs in this Gospel of the stilling of the tempest (Matthew 8.23-27), when the waves not only buffet the ship, but actually engulf it. It appears that the ship must go down and sink. All this time Christ is lying asleep. There is no hope of life here: death is on top and has scored a victory. Life is lying vanquished. But this is only how matters stand if one judges solely by appearances. As disciples of Christ we must not draw conclusions and act simply on appearances, but by faith.

SL.XI.500,6

PRAYER: Dear Lord Jesus, appearances and experiences in this world so often belie our hopes as your disciples. At such times fill our hearts with courageous faith and hope which never falter but cling even more firmly to you when dark clouds hover above us. Amen.

80

THE WEEK OF EPIPHANY IV

THURSDAY

LESSON: HEBREWS 4.14-16

And the men marvelled, saying, "What sort of man is this, that even winds and sea obey him?"   Matthew 8.27

In the Gospel of the stilling of the tempest (Matthew 8.23-27), we are reminded where to seek consolation and help in the hour of need. This is not available to us in the world; human skill and might offer no protection.

Christ alone is the helper in the hour of need. We must turn to Him in all our needs with trust and confidence, as the disciples do here. Had they not believed that He would help them, they would not have awakened Him and cried to Him for help. True, their faith was still weak and mixed with much unbelief. They experienced a certain amount of hesitation in committing their safety and lives into His keeping. They were not so sure that He could rescue them in the midst of the sea and snatch them from the jaws of death. The disciples could not command or demand help because of their faith.

From all this we can conclude that God's Word has no master or judge; it requires no protector apart from God Himself. It is His Word. Therefore, just as He has sent His Word forth without human merit or counsel, so He also wants to operate with it and protect it without human help and strength. The man who puts his faith in human help loses out in two directions: he finds no help from God or men.

SL.XI.503,14

PRAYER: Be near us and help, Lord Jesus, in every hour of need, especially when our faith weakens, for the sake of your mercy, truth and grace. Amen.

FRIDAY

LESSON: PSALM 31.1-8

When I am weak, then I am strong.   2 Corinthians 12.10

The Gospel (of the stilling of the tempest) consoles and emboldens us in two ways. When we encounter persecution for the sake of God's Word, we may say, "Christ is in the ship, and therefore the sea and the wind rage and the waves fall on the ship and try to sink us. But let them rage! God's purposes stand fast: the wind and the sea owe Him obedience. Persecution will last no longer than He wills it. Even if persecutions come upon us, they must still be subject to Him. He is Lord of all things, and hence nothing can really harm us. O that He would help us, so that we do not become faint-hearted in unbelief! Amen."

The fact that the men marvelled and praised the Lord because wind and sea were subject to Him, indicates that the Gospel, God's Word, spreads further and further and becomes stronger through persecution. Faith also increases under such conditions.

This seems very strange when we compare this situation with secular benefits. These decline when misfortune strikes and opposition is encountered; they increase under good fortune and peaceful conditions. Christ's kingdom is strengthened in tribulation and declines under peace and comfortable conditions as St. Paul says in his letter to the Corinthians: "**My power is made perfect in weakness**". 2 **Corinthians 12.9**.

SL.XI.504, 16-17

PRAYER: Lord God, our loving heavenly Father, make true the assurances of help and support which you have so often given us in your Word so that in every need we cling to these assurances in and through Jesus Christ our Saviour. Amen.

SATURDAY

LESSON: 1 CORINTHIANS 12.4-11

God is able to provide you with every blessing in abundance, so that you may always have enough of everything and may provide in abundance for every good work.   2 Corinthians 9.8

To impute absolute perfection and sinlessness to the saints is a fruit of carnal thinking and devotion. On this basis, men do not measure the saints by God's grace, but according to their own person, worthiness and grandeur. This is quite contrary to the way in which God measures men. God measures men in accordance with His gifts. God never allowed John the Baptist to perform any miracle such as many lesser saints are reported to have performed (John 10.41). In short, He has often performed through lesser saints what He has not done through the great saints.

When Christ was twelve years old He concealed Himself from His mother and allowed her to be mistaken and lacking in knowledge (Luke 2.43). On Easter Day He showed Himself to Mary Magdalene before He showed Himself to His mother and the apostles (John 20.14). He spoke to the Samaritan woman (John 4.7), and even with the woman taken in adultery (John 8.10), in a more friendly manner than He showed towards His mother. Peter falls and denies Christ, but the murderer on the cross acknowledges Him and believes in Him.

In these and similar remarkable examples He wants us to estimate the saints according to His indwelling Spirit so that we should not simply judge them according to their person. He wants to dispense His gifts freely, according to His good pleasure, as Paul declares (1 Corinthians 12.11), and not according to our ways of thinking.

SL.XI.484,14-15

PRAYER: All that we are and have, O Lord, is of your mercy and grace alone. Pour out your Spirit upon us that we may ever continue to live in the light of your grace, in and through our Saviour Jesus Christ. Amen.

SUNDAY

LESSON: MATTHEW 13.24-30

The kingdom of heaven may be compared to a man who sowed good seed in his field; but while men were sleeping, his enemy came and sowed weeds among the wheat, and went away.   Matthew 13.24,25

This Gospel teaches us how the kingdom of God, or Christianity, fares in this world, especially with respect to its doctrine. It must never be our hope and expectation that there will be nothing but orthodox Christians and the pure doctrine of God's Word on this earth.

There must also be false Christians and heretics so that the genuine Christians may be proved, as Paul reminds us when he says to the Corinthians, "**There must be factions among you in order that those who are genuine among you may be recognized**". 1 Corinthians 11.19.

This parable does not speak of the false Christians who are failures as Christians only outwardly, in their lives. He is speaking of those who are false to Christianity in their doctrine and faith, who go under the name of Christians, who make a fine show in playing the hypocrite and are really injurious. It is a question of conscience, not just of outward action. The servants who can recognize the weeds among the wheat must be enlightened by the Holy Spirit.

The whole point here is that we should not be surprised or dismayed if false doctrine and wrong faith of various kinds make their appearance in our midst. The devil is always present in some way or other among the sons of God (Job 1.6).

SL.XI.506,3

PRAYER: Sanctify our hearts and lives in such a way, O Lord, that we may not harm your kingdom in any way by hypocrisy, but in all things prove ourselves good seed, for Christ the Saviour's sake. Amen.

MONDAY

LESSON: PSALM 145.13-21

Let both grow together until the harvest.   Matthew 13.30

The Gospel (of the weeds among the wheat) shows us what action we should take against heretics and false teachers. It is not always possible to eradicate them and destroy them. Christ expressly declares that we must allow the weeds and the wheat to grow together.

We must base our whole action here on the Word of God alone. In this connection it is possible that the one who is in error today may be right tomorrow. Who knows when God's Word will touch a man's heart? If he is burnt or otherwise dispatched it becomes quite impossible for him to be corrected; he is removed from all influence of the Word of God and a man is lost who might otherwise have been saved.

This is the reason why the Lord says that precautions should be taken, so that when the weeds are gathered the wheat should not be rooted out with them. This would, indeed, be a horrible thing for which we could not answer before God.

What foolish people we were for so long for believing that we could force the Turks to believe with the sword, the heretics with the fire, and the Jews with death, trying to root out the weeds with our own strength and power! We acted just as if we were empowered to control men's hearts and spirits and make them godly and orthodox when God's Word alone can do this.

SL.XI.506,4-5

PRAYER: Grant us both knowledge and grace, O Lord, that we may never presume to interpose ourselves in any context where your Word alone should be the one and only factor that can help our fellowmen and your kingdom, for Jesus' sake. Amen.

TUESDAY

LESSON: MATTHEW 12.1-8

Confess your sins to one another.   James 5.16

As Christians we confess our sins not only to God but also to our neighbour. This is a confession of love as the first is a confession of faith. James writes of this confession to our neighbour when he says, **"Confess your sins one to another"**. In this confession you acknowledge the wrongs you have done to your neighbour. Christ has outlined the procedure which we are to follow in His Sermon on the Mount: **"If you are offering your gift at the altar, and there remember that your brother has something against you, leave your gift there before the altar and go; first be reconciled to your brother, and then come and offer your gift. Make friends quickly with your accuser, while you are going with him to court."** Matthew 5.23-25.

Christ here gives instructions to both parties. The one who has given offence should ask for forgiveness; the one who has been offended should be ready to forgive. This confession is necessary and commanded like confession to God. God will not bestow His grace on anyone and forgive him his sins if he is not prepared to forgive his neighbour. Our faith is not right if it does not produce this fruit, namely, forgiving the neighbour and requesting his forgiveness. Otherwise we must not come before God. If this is not a fruit of your faith, your faith as well as your confession to God is not in order.

SL.XI.585,6

PRAYER: Bestow your grace upon us in such measure, O God, that we are duly humbled and readily confess our sins to our neighbour, forgiving him his sins against us, in and through our Saviour Jesus Christ. Amen.

WEDNESDAY

LESSON: EPHESIANS 4.25-32

For freedom Christ has set us free; stand fast therefore, and do not submit again to a yoke of slavery.   Galatians 5.1

Private or auricular confession has become established in the church without any direct command in the Word of God. In enforcing this upon all members of the Church, the leaders of the Church have at times imposed heavy burdens on the consciences of men and caused much spiritual harm.

No one should be forced or compelled to private confession; and no man should be prevented from confessing his sins privately, if he so desires. If you confess your sins privately because you have been forced into it by threats or routine procedures, this cannot possibly be pleasing to God.

If you cannot practise private confession of your own free will and without compulsion you are better off without it. If you do this in compliance with regulations or any other human directions, you are not acting correctly. The whole world flocks to this confession during Easter week because it has been commanded under various ecclesiastical penalties. This week would be more correctly called a week of ordeals and torments in which the conscience of men is plagued and tormented, with much spiritual damage and ruin resulting, and in which Christ Himself is plagued and tormented much more disgracefully than when He hung upon the cross.

We should raise our hands in thankfulness to God that He has enlightened us in this connection. For although the fruits of our faith may be limited, and we are still far from perfect, we have nevertheless received a correct understanding of matters. It is much better for us to stay away from confession and the Sacrament than to be forced to take part in them under compulsion and threats.

SL.XI.585,7

PRAYER: O God, our heavenly Father, help us to stand fast at all times in the freedom wherewith Christ has made us free, so that we always act in your presence as free men redeemed by the blood of Christ. Amen.

THURSDAY

LESSON: MATTHEW 18.23-35

If we confess our sins, he is faithful and just, and will forgive our sins and cleanse us from all unrighteousness.
1 John 1.9

As stated above, no one should ever be forced to private confession; but for various reasons it is still good and advisable. You should never despise the Word of God no matter how often you hear it, but be eager at all times to receive and accept it. God has brought it about that His Word has gone forth into all the world, filling all corners, so that wherever you may go you will find God's Word everywhere. Whenever I proclaim the forgiveness of sins, I am proclaiming the true Gospel. For the sum and substance of the Gospel is that he who believes in Christ will obtain the forgiveness of sins.

Every time a Christian preacher opens his mouth, he is bound to speak a word of absolution. We should always be eager to accept this proclamation with joy wherever and whenever we hear it, and thank God from the bottom of our hearts that we can hear this proclamation in so many places.

This is also the important factor in private confession. It is not your act that is the important thing here, but what the pastor proclaims to you in this act; his declaration that your sins have been forgiven, his absolution. It does not matter whether this absolution comes from a pastor in the course of his duties or from any other Christian. The Word which is proclaimed to you here is not man's word but God's Word. Here, in the context of absolution, it is just as though God Himself were speaking to you through your pastor or your Christian brother. SL.XI.586,8-9

PRAYER: Awaken in us such reverence and respect for your saving Word, O God, that we value it wherever and whenever it is offered, especially also in the simple word of absolution heard from a Christian brother, for Christ our Saviour's sake. Amen.

FRIDAY

LESSON: MATTHEW 18.15-20

If you forgive the sins of any, they are forgiven; if you retain the sins of any, they are retained.   John 20.23

In confession you have the advantage that the Word is applied to you personally, as is also the case in the Sacrament. In the sermon, the Word is proclaimed to the whole congregation, and although it may have impressed you in various ways it may not have struck you in its full import. But in confession the Word is directed to you alone; it cannot miss you.

Should you not be very happy to discover a place where God speaks to you individually? If we could actually receive a message directly from an angel, we would all probably be prepared to rush to the very ends of the earth.

Are we not crazy, wretched, and ungrateful for closing our ears to the message that is always so readily available to us? We have the Scriptures which attest that God speaks through us, and that when God speaks to us through men in the Scriptures it is just as though God Himself were speaking to us from His own mouth. Christ declares: **"Where two or three are gathered in my name, there am I in the midst of them"**. Matthew 18.20. He has also given us the assurance:**"If you forgive the sins of any, they are forgiven; if you retain the sins of any, they are retained"**. John 20.23. It is God Himself who pronounces the absolution, just as it is God who baptizes a child.

Will you claim that you have no need for confession? Even though you receive the assurance of forgiveness in the Sacrament, you should nevertheless still practise confession, because here God is dealing with you personally.

SL.XI.587,10

PRAYER: We thank you, Lord Jesus, for the personal comfort of forgiveness which you have made so readily available to us in the words of absolution, both collectively and individually, for your mercy's sake. Amen.

SATURDAY

LESSON: JOHN 17.20-26

I do not pray for these only, but also for those who believe in me through their word.   John 17.20

Another advantage of confession is that it provides you with an opportunity to confess your errors and mistakes, and to seek counsel for them. Even if there were no other reasons for it, and God did not at the same time speak to us there, I would not like to do without confession for the simple reason that it provides me with a good opportunity to open up to my brother and make my complaints and concerns known to him. It is a wretched thing for conscience to be burdened in the grip of fear, without knowing where to turn for consolation.

It is very comforting for two people to get together and help each other with advice and consolation. This is a brotherly procedure and also a mark of Christian love. The one discloses his troubles; the other heals the wounds that have opened up before him. I would not trade this for the wealth of the whole world.

This confession should not be commanded and recommended in such a way that people are going to develop a bad conscience by gaining the impression that they must practise this confession before attending Communion. On the other hand, we should not disregard this confession. We can never hear too much of God's Word and have it so firmly established in our hearts that it becomes impossible to establish it more firmly.

SL.XI.588,11

PRAYER: Make your Word a bright and shining light for us, O Lord, a true means of salvation, in and through our Saviour Jesus Christ. Amen.

SUNDAY

LESSON: MATTHEW 17.14-21

Faith is the assurance of things hoped for, the conviction of things not seen.   Hebrews 11.1

A significant feature of the strong faith of men like the centurion of Capernaum (Matthew 8.5-13) is that he knows that his salvation is not dependent on the bodily presence of Christ. This does not necessarily help us. Our salvation is dependent on the Word and on faith. At that time the apostles did not yet know this, and perhaps even Christ's mother was not quite clear on this issue. They held firmly to His bodily presence, and did not take kindly to the idea of Christ's departure from them (John 16.6). They did not cling simply to His Word.

But this heathen is so fully satisfied with His Word that he does not desire Christ's presence and does not regard himself worthy of it. His example also demonstrates his strong faith. "I am a man under authority", he says, "and with one word I can do whatever I want to do. Cannot you, then, with one of your words, do whatever you want to do? I am certain, as you have also demonstrated, that health and sickness, death and life are subject to you, just as my servant is subject to me." Hence his servant also is healed from that hour by the power of this faith.

SL.XI.485,18

PRAYER: Lord God, our heavenly Father, give us such trust and confidence in the promises and assurances of your Word that we never waver in faith, through Jesus Christ our Lord. Amen.

MONDAY

LESSON: ROMANS 13.8-10

Do not use your freedom as an opportunity for the flesh, but through love be servants of one another.   Galatians 5.13

After we have eaten and drunk the body and blood of Christ our Lord in the Holy Supper, we should offer ourselves to be eaten and drunk to our neighbour and say to him, "Take, eat and drink". I am not saying this derisively but in all seriousness.

You should give yourself to your neighbour with your whole life, just as Christ does in the words of the Sacrament with all that He is. It is as though Christ were saying: "Here am I, who am given for you. This treasure I present to you here. All that I have, you shall also have. If you are in need, I shall also be in need. Here you have My righteousness, life and salvation, so that neither sin, death, hell nor any misfortune will ever overwhelm you. As long as I remain justified and live, so long you will also remain in piety and life."

Thus He speaks to us. These words we must also take up and speak to our neighbour, not only with our mouths but also with deeds. We should say to our neighbour: "Dear brother, I have received my Lord and He is mine. I now have more than enough of everything. Take what I have; it is all yours. I place it at your disposal. If it is necessary for me to die for you, I will also do that."

This is the goal set before us in the Holy Sacrament. Proof of our faith in our whole attitude and bearing to our neighbour should shine forth clearly in those who use this Sacrament correctly.

SL.XI.596,24

PRAYER: Lord God, heavenly Father, in the strengthening of our faith in the Holy Supper enable us especially to manifest our faith and love towards our needy neighbour, for Christ's sake. Amen.

TUESDAY

LESSONS: GALATIANS 5.13-17

Immediately the father of the child cried out and said, "I believe; help my unbelief!"   Mark 9.24

It is true that we will never bring it to pass that we reach such a stage of perfection that we actually surrender our soul, body, property and honour for someone else. We still live in the flesh which is so deeply rooted in us that we cannot provide such a pure sign and demonstration of what the Sacrament should actually produce in us. Because of our shortcomings and failures, Christ has instituted His Sacrament for our use, so that from this source we may make good our shortcomings.

To what other source can you turn when you become aware of your failures and shortcomings? You must pour out your complaints to the Lord and say, "My trouble here is that you bestow such an abundance upon me that I cannot possibly do the same thing to my neighbour. That is my complaint! And now I beseech you to permit me to become so rich and powerful that I can do likewise."

Although it is impossible for us to become as perfect as Christ, we should nevertheless have an earnest desire for such perfection. Although there will always be a lack of perfection in all our desires and efforts, we should not despair as long as the earnest desire for improvement in this respect stays with us.

SL.XI.597,25

PRAYER: Undergird and strengthen all our feeble efforts to serve you and our neighbour, dear heavenly Father, so that by your grace we are always permitted to bring forth the fruits of faith that please you, in and through our Saviour Jesus Christ. Amen.

WEDNESDAY

LESSON: LUKE 10.25-37

You shall love your neighbour as yourself.   Matthew 19.19

If you want to be quite sure that you have made a profitable use of the Sacrament, you should pay close attention to the way in which you treat your neighbour. Your devotional poses and reveries and your own pious thoughts and reflections can mislead you here. You may well have very pious thoughts, but this is no absolute criterion; you are still subject to error despite all your pious thoughts. But in the way in which you treat your neighbour you have very powerful evidence of the power of the Sacrament in your life.

If you find that the words and the sign of the Sacrament are softening your heart and moving you to be kind to your enemy, to receive your neighbour, and to help him bear his distress and sorrow, all is well. If this is not the result of your partaking of the Sacrament, you cannot be certain that you have profited from the Sacrament, even if you were to partake of it a hundred times a day with the greatest of devotion and were overwhelmed with tears of joy. Such wondrous devotion which carries on in this manner counts for nothing with God. It is also very dangerous, because it is so completely self-centred and misleading.

Before all else we must actually know what we are doing in partaking of the Sacrament as St. Peter reminds us when he declares: **"Brethren, be the more zealous to confirm your call and election", 2 Peter 1.10**, namely, by your good works.

SL.XI.599,29

PRAYER: May your Word and Sacrament, heavenly Father, always be a real power in our lives, producing many good works of love toward our neighbours, for Jesus' sake. Amen.

THURSDAY

LESSON: PSALM 71.12-16

Thou hast delivered my soul from death.   Psalm 56.13

There is certainly a big difference between facing death boldly, suffering death patiently, or bearing any other pain willingly, and the idea that we can blot out sin through such death or suffering and obtain grace before God. Heathen have often died boldly and bravely, and many a scoundrel and uncouth person still does so today. But the idea that we blot out sin by death and suffering is a poisonous and deadly addition of the devil, like all other lies whereby he bases confidence and consolation on our own doing and works.

We must be on our guard against this. For just as strongly as I must guard against anyone who tells me that I must enter a monastery if I want to save my soul, so strongly also must I offer resistance at my life's end to anyone who directs me to my own death and suffering for consolation and hope, as though these could wash away my sins.

This is a denial of God and His Christ, blasphemy of His grace, and distortion of His Gospel. Those do much better who hold a crucifix up before a dying person to remind him of the suffering and death of Christ.

SL.XI.528,6

PRAYER: In your cross alone, O Lord, is all our hope of salvation, eternal life and blessedness. May we never lose these blessings by trusting wholly or in part in our own works and feelings, but continue to hope and trust in you alone. Amen.

FRIDAY

LESSON: 1 THESSALONIANS 4.9-12

Do not neglect to do good and to share what you have.
Hebrews 13.16

Faith brings Christ to you and gives Him to you as your own with all His blessings. Love gives you your neighbour with all your blessings. In these two respects you have the Christian life pure and complete.

You may ask here: What are the good works which I am to perform for my neighbour? The answer is that they have no special name, just as the good works which Christ does for us have no special name.

How then can we recognize these works? They have no names, so that we do not begin making distinctions here, performing some of them but not others. We must give ourselves completely to our neighbour with all that we are, just as Christ gave Himself completely for us with all that He was. Christ did not only pray or fast for us. He gave Himself for us wholly with praying, fasting, all His works and suffering, so that there is absolutely nothing in Him which is not ours and at our service.

It is not a good work on your part merely to make your neighbour a charitable offering or to pray for him. It is a good work if you give yourself wholly to your neighbour with all that you are and have, and render him whatever service you can. This service could take the form of almsgiving, prayer, work, fasting, counsel and comfort, as well as teaching, admonishing, punishing, defending, clothing, feeding, and even suffering and dying for your neighbour.

SL.XI.17,39-41

PRAYER: Lord Jesus, fill our hearts with true love for our neighbour that we may learn to give ourselves for him, as you have given yourself for us. Amen.

SATURDAY

LESSON: PSALM 95.1-7

By this my Father is glorified, that you bear much fruit, and so prove to be my disciples.   John 15.8

You should note very carefully that you can never perform any good work for the benefit of God or His saints. You can obtain, seek, beseech and receive good from God only through faith. Christ has done and performed everything for you, paid for your sins, and obtained grace, life and salvation for you. Be satisfied with Him.

Your only concern must be to bring more and more of Him into yourself and to strengthen your faith in Him. Hence, do all the good that you can, and arrange your whole life so that it is really good. It is a good life if it is useful to others and not merely to yourself.

Christ has already done everything for you and given you all that you could possibly seek or desire for yourself here and yonder, whether it be the forgiveness of sins, the attainment of salvation, or whatever it may be called. If you find that there is something in you that you have done for God, or His saints, or for yourself and not wholly for your neighbour, know for sure that it is not a good work.

Accordingly, the husband should serve his wife and child, the wife her husband, children their parents, servants their masters, masters their servants, the government its subjects and subjects the government. Every man should serve the other man, even his enemy, and live, speak, act, hear, suffer and die for his neighbour in service and love. He must always be the hand, mouth, eye, foot and even the heart and courage of his neighbour.

SL.XI.20,47

PRAYER: Grant us the grace and love, O Lord, that our lives may at all times be good and useful lives for all our fellowmen, for your sake. Amen.

SUNDAY

LESSON: MATTHEW 20.1-16

Now when the first came, they thought they would receive more; but each of them also received a denarius.
Matthew 20.10

The Gospel comes with a levelling action and makes all men equal in sin, so that those who perform many works count for no more than the open sinners, and must also become sinners and hear themselves described in Paul's words, **"All have sinned "**. **Romans 3.23.** No one can be justified before God by what he himself does, by his works.

At this stage men look around and begin to despise those who have done practically nothing. They ask themselves why all their pain and labour should count for no more than the laziness and loose living of others.

They also begin to complain to the householder because they do not think it is fair. They actually blaspheme against the Gospel and become quite hardened in their work-righteousness. They love the favour and grace of God, and have to content themselves with their temporal reward. They must trudge off with their denarius into condemnation because they served merely for their hire — they were not concerned about any eternal blessing. So they receive this hire and nothing more.

The others, however, must acknowledge that they have not merited either the denarius or the favour shown to them; they received more than they bargained for. These remain in faith and are saved, and in addition they also have enough here for their temporal needs. For all depends on the goodwill of the householder.

SL.XI.511,6

PRAYER: Preserve us, O Lord, from the hypocritical notion that we can become much better than others, and thus reach a position where we may claim your blessings and mercies as merits. Keep us ever mindful of Christ's death, not for the righteous, but for sinners. Amen.

MONDAY

LESSON: MATTHEW 6.25-33

Seek first his kingdom and his righteousness, and all these things shall be yours as well.   Matthew 6.33

The denarius represents the temporal welfare of men, and the favour of the householder their eternal welfare. Both groups in the parable receive a denarius, an equal amount for their earthly sustenance.

Those described in the parable as "the last" did not seek as much pay as the others; all this was an additional gift to them because they sought the kingdom of God first (Matthew 6.33). On top of all this, they also receive the grace which brought them eternal life and they were happy and joyful.

"The first", however, seek what is temporal; they accept the engagement and work for this only. For this reason they miss out on grace and earn hell with all their heavy toil. For the former, "the last", do not suffer from the presumption that they have actually earned the denarius; yet they get everything. When "the first" see this, they delude themselves into thinking that they should obtain much more, and they miss out on everything.

As we see clearly when we examine the hearts of those two groups, "the last" do not pay attention to their merits or deserts, but they partake of the Lord's goodness. "The first", however, pay no attention to the Lord's goodness, but look only to their own deserts and regard the payment as due for their service, and complain about the householder's goodness.

SL.XI.512,8

PRAYER: Thanks be to you, Lord Jesus, for your undeserved and full salvation which you bestow on us freely and without cost through the ministrations of your holy Church. Amen.

TUESDAY

LESSON: ROMANS 11.33-36

The last will be first, and the first last.   Matthew 20.16

We must understand the two words "last" and "first" in two respects: in respect to God and in respect to men.

"The first" before men and those who consider and conduct themselves as those who are closest to God, "the first" before God, quite paradoxically are regarded as "the last" before God and the farthest removed from Him.

On the other hand, those who are "the last" in the eyes of men, who regard and conduct themselves as those farthest removed from God and "the last" before Him, are paradoxically the closest to God and "the first" before Him.

He who wants to be secure should closely follow the saying, **"Whoever exalts himself will be humbled". Matthew 23.12.** For here in this Gospel we are clearly reminded that "the first" before men is "the last" before God and "the last" before men is "the first" before God. Similarly, "the first" before God is "the last" before men and "the last" before God is "the first" before men.

SL.XI.512,9

PRAYER: You have shown us, heavenly Father, that our salvation in Christ is beyond all human understanding, and confronts man with much that seems absurd to human reason. Humble us by your grace, that we never presume to judge you and your ways with us by our own weak reason and understanding. May we always remain firmly established in your Word of truth, for Christ's sake. Amen.

WEDNESDAY

LESSON: PSALM 138.1-6

God opposes the proud, but gives grace to the humble.
1 Peter 5.5

The Gospel (Matthew 20.1-16) does not simply speak of those who are "first" and "last" in an ordinary sense as, for example, the mighty ones of this world, who are heathen and know nothing of God, are nothing in God's sight. It speaks of those who have persuaded themselves that they are the "first" or "last" before God.

There it aims very high and hits some very important people; indeed, it is most disturbing for the greatest of the saints.

This is why Jesus told this parable to His apostles. For it can happen that one who is quite poverty-stricken in the eyes of the world, weak and despised, who has even suffered something for God's sake and gives no appearance at all of amounting to anything, still nurtures secret ideas of self-satisfaction and begins to think that he is the "first" before God when he is actually the "last".

On the other hand, even if any one is so despondent and weak that he regards himself as the "last" before God, despite the fact that in the world he enjoys money, honour and good things, he is the "first".

SL.XI.512,10

PRAYER: Empty us, O Lord, of all false pride and self-righteousness that, firmly trusting in your grace and mercy, we may always rank as those who are "first" in your sight, in and through Jesus Christ our Lord. Amen.

THURSDAY

LESSON: MICAH 6.6-8

A man's pride will bring him low, but he who is lowly in spirit will obtain honour.   Proverbs 29.23

It is very necessary that this Gospel (Matthew 20.1-16) should be preached to those in our time who know the Gospel, like me and others like me, who are teachers of the whole world and become its masters. We are very prone to develop the idea that we are closer to God than others, and that we have devoured God's Spirit with feathers and legs.

How does it come to pass that so many sects have arisen, the one undertaking this, the other that, in connection with the Gospel? Without a doubt, the reason is that more of these really think that the statement applies to them, "The first will be last", or, if it does apply to them they are secure and without fear and regard themselves as "the first".

Their experience will have to tally with this statement; they must become "the last". They simply go ahead and set up much disgraceful doctrine and blasphemy against God and the Word.

SL.XI.513,12

PRAYER: Open our eyes, O God, that we always recognize that we are paupers in your sight, absolutely dependent on your grace for all that we need as your children, for Jesus' sake. Amen.

FRIDAY

LESSON: PSALM 25.1-10

He has put down the mighty from their thrones, and exalted those of low degree.   Luke 1.52

No one is so high, or will ever reach such a height, of whom it is not to be feared that he could become the lowliest. On the other hand, no one has ever fallen so deeply, or will fall so deeply, that he cannot entertain hopes of becoming the highest.

The reason for these paradoxes is that all merits are set aside and God's goodness alone is praised. The first will be last, and the last first.

When God declares that **"the first will be last"**, He takes away all your presumptions and forbids you to exalt yourself, even above a whore, even if you were Abraham, David, Peter, or Paul. But when He says, **"The last will be first"**, He bids you cast off all despair and not to regard yourself unfavourably even in comparison with the saints, even though you were Pilate, Herod, Sodom and Gomorrah.

For just as we have no reason at all for presumption, so also we have no reason for despair.

SL.XI.515,14

PRAYER: Heavenly Father, in your Son and His work of salvation we have all that we need for our faith and life as your children. Keep far from us all presumption and pride, that we always trust in your mercy and grace alone, through Jesus Christ our Lord. Amen.

SATURDAY

LESSON: 1 PETER 3.13-17

As he said this, a woman in the crowd raised her voice and said to him, "Blessed is the womb that bore you, and the breasts that you sucked!" But he said, "Blessed rather are those who hear the word of God and keep it!"

Luke 11.27,28

Here Jesus meets the carnal devotion of these people and teaches all of us that we should not just gape like yokels at the works and superior worth of the saints, but concentrate on God's Word — we should hear and keep God's Word. For the holiness and worthiness of the mother of this child (Mary) is of no great consequence to us and confers nothing at all upon us; nor does it matter how noble her child and the fruit of her womb is.

The only thing that really matters here is what this child has done for us: that He has rescued us from the devil, without any contribution or merit from us. This is portrayed for us by God's Word, which we should hear and keep in firm faith. Then we, too, will be saved like this mother and her child. Although this word and work will inevitably be blasphemed, we shall endure this and reply with "gentleness" (1 Peter 3.15), for the improvement of others.

SL.XI.557,13

PRAYER: Lord God, we thank and praise you for the clarity with which you have revealed your Gospel of salvation by grace alone without any works — even those of the holiest of men — solely and alone through Jesus Christ our Lord. Amen.

SUNDAY

LESSON: LUKE 8.4-15

The ones along the path are those who have heard; then the devil comes and takes away the word from their hearts, that they may not believe and be saved.   Luke 8.12

The first group are those who have heard the Word, but do not really understand it or pay attention to it. These are not the bad people on this earth but the greatest, cleverest, holiest, and also the largest group.

Jesus is not speaking here of those who persecute the Word and do not hear it, but of those who hear it and are its pupils. They also want to be regarded among "the first", live among us in the Christian congregation, and partake with us of Baptism and the Sacrament. But their hearts are carnal and remain so. They do not absorb the Word; it goes in one ear and out of the other. The seed on the path does not penetrate, but lies on top of the path; for the path is beaten down hard by the feet of men and beasts.

Jesus says that the devil comes and takes the Word out of their hearts, so that they do not believe it for their salvation. The devil exerts his power here not only by hardening their hearts with worldly ideas and living, so that they lose the Word and let it go without really understanding it or recognizing it, but the devil also sends them false teachers in place of God's Word who tread God's Word underfoot with the doctrine of men.

SL.XI.516,2-3

PRAYER: Give us at all times a firm understanding of your Word, O God, that we may hold it fast in firm and steadfast faith and resist all the might of Satan in his efforts to rob us of your Word, in Jesus' name. Amen.

MONDAY

LESSON: 2 TIMOTHY 3.10-17

Give no opportunity to the devil.   Ephesians 4.27

Heretics, factionaries and fanatics understand the Gospel carnally, and interpret it in whatever way they wish according to their liking. All these people hear the Gospel, but bring forth no fruit; they are ruled by the devil and are more under the domination of the ordinances of men than they were before they heard the Gospel.

It is really a horrifying statement which Christ makes in the Gospel (Luke 8.4-15) that the devil takes the Word out of their hearts. He thereby testifies that the devil rules mightily over their hearts, despite the fact that they are called Christians and hear the Word.

Likewise, it sounds pitiable that they should be trodden underfoot and be subjected to the doctrines of men, through which also, under the semblance and name of the Gospel, the devil cunningly takes the Word from them so that they never understand it to their salvation, but are lost for ever.

This is how fanatics operate today in all countries. For where this Word does not remain, there is no salvation; not even great works and holy lives will help them here. When Jesus says that they will not be saved because the Word has been taken from them, He clearly demonstrates that not works, but faith, saves through the Word alone, as Paul also declares (Romans 1.16).

SL.XI.517,4

PRAYER: Grant us true steadfastness and firmness of faith, O Lord, that we both know what we believe and continue therein, walking as closely as possible to the Gospel of our Lord and Saviour Jesus Christ, in whose name we also ask this. Amen.

TUESDAY

LESSON: 1 PETER 1.3-9

The ones on the rock are those who, when they hear the word, receive it with joy; but these have no root, they believe for a while and in time of temptation fall away.   Luke 8.13

This group receive the Word with joy but they are not persistent. These also form a large number. They hear and accept the Word without sects, factions or fanatics. They also rejoice in their knowledge of the unimpaired truth, that one is saved without works, through faith, and that they have been freed from the imprisonment of the law, conscience and the doctrine of men.

When a crisis comes, however, and they have to suffer injury, disgrace, loss of life or property, they fall away and deny the Word. They do not have sufficient root and do not stand deep enough. They resemble the seed on the rock, which grows up quickly and becomes green, so that it is a pleasure to behold and gives good promise, but when the sun shines hotly, it withers away because it lacks moisture.

That is also what these hearers do. In time of persecution they deny the Word or keep quiet and do, speak and endure all that their persecutors order them or want them to do. Prior to this, when there was still peace and no heat, they spoke readily, and joyfully confessed the Word so that there was hope that they would bring forth much fruit and be very useful Christians.

These fruits are not works alone, but even more the confession, preaching and spreading of the Word, so that many others are taught and the kingdom of God is extended.

SL.XI.517,5

PRAYER: Strengthen us in the hour of trial and temptation, O Lord, so that by such chastenings we may always come forth stronger in faith, in and through our Saviour Jesus Christ. Amen.

WEDNESDAY

LESSON: MARK 10.17-27

As for what fell among the thorns, they are those who hear, but as they go on their way they are choked by the cares and riches and pleasures of life, and their fruit does not mature.   Luke 8.14

The third group are those who hear the Word and understand it, but still fall out on the other side, namely, among the pleasures and comforts of this life so that they, too, achieve nothing with the Word. This is also a very large number.

Although they do not introduce heresy like the first group, but always retain the Word unalloyed and pure, and are not assailed on the left like the second group with opposition and persecution, they still fall away on the right. Their undoing is that they have peace and good times. They do not really give themselves to the Word in all earnestness, but become lazy. They immerse themselves in cares, riches and pleasures of this life, and their fruit does not mature.

They resemble the seed that fell among the thorns. Although there is no rock there but good earth, no hard-packed path but land ploughed deep enough, the thorns still prevent the seed from coming up, or they choke it.

These people have all that will serve them for salvation in the Word, but they do not make use of it; they rot away in this life, in the flesh. To this number belong those who hear the Word but never tame the flesh. They know what is right, but do not act accordingly. **"Their fruit does not mature."**

SL.XI.518,6

PRAYER: Forgive us, O Lord, all the wasted opportunities that we miss amidst the many pressures and tensions of our daily lives. Grant us grace both to hear your Word with open hearts and, with a ready will, act in accordance with it. Amen.

THURSDAY

LESSON: MATTHEW 10.34-39

As for that in the good soil, they are those who, hearing the word, hold it fast in an honest and good heart, and bring forth fruit with patience.   Luke 8.15

The fourth group are those who grasp the Word and hold on to it with a good heart and bring forth fruit with patience, that is, those who hear the Word and steadfastly hold on to it, so that they risk and give up everything for it.

The devil does not succeed in taking the Word from them, or mislead them in any way in their connection with the Word. The heat of persecution does not drive them from the Word. The thorns of pleasant living and the greed of this world prove no hindrance to them. They bring forth fruit that they may also teach the Word to others and enlarge the kingdom of God. They also do good to their neighbour in accordance with the Word. Hence, Christ says here that they **"bring forth fruit with patience"**.

They certainly also suffer much for the sake of the Word: insults and shameful treatment from the factionaries and heretics; hatred, jealousy, injury to body and property from the persecutors, in addition to what the thorns and their own temptations of the flesh cause.

The Word is well called the Word of the cross, for he who would keep it must bear and overcome cross and misfortune with patience.

SL.XI.519,7

PRAYER: You have often reminded us, Lord Jesus, that as your disciples we will have to bear a cross. Pour your grace and strength upon us that this cross may never crush us, but draw us ever closer to your cross and ultimate victory. Amen.

FRIDAY

LESSON: PSALM 31.15-24

O send out thy light and thy truth; let them lead me, let them bring me to thy holy hill and to thy dwelling!
Psalm 43.3

After hearing the Word, large numbers fall away from it and bring no fruit to perfection. We are told this for our learning so that we should not be led into error.

It is certainly unpleasant to preach to those who treat the Word so disgracefully, and especially set themselves against the Gospel. For this is preaching which is to become so general that it is to be presented to all creatures, as Christ declares, **"Preach the gospel to the whole creation"**, **Mark 16.15**, and as the psalmist puts it, **"Their voice goes out through all the earth, and their words to the end of the world". Psalm 19.4.**

What if many do despise the Word? It must be that many are called but few chosen. For the sake of those who are good seed and who bring forth fruit with patience, seed must also fall in vain on the path, on the rock and among the thorns.

Of one thing we can be sure, and that is that God's Word never departs without producing fruit. It always finds some good ground, as the Gospel also says here, that some of the sower's seed fell on good ground and not only on the path, among the thorns, and on the rock. For wherever the Gospel reaches, there are Christians. **"My word shall not return to me empty." Isaiah 55.11.**

SL.XI.520,10

PRAYER: Grant, O Lord, that the saving power of your Gospel may always be a real incentive for us to spread the teachings of the Gospel in word and deed, for Christ our Saviour's sake. Amen.

SATURDAY

LESSON: EPHESIANS 3.7-13

To you it has been given to know the secrets of the kingdom of God. Luke 8.10

What does He mean when He says: **"To you it has been given to know the secrets of the kingdom of God"**? What is a "secret" here? If one cannot know it, why does one preach it?

"Secret" means a hidden, concealed matter which one does not know, and **"the secrets of the kingdom of God"** are the matters in God's kingdom which are hidden. Christ, with all the grace He has manifested to us as Paul describes Him, is one of these "secrets". He who knows Christ aright, knows what God's kingdom is and what it contains.

This is called a "secret" because it is spiritual and concealed, and remains so unless the Spirit reveals it. For there are many who see it and hear about it but who do not accept it.

There are many today who preach Christ and hear how He was given for us. But this is often only a matter of the tongue, not of the heart. They do not believe it themselves and have no real experience of it, for as Paul declares, **"The unspiritual man does not receive the gifts of the Spirit of God"**. 1 Corinthians 2.14.

So Christ says here, **"To you it has been given"**, that is, the Holy Spirit has enabled you not only to hear and to see, but to recognize and to believe with your hearts, and therefore it is no longer a "secret" for you.

SL.XI.523,19

PRAYER: Thanks and praise be to you, O heavenly Father, for the revelation of the mystery of your grace in Christ Jesus our Lord which you have made known to us in the Gospel. Establish us in this grace that we may witness to it before our fellowmen, for Christ's sake. Amen.

SUNDAY

LESSON: MATTHEW 26.1-13

The next day he saw Jesus coming toward him, and said, "Behold, the Lamb of God, who takes away the sin of the world!"   John 1.29

In many people the passion of Christ arouses little more than sympathy. They lament and bemoan the fact that He suffered innocently. A great multitude of women followed Jesus near the end of His public ministry "who bewailed and lamented him". Jesus tried to set them right when He said to them, **"Daughters of Jerusalem, do not weep for me, but weep for yourselves and for your children".** Luke 23.28.

Along these lines many make rather wide excursions during the passion season. They make a lot of the sad farewell of Jesus from His friends at Bethany with rather liberal portions of the pains and sorrows of the Virgin, but they hardly get any further than this. In this way Christ's passion is inordinately delayed so that God only knows whether it was thought up to put men to sleep rather than to keep them awake. In this same group we must place those who teach that much benefit is derived during the passion season from various holy exercises, fasts and special devotions.

If we are not reminded of Christ's sufferings on our behalf in all this, it becomes nothing but an unfruitful work, no matter how good and worthy it may be in itself. What does it help you for God to be God, if He is not God for you? What use is there in the healthiness and goodness of eating and drinking if it is not healthy for you? This is exactly the situation in regard to special Lenten exercises when men do not seek the correct benefit from them.

SL.XI.576,3

PRAYER: Dear Lord, instruct our faith so that we always view your passion as a suffering for us and on our behalf, a work of love which you assumed as our Saviour and Redeemer. Amen.

MONDAY

LESSON: MATTHEW 26.14-25

Thanks be to God for his inexpressible gift!
2 Corinthians 9.15

If we are considering the passion of Christ in the correct way, its immediate effect on us should be a feeling of deep shock and an uneasy conscience. We should be deeply shocked when we see the harsh wrath of God and His unrelenting seriousness in dealing with sin and sinners. He is not prepared to release sinners to His only and dearly beloved Son unless this Son assumes a very heavy penalty on their behalf. He Himself tells us through the prophet that this Son was "**stricken for the transgression of my people**". **Isaiah 53.8**.

What can ever befall the sinner after the most beloved Son has been smitten in this way? There must have been unspeakable and unrelenting seriousness here if it required such an immeasurably great Person to render satisfaction and to suffer and die in this connection.

If you ponder the matter deeply enough and remember that it is God's own Son, the eternal wisdom of the Father, who is suffering here, you will be shocked, and the deeper you ponder it, the more deeply you will be shocked.

Fix it firmly in your heart and mind and have no doubt at all that it was you who brought all this suffering upon Christ. Your sins were responsible for the sufferings of Christ.

SL.XI.576,4

PRAYER: Dear heavenly Father, we can only stutter in response to the unspeakable grace and mercy which you have bestowed upon us in the suffering and death of your dearly beloved Son. Accept this stuttering in the name of Jesus Christ our Saviour. Amen.

TUESDAY

LESSON: MATTHEW 26.26-35

Then Jesus told his disciples, "If any man would come after me, let him deny himself and take up his cross and follow me".   Matthew 16.24

This life is nothing else but a life of faith, love, and the holy cross. But these three never reach a stage of perfection in us as long as we live here on earth, and no one ever reached perfection in this respect except Christ. He is the Sun and has been given to us and set up for us as an example whom we must imitate.

There are always some to be found in our midst who are weak, others strong, and still others who are stronger. Some can suffer only a little and others much. But we must all continue in the likeness of Christ. For this life follows a course in which we proceed continually from faith to faith, from love to love, from patience to patience, from cross to cross.

It is not a matter of being righteous but of being justified. We have not yet reached our goal; we are all on the path and on the way, but some are further along than others. God is satisfied when He finds us at work with a definite purpose. If He so wills it, He comes quickly and strengthens our faith and love and He can translate us in a moment from this life into heaven. But as long as we are on this earth we must bear with each other as Christ bore with us, always remembering also that none of us is ever quite perfect.

SL.XI.600,31

PRAYER: You know all our weaknesses, shortcomings, failures and sins, heavenly Father. Help us in your means of grace to the improvement and progress which is a characteristic of your children, through Christ Jesus the Saviour. Amen.

ASH WEDNESDAY

LESSON: PSALM 32.1-7

If thou, O Lord, shouldst mark iniquities, Lord, who could stand? But there is forgiveness with thee, that thou mayest be feared.   Psalm 130.3,4

David says in the psalm, "**I acknowledged my sin to thee, and I did not hide my iniquity; I said, 'I will confess my transgressions to the Lord'; then thou didst forgive the guilt of my sin**". **Psalm 32.5.** No one can stand before God without bringing this confession of sins with him. That is why the psalmist also declares: "If thou, O Lord, shouldst mark iniquities, Lord, who could stand? But there is forgiveness with thee, that thou mayest be feared." **Psalm 130.3,4.**

Anyone who really wants to stand before God must be quite sure that this confession of sins really comes from his heart and firmly believe that, unless the Lord is merciful to him, all is lost, no matter how pious he is in himself. Even all the saints must acknowledge the need of God's continual grace and mercy and in all humility confess their sins before Him.

There is no difference here, for all have sinned. If anyone has received special grace, thank God for it and do not boast. If anyone has fallen into sin, it simply demonstrates that he is flesh and blood. But no one has fallen so deeply that one who still stands may not fall ever deeper. As far as we are concerned, there is no difference between us and others; it is God's grace alone that divides us from others.

This confesson of sin is so necessary that we dare not overlook it for a moment. It must be our concern during our whole life as a Christian. Without ceasing we must evermore praise God's grace and recognize that all boasting on our part is vain before God.

SL.XI.584,4-5

PRAYER: Because of your wonderful grace, Lord God, loving heavenly Father, we poor sinners can stand before you confessing our sins. When we do this, give us the assurance of the forgiveness of sins, in and through our Saviour Jesus Christ. Amen.

THURSDAY

LESSON: MATTHEW 26.36-46

He was wounded for our trangressions, he was bruised for our iniquities.   Isaiah 53.5

Christ's passion should help us to a knowledge of self, to be horrified at ourselves and to bring us to contrition. If this is not the result of Christ's passion as far as we are concerned, it has not yet achieved its purpose in us. In His passion, Christ placed Himself on an equal footing with us, so that as He suffered in body and soul in a wretched manner because of our sins, so we must also suffer with Him in the knowledge of our sins. This is no matter for many words, but for deep thinking and a proper estimate of our sins.

Consider this illustration! If a criminal was convicted of murdering the child of a prince or a king, and you were quite unconcerned, sang and played as though you were quite innocent until a terrible attack was launched upon you and it was proved that you had prevailed upon the criminal to commit his crime, the world would become too narrow for you, especially if your conscience left you in the lurch.

You should become much more anxious when you ponder the sufferings of Christ. For although the Jews, the criminals, have come under God's judgement and have been cast off, they were merely the ministers of your sin. You are really the one who through your sin throttled and crucified God's Son.

SL.XI.578,8

PRAYER: My sin and guilt, Lord Jesus, were no small part of your passion, suffering and death: I thank you, Lord, for the riches of your grace and mercy and, above all, for your wonderful love to me and all other sinners. Amen.

FRIDAY

LESSON: MATTHEW 26.47-56

Rejoice in so far as you share Christ's sufferings, that you may also rejoice and be glad when his glory is revealed.
1 Peter 4.13

Anyone who remains so completely unmoved and hard-boiled that the sufferings of Christ do not horrify him and bring him to his senses, has cause to be afraid. For it cannot be otherwise; you must become conformed to the image and suffering of Christ either in this life or in hell. At the very least, you must be terrified in the face of death, tremble and quake, and feel everything that Christ suffered on the cross.

It is a gruesome experience to witness agony on a death-bed. Therefore you should pray God to soften your heart and permit you to ponder the suffering of Christ fruitfully. It is impossible for us of ourselves to ponder the sufferings of Christ thoroughly unless God Himself implants the resolution in our hearts. Pray God that this contemplation of Christ's sufferings may not result in any doctrine or teaching which you hurry to accomplish of yourself before you have earnestly sought God's grace so that you accomplish it by His grace and not of yourself.

Here we see why so many have gone astray in regard to the sufferings of Christ. They do not pray to God for His grace to profit from Christ's passion, but they try to attain their end in their own strength and by their own methods. They operate in a thoroughly human and unfruitful manner.

SL.XI.579,9

PRAYER: Soften our hearts, O God, by your grace that we may fruitfully ponder the sufferings of Christ and see in them the stripes whereby we are healed, for the sake of Jesus our Saviour. Amen.

SATURDAY

LESSON: MATTHEW 26.57-58

If any one is in Christ, he is a new creation; the old has passed away, behold, the new has come.

2 Corinthians 5.17

We have no hesitation at all in declaring that anyone who contemplates God's sufferings for a day, an hour, a quarter of an hour, does better than fasting for a whole year, praying a psalm every day, and hearing a hundred masses. For such contemplation changes a man quite basically and is very close to the new birth of baptism. Here the sufferings of Christ perform their true and noble work. They choke the Old Adam and dispel all pleasure, joy and confidence in creatures, even as Christ was forsaken by all and even by God.

Because this work is not under our control, it happens that at times we must pray for it. The result does not follow immediately. Nevertheless, we must not lose heart and desist from our efforts. Sometimes it happens that we do not pray in accordance with God's will. God acts in freedom and will not become our captive. And so a man may become saddened in his conscience and very dissatisfied with his life without realizing that it is Christ's sufferings of which he thinks very little that are influencing him in this way just as others can ponder Christ's sufferings almost continuously without ever coming to self-knowledge. With the former, the sufferings of Christ are a hidden but genuine factor, with the latter they are merely apparent and deceptive. In this way God often brings the unexpected to pass.

SL.XI.579,10-11

PRAYER: Keep us ever mindful, heavenly Father, of the grim reality of the suffering and death of our Lord, and grant us your grace fully to accept all that our Lord gave and suffered for us, in our stead. Amen.

SUNDAY

LESSON:MATTHEW 4.1-11

We are his workmanship, created in Christ Jesus for good works, which God prepared beforehand, that we should walk in them.   Ephesians 2.10

It is customary to read the Gospel of Christ's temptation by the devil at the beginning of the season of Lent to set Christ's example before Christians and encourage them to fast as Christ fasted.

This is utter tomfoolery!

In the first place, no one can ever measure up to such an example and fast without any food at all for forty days and nights as Christ did. Christ, moreover, followed the example of Moses, who also fasted for forty days and nights when he received God's law on Mount Sinai. Accordingly, Christ also wanted to fast when He was about to bring us the new law and to publish it.

In the second place, our fasting is a complete mistake instituted by men. Although Christ fasted for forty days, there is nothing at all in His Word in which He orders us to do likewise. He probably also did other things that He does not want us to do. But what He tells us to do and not to do we should keep carefully in mind, and act according to His Word.

Our worst mistake of all was to regard and practise our fasting as a good work. We did not fast to discipline our flesh, but to acquire merit before God, to blot out our sins and to obtain grace.

SL.XI.532,1-2

PRAYER: You have bound us, O Lord, as your children to your Word as our rule of faith and life. In this Word you assure us we shall know the truth and the truth will set us free. This we also pray in your name. Amen.

MONDAY

LESSON: ROMANS 8.12-17

Then Jesus was led up by the Spirit into the wilderness to be tempted by the devil.   Matthew 4.1

There is a reason why the evangelist with considerable care states right at the beginning of this Gospel that Jesus was led by the Spirit into the wilderness, that He fasted there and was tempted. The reason for this is that no one should ever presume to follow Christ's example by his own choice and make a selfish fast of it, decided by his own will alone. He should wait for the Spirit, who will send him quite enough fasting and temptation.

Anyone who deliberately courts the danger of hunger or any other temptation when, under the blessing of God, he can eat, drink and enjoy the other comforts of life, is tempting God. We should never seek out shortages and temptation. They will doubtless come of themselves to give us ample opportunity to do our best in noble fashion.

We read that **"Jesus was led by the Spirit into the wilderness"**, not "Jesus chose the wilderness for Himself". Paul also says, **"All who are led by the Spirit of God are the sons of God". Romans 8.14**. God gives His blessings for us to use them with thanksgiving and not to despise them. He does not bless us so that we should tempt Him.

SL.XI.534,4

PRAYER: Enlighten us and guide us by your Holy Spirit, heavenly Father, that we never presume to tempt you in disregard of your blessings but use them to your greater glory, in and through Jesus Christ our Saviour. Amen.

TUESDAY

LESSON: LUKE 12.22-31

**Although he was a Son, he learned obedience through
what he suffered; and being made perfect he became the
source of eternal salvation to all who obey him.**

Hebrews 5.8,9

The account of Christ's temptation has been written both
for our learning and admonition.

First, we should learn here how Christ by His fasting,
hunger, temptation and victory served us and helped us.
Accordingly, he who believes in Christ shall suffer no want,
and no temptation can harm him. He will have sufficient in
the midst of need, and he will be safe in the midst of
temptation. His Lord and head has conquered for him and for
his benefit in all these respects. Of this he is quite sure, for
his Lord has declared, **"Be of good cheer, I have overcome
the world"**. **John 16.33**. If God could nourish Christ for forty
days without food, He can also nourish His Christians.

Secondly, this example also admonishes us to endure want
and temptation gladly in the service of God and for the good
of our neighbour, as Christ did for us, as often as the need
arises. It will certainly arise if we are to teach and confess
God's Word. Therefore, this Gospel is a wonderful
consolation and strengthening against our unbelieving and
shameless flesh. It establishes and strengthens our
conscience that we do not plague ourselves with worry about
our bodily welfare, but are certain that He will and can
nourish us.

SL.XI.534,5-6

*PRAYER: Thanks and praise be to you, O Lord our
Saviour, for all that you suffered in our stead and on our
behalf. Bless us at all times with your gifts that we gladly
suffer in the service of God and for the benefit of our
neighbour, for your mercy's sake. Amen.*

WEDNESDAY

LESSON: MATTHEW 26.36-41

If you are the Son of God, command these stones to become loaves of bread.   Matthew 4.3

After approaching Christ, the devil assails Him by confronting Him with His bodily welfare and casting doubt on God's goodness, saying, **"If you are the Son of God, command these stones to become loaves of bread"**.

It is as though he meant to say: "Rely on God and don't bake; wait until a roasted rooster flies into your mouth. Do you now claim that you still have a God who cares for you? Where now is your heavenly Father, who looks after you? I am telling you, He is leaving you in the lurch. Eat up now and drink in faith and let us see how satisfied you will be, especially if they are stones. What a fine Son of God you are! What a Father He is to you, when He does not even send you a crust of bread, and lets you be so poor and needy. Just keep on believing that you are His Son and He is your Father."

With such thoughts the devil assails all the children of God. Christ certainly experienced all this. He was no stock or stone, although He was pure and without sin and remained so, as we cannot be.

SL.XI.536.8

PRAYER: For our sakes, O Lord, you suffered yourself to be tempted by our enemy, the devil, and overcame him with the powerful testimony of your Father's holy Word. Enable us, your disciples, to gain a similar victory over the devil whenever we are assailed by him, for your truth's sake. Amen.

THURSDAY

LESSON: EPHESIANS 6.10-17

Jesus said to him, "Again it is written, 'You shall not tempt the Lord your God'."   Matthew 4.7

The devil's second temptation is quite different from the first one, but quite similar to it in its absurdity.

Here the devil teaches us to tempt God, just as he urged Christ to throw Himself from a pinnacle of the temple. This was quite unnecessary in any case, because there would probably have been a good set of stairs available on which He could have climbed down. That the devil here tried to induce Christ to a temptation of God is quite clear from Christ's reply.

Wherever the devil comes upon a heart that trusts God in the hour of want and need, he quickly abandons concerns for bodily welfare and greed and makes his assault from quite a different angle. "If you want to be all spiritual and trusting", he says, "I'll give you some help". He proceeds to come at you from another direction: he tries to get you to put your faith into something that God has not commanded you to believe and does not want you to believe.

It may be that God has supplied your house with bread, as He does annually throughout the whole world, and you refuse to make use of it, making want and need for yourself, declaring, "We are to put our faith in God. I will not eat the bread, but wait till God sends me bread from heaven." That would be tempting God. For He does not tell you that you must still hope for what you already have and keep on working for it. How can you hope for something you already have?

SL.XI.539,17-18

PRAYER: Lord God, heavenly Father, our old evil foe, the devil, was cunning enough and brazen enough to attack even your Son, our Lord Jesus Christ. When he tempts us into unbelief and wrong beliefs, you have shown in your Son's example how to overcome the devil's temptations. Grant us your grace and strength to do this in the name of Jesus. Amen.

123

FRIDAY

LESSON: JAMES 4.5-10

Again, the devil took him to a very high mountain, and showed him all the kingdoms of the world and the glory of them; and he said to him, "All these I will give you, if you will fall down and worship me".   Matthew 4.8,9

The third temptation is concerned with temporal honour and power.

Those who fall away from the faith for the sake of honour and power, are victims of this temptation. They want to enjoy nothing but good days here on earth, and believe only as far as honour and glory will permit. To this class belong also the heretics, who cause sects and factions among Christians so that they may go their way before the world and float about in honour.

You can place this third temptation on the right-hand side and the first one on the left-hand side. The first temptation concerns misfortune which stirs up anger, impatience and unbelief in us; the third and last is a temptation of good fortune in which one is urged to seek pleasure, honour, joy and everything exalted.

The second, middle temptation is altogether spiritual, and concerns itself with freakish pranks and error to mislead us in our understanding and to draw us away from faith.

SL.XI.542,23

PRAYER: Lord, preserve us by the power of your Word against all the ragings and ravings of our old evil foe, Satan, and all his machinations, in the name of Jesus our Saviour. Amen.

SATURDAY

LESSON: PSALM 34.1-10

Then the devil left him, and behold, angels came and ministered to him.   Matthew 4.11

Finally, the angels came to Him and ministered to Him. This must have taken place in a bodily manner. They appeared as bodily ministrants and brought Him food and drink and ministered to His needs at the table and in all other ways. They rendered external services to His body.

The devil, His tempter, without a doubt also appeared in a bodily form, perhaps also as an angel. For he must have been something higher than a human being to place Him on a pinnacle of the temple and to show Him all the kingdoms of the world in a moment. That the devil was something higher than a man is also apparent in his offer of all the kingdoms of the world, and the suggestion that Christ should worship him. He certainly did not appear here in his true colours, for when he wants to lie and deceive he tries to look beautiful. St. Paul says that he **"disguises himself as an angel of light"**. **2 Corinthians 11.14.**

What we read in the Gospel is for our comfort. We should learn that where one devil assails us, many angels can minister to us. If we fight manfully and resist the devil, God will not let us suffer want. He will send His angels to minister to us and at times they can even serve us as our bakers, butlers and cooks, and help us in our every need. This was not written for Christ's sake: He did not need this. If the angels ministered to Him, they can also minister to us.

SL.XI.544,27

PRAYER: Lord God, our heavenly Father, send your holy angels to us that by their ministrations we may be protected from all harm and danger and ever rest in your grace, in and through our Saviour Jesus Christ. Amen.

SUNDAY

LESSON: MATTHEW 15.21-28

Immediately a woman, whose little daughter was possessed by an unclean spirit, heard of him, and came and fell down at his feet.   Mark 7.25

In this Canaanite woman we see that true faith is confidence of the heart in the grace and goodness of God, revealed and experienced through God's Word. St. Mark tells us that she had "heard" of Jesus: a report about Jesus had somehow or other reached her. What kind of report? Without a doubt, it was a good report that was being noised about: that Christ was a godly man who readily helped everyone. Such a report about God is real gospel and a word of grace. It awakened faith in this woman, for if she had not believed, she would not have followed after Jesus.

How does it come to pass that many more heard this good report about Christ, who did not follow after Him and paid no attention to this good report? The answer is that the physician is useful and welcome to the sick, but those who are well pay no attention to Him. The Canaanite woman, however, felt her need, and so she followed this sweet report.

Moses must also precede here and teach men to recognize their sins so that grace may become sweet and welcome. It is labour lost to portray Christ in the most friendly and lovable manner, unless men have been humbled previously by self-knowledge and hunger for Christ, as the Magnificat also declares, **"He has filled the hungry with good things, and the rich he has sent empty away"**. Luke 1.53.

This is all said and written for those who are distressed, poor, needy, sinful and despised, so that in all their needs they may know to whom they should flee to seek consolation and help.

SL.XI.544,1-2

PRAYER: We know full well, O Lord, that of ourselves and by our merits we are poor, lost and condemned sinners. Eternal thanks and praise be to you for the sweet news of salvation which you have revealed to us in your Gospel of salvation, in and through Jesus Christ our Saviour. Amen.

MONDAY

LESSON: 1 PETER 1.16-21

Behold, a Canaanite woman from that region came out and cried, "Have mercy on me, O Lord, Son of David; my daughter is severely possessed by a demon". But he did not answer her a word. Matthew 15.22,23

Note how Christ hammers and drives faith into His believers so that it becomes strong and firm! First, when the Canaanite woman follows the good report she has heard about Christ and cries to Him in the sure confidence that in accordance with this report He will also treat her graciously, Christ presents a completely different picture to the woman.

She soon had grounds for believing that her faith and good confidence in Him were quite misplaced. She had every reason to ask: "Is this the good, friendly man?" or, "Are these the good words I heard reported of Him and on which I relied? It cannot be true. He is your foe. He does not want to have anything to do with you. He might as well tell me outright: I don't want to have anything to do with you! But now He is as silent as a stone."

This is a heavy rebuff when God presents such a stern and angry face and completely hides His grace, as those well know who feel and experience in their hearts the thought that God will not keep what He has spoken and will allow His Word to prove itself false. This happened to the children of Israel at the Red Sea. In other ways it has been the experience of many other saints.

What does this woman do in such a situation? She simply disregards the unfriendly countenance of Christ and does not let any of this lead her astray. She does not take it all according to the letter. She remains absolutely firm in her reliance on the good report she has received and will not be removed from it.

SL.XI.546,3

PRAYER: Heavenly Father, we thank and praise you for the certainty of truth and salvation which you have revealed to us in your Gospel of salvation. We pray for the grace to keep us ever firmly fixed in our faith in you and your Gospel, in and through Jesus our Saviour. Amen.

TUESDAY

LESSON: COLOSSIANS 1.21-23

His disciples came and begged him, saying, "Send her away, for she is crying after us". He answered, "I was sent only to the lost sheep of the house of Israel".

Matthew 15.23,24

When the cries and faith of the Canaanite woman prove fruitless, the disciples of Christ lodge an appeal on her behalf in the belief that they will certainly be heard. But when they suggest that Christ should become more lenient, He actually becomes harder and renders the faith and prayer of both parties ineffective — as it seems to their feelings. For He does not remain silent here and leave them in doubt; He declines their plea and declares, "**I was sent only to the lost sheep of the house of Israel**".

This rebuff is even more severe, for not only are our own persons rejected; the only consolation still available to us is also cut off, namely, the consolation and intercession of godly and holy people on our behalf. For when we feel that God is no longer gracious to us, and we find ourselves entangled in a very distressing situation, it is our last resort to turn for counsel and help to godly men who are led by the Spirit of God. If these men are willing to do for us what love demands of them, but nothing comes of all their efforts, and they have not even been given a hearing, we really find ourselves in a worse plight than before their intervention on our behalf.

Even this rebuff did not weaken the faith of this Canaanite woman. She still believed and trusted in the good report she had heard of Christ.

SL.XI.547,5

PRAYER: Your promises and assurances to us, O Lord, are true and steadfast. Grant us at all times such confidence in the declarations of your Gospel that we never waver in faith, but ever stand fast in your grace, for Christ's sake. Amen.

WEDNESDAY

LESSON: LUKE 11.5-13

We share in Christ, if only we hold our first confidence firm to the end.   Hebrews 3.14

When we hear how Christ answered the Canaanite woman in the Gospel (Matthew 15.21-26), we are in a way reminded of quite a number of remarkable statements that He made to His disciples on various occasions. He said to them, **"If two of you agree on earth about anything they ask, it will be done for them by my Father in heaven".** Matthew 18.19. In Mark we read, **"Whatever you ask in prayer, believe that you receive it, and you will".** Mark 11.24. There are also many other passages of this kind.

What has come of all these promises here? He soon answers and says, "It is true that I hear all prayers; but such promises I have made only to the house of Israel".

Is this not a real thunderclap which shatters both heart and faith into a thousand pieces? The Word of God, on which the woman has built her faith, is not spoken to her, it concerns others. Here all saints and all intercession must become silent; here the heart must let the Word go, if it is to allow the feelings to decide the matter.

But what does the woman do? She does not give up. She still clings to the Word, even though it seems that an attempt is being made to force her to give it up. She does not heed the stern words of Christ. She still has the firm conviction that somehow or other Christ's goodness is still concealed under all this. She is still not prepared to form the judgement that Christ is ungracious or that He can be ungracious. This is what it means to hold fast!

SL.XI.547,6-7

PRAYER: Grant us a full measure of your grace, heavenly Father, so that despite all the obstacles our faith meets in a world where there is much sin and opposition to your holy will, we may still maintain a firm and unwavering faith in and through our Saviour Jesus Christ. Amen.

THURSDAY

LESSON: ROMANS 9.14-24

She came and knelt before him, saying, "Lord, help me".
Matthew 15.25

The Canaanite woman came to Jesus in a house, as Mark tells us, **"and fell down at his feet", Mark 7.25,** and made her plea: **"Lord, help me!"**

It was now that she received the mortal blow. Before all present, she was told in so many words that she was a dog, not worthy to partake of the children's bread. What will she say to this? Here she has heard the very worst. She is one of the lost who have been damned, who are not to be reckoned with the elect.

This is a final, irrevocable reply and no one can debate it. But she does not desist. She concurs with Christ's judgement and agrees with it. She is a dog, and she wants no more than a dog, namely, to eat the crumbs which fall from the master's table.

Is this not a master-touch? She takes Christ captive with His own words. He compares her with a dog. She accepts the comparison and asks for no more than permission to be such a dog, as He Himself has judged her to be. Where was He to turn? He was caught. One lets a dog have the crumbs under the table; these are his right.

He now opens up to the woman and grants her what she wishes. She is now not a dog but also a child of Israel.

SL.XI.548,8-9

PRAYER: Thanks and praise be to you, our loving heavenly Father, for the mercy and grace which brought us to faith in you and your promises and which has kept us in this faith, in and through Jesus Christ our Saviour. Amen.

FRIDAY

LESSON: PSALM 46

Let us hold fast the confession of our hope without wavering, for he who promised is faithful.   Hebrews 10.23

What we are told about the Canaanite woman and her faith (Matthew 15.21-28) has been written for our comfort and instruction, that we may learn how deeply God at times hides His grace from us. We should not form our estimate of Him according to our feelings and speculations, but hold absolutely and completely to His Word.

Here we see that although Christ takes up a very inflexible position, He does not make any final judgements by expressly saying "No". His replies all seem to be negative, but they do not contain a final "No". They hang and float in the air.

He does not say, "I will not listen to her", but remains silent, saying neither "Yes" nor "No". Nor does He say that she is not from the house of Israel. He simply states that He is sent only to the house of Israel. He lets the matter hang and float between "Yes" and "No". Nor does He say, "You are a dog; you should not receive any of the children's bread". He says, "It is not fair to take the children's bread and throw it to the dogs". He lets it hang and float whether she is a dog or not. But all his replies seem to imply a "No" rather than a "Yes", and yet there is more of "Yes" in his replies than "No".

There is "Yes" here and nothing but "Yes", but it is deep and hidden and seems to be "No".

SL.XI.548,10

PRAYER: There are times, heavenly Father, when we feel that you are far away from us and that your grace is hidden from us. Open our eyes at such times with the light of your truth so that we see clearly that your grace and love are steadfast and unchanging and ever available to us in and through our Saviour. Amen.

SATURDAY

LESSON: PSALM 33.13-22

Cast your burden on the Lord, and he will sustain you.
Psalm 55.22

That God nourishes the whole world by means of bread and not only through the Word without bread, has its special reason. God is concealing His work under this procedure in order to exercise our faith.

In the case of the children of Israel also, He issued orders for them to arm themselves and fight, but He did not want them to gain the victory through their sword and their own deeds. He Himself wanted to defeat their enemies and gain the victory under their sword and through their deeds. Here He could also have said, "The warrior does not gain the victory through his own sword alone, but through every word which proceeds from the mouth of the Lord".

David also says, **"Not in my bow do I trust, nor can my sword save me".** Psalm 44.6. **"His delight is not in the strength of the horse, nor his pleasure in the legs of a man."** Psalm 147.10.

He still makes use of man and horse, sword and bow, but He fights and He accomplishes everything without the power and might of the man and the horse. The latter are merely curtains and coverings for His might and power. This is proved by the fact that He has often acted, and still often acts daily, without man and horse where necessity demands it, and where there is no possibility of a temptation of Himself being involved.

SL.XI.538,15

PRAYER: Lord God, heavenly Father, our stay and support in all our needs, grant us such an understanding of your Word, and trust in its teachings, that we always accept all its consolations in firm assurance, in and through Christ our Lord. Amen.

SUNDAY

LESSON: LUKE 11.14-28

He was casting out a demon that was dumb; when the demon had gone out, the dumb man spoke.   Luke 11.14

This is a beautiful Gospel in which we learn a great deal about many different things and in it there is portrayed almost all that Christ, His kingdom and Gospel are. We learn what the Gospel achieves and how it makes its way in the world.

First of all, as do all the Gospels, it teaches us faith and love, for it holds up Christ before us as a saviour and helper in all needs, out of His great love. He who believes this is saved.

Here we see also that He has nothing to do with those who are well, but with the poor man who is ailing under many troubles. He was blind, as Matthew tells us (12.22), and dumb and possessed by a demon, as Luke says. Most of the deaf are also dumb, so that in Greek the same word is used for deaf and dumb.

The concern of Jesus for this poor man is an incentive for us to turn to Him in every need, expecting from Him all that is good. After experiencing good at His hands, we should follow Him in love and do good to others, as He has done good to us. This is the common and most delightful teaching of this Gospel and of all the Gospels throughout the whole church year.

This poor dumb man, moreover, did not come to Jesus without the Word. Those who brought him to Jesus must have heard of Christ's love, and this moved them to put their trust in Him. Let us always remember that faith comes through the Word.

SL.XI.552,1

PRAYER: Lord Jesus, your love and compassion for men in their trials and troubles was truly wonderful. Be to us a helper and saviour also today, for your mercy's sake. Amen.

133

MONDAY

LESSON: COLOSSIANS 4.2-6

But some of them said, "He casts out demons by Be-elzebul, the prince of demons" . . . But he, knowing their thoughts, said to them, "Every kingdom divided against itself is laid waste, and house falls upon house. And if Satan also is divided against himself, how will his kingdom stand? For you say that I cast out demons by Be-elzebul."

Luke 11.15,17,18

What did these slanderers reply to this clear logic of Jesus? Their mouth was stopped and their heart was hardened so that they put forward no more questions. For a hardened heart is no longer open to instruction, no matter how brightly and clearly the truth is set forth. But the faith of the godly is strengthened hereby when they see that the ground for their faith is true and good.

For the sake of the godly, answers must at times be given to those who are hardened, and their mouths stopped. Even though they are not converted or silenced, it serves a good purpose to have their stubborn folly revealed, showing that the longer they speak the more their folly increases.

From this it also can be deduced that their cause does not even have the appearance of being good and true as Solomon also says, "Answer a fool according to his folly, lest he be wise in his own eyes". Proverbs 26.5. His meaning is that we should answer him according to his folly, to put him to shame, for the sake of others, so that they do not follow him and are not deceived by him, as though he were in the right.

Otherwise, where there is no such special reason, it is better to be silent, as Solomon says in the same context, "Answer not a fool according to his folly, lest you be like him yourself". Proverbs 26.4.

SL.XI.553,4

PRAYER: O Lord, give us at all times the courage to speak out boldly for the sake of others and wisdom to be silent lest we increase the folly of others by our speaking. Amen.

TUESDAY

LESSON: TITUS 3.8-11

Jesus rebuked him, saying, "Be silent, and come out of him!" And the unclean spirit, convulsing him and crying with a loud voice, came out of him.   Mark 1.25,26

No one should imagine that the evil spirits at times present an appearance of disunity and that one yields to the other to deceive men. For it is quite evident that they offer resistance, demur, cry out and storm, tear and rage when they sense that an earnest effort is being made to drive them out. They are opposed to Christ and at variance with Him, yielding to Him under compulsion and unwillingly. Nothing is left here but the patent and blasphemous lie in which they are held fast and disgraced, so they seize upon God's work out of poisonous hatred and jealousy in the interests of the devil.

From this we should learn not to be unduly surprised if our doctrine and conduct is blasphemed, and if hardened hearts are never satisfied and converted, even though they have been overcome by palpable truth and their mouths have been stopped.

It is enough that their hardened folly has been disclosed by our answer before the godly, recognized for what it is, and brought to naught so that the godly may not be misled by any mere appearance of good. Thereafter, let them go their own way. Such people are perverted and sinful and even "self-condemned", as Paul reminds Titus (3.11).

SL.XI.553,5

PRAYER: In your mercy and grace, O Lord, direct and govern all our efforts as your disciples, that the best interests of your kingdom are always served and our neighbour's welfare is promoted, in the name of Jesus our Saviour. Amen.

WEDNESDAY

LESSON: 1 CORINTHIANS 2.1-5

Therefore, they [your sons] shall be your judges. But if it is by the finger of God I cast out demons, then the kingdom of God has come upon you.   Luke 11.19,20

When Jesus tells the Jews, who question His authority to cast out demons and ascribe it to the devil, that their sons will be their judges, He means to say that He is appealing to these sons. These sons will be forced to pronounce the judgement that they are slandering Him unjustly, and condemning themselves in doing so.

If one devil does not drive out another devil, there must be another power operative here which is neither devilish nor human, namely, divine power. Jesus continues, "But if it is by the finger of God that I cast out demons, then the kingdom of God has come upon you". This **"finger of God"** Matthew clearly designates as **"the Spirit of God"**, for in describing this same event he reports Jesus as saying, **"If it is by the Spirit of God that I cast out demons . . ."** **Matthew 12.28.**

In short, Christ here wants to say, "If the kingdom of God is to come to you, the devil must be driven out, for his kingdom is opposed to God's kingdom, as you yourselves must confess. But the devil is not driven out by a devil, much less by men or through the power of men. He is driven out only through the Spirit and the power of God."

SL.XI.554,7

PRAYER: According to your Word and promises, O Lord, let your kingdom of grace come to us and be established in our midst, through the active working of your Holy Spirit in the means of grace, for the Saviour's sake. Amen.

THURSDAY

LESSON: EPHESIANS 6.12-17

If Satan also is divided against himself, how will his kingdom stand? . . . If it is by the finger of God that I cast out demons, then the kingdom of God has come upon you.
Luke 11.18,20

From Christ's words in this Gospel it follows that where God's finger does not drive out the devil, the devil's kingdom still stands, and where the devil's kingdom is, there is no kingdom of God. It follows quite conclusively that as long as the Holy Spirit has not come to us, we are not only incapable of accomplishing what is good, but are of necessity in the devil's kingdom.

If we are in the devil's kingdom, we cannot possibly do anything else but what pleases the devil; otherwise it could not be called his kingdom. Paul suggests that such people are caught in the snare of the devil, being captured by him to do his will (2 Timothy 2.26). How could the devil permit the subjects of his kingdom to follow their own inclinations in doing what is against his kingdom and not for his kingdom?

Christ here makes a most striking, shocking but important statement when He assigns a kingdom to the devil that cannot be avoided when the Holy Spirit is absent. He also declares that God's kingdom cannot come unless the devil's kingdom is driven from us with God's own power from heaven.

SL.XI.555,8

PRAYER: Dear Lord Jesus, in your glorious resurrection from the dead you proclaimed your victory over sin, death and the devil. Fill our hearts with such trust in your victory that we go from strength to strength in the power of your truth, for your love's sake. Amen.

FRIDAY

LESSON: ROMANS 16.17-20

When a strong man, fully armed, guards his own palace, his goods are in peace; but when one stronger than he assails him and overcomes him, he takes away his armour in which he trusted, and divides his spoil.   Luke 11.21,22

In this illustration taken from everyday life Jesus demonstrates that no one but God alone can really overcome the devil. No one is ever in a position to boast that he can of himself drive out sin and the devil.

Note well how He describes the devil. He calls him "**a strong man**" who is fully armed and guards his own palace. That is, the devil not only has possession of the world as his own kingdom, but he also has it guarded and supported so that no one can take it from him. It is also a kingdom with inner peace that carries out his will.

Just as little as a house or court may successfully oppose or guard itself against a tyrant who really has possession of it, so little can free will or human might avail against sin and the devil. It can avail nothing at all — it must be subject to sin and the devil.

Just as the house must be conquered by a "**stronger**" man and be taken away from the tyrant, so also must man be saved and rescued from the devil through Christ.

We see here once again that in the matter of our salvation, our doing and righteousness avail nothing at all, but that it is God's grace alone that bestows salvation upon us.

SL.XI.556,10

PRAYER: Keep us ever mindful, heavenly Father, that in our battle against sin and the devil, success awaits us only if we contend against our old evil foe with all the resources which you in your grace provide for us, in and through the "stronger" man, Jesus Christ our Saviour. Amen.

SATURDAY

LESSON: LUKE 9.46-50

He who is not with me is against me, and he who does not gather with me scatters.   Luke 11.23

The Gospels are replete with many fine sayings which set forth very important teachings. This is also the case in Christ's words at the end of the Gospel concerning the healing of the dumb demoniac: "**He who is not with me is against me, and he who does not gather with me scatters**". "The devil is not with me, for I drive him out. And so he must certainly be against me."

However, this saying refers not only to the devil, but to the blasphemers, on whom also He passes sentence and condemnation here. They are against Him because they are not with Him.

To be with Christ means to think with Christ, that is, to believe in Christ, to believe that His works and not our works help us. That is Christ's position, and that is what He teaches. To "**gather**" with Christ is to do good in love and to be rich in good works.

He who does not believe in Christ is compelled to rely on his own works. Such a man is not with Christ but against Christ. He denies Christ because he builds on his own works. A man who does not love, does not gather with Christ, but performs vain works whereby he becomes worse and gets further away from faith.

SL.XI.556,11

PRAYER: Lord God, our loving, heavenly Father, grant us at all times such an understanding and clarity of faith that we are always absolutely with Christ and not against Him, gathering with Him and not scattering. Amen.

SUNDAY

LESSON: JOHN 6.1-15

Seek first his kingdom and his righteousness, and all these things shall be yours as well.   Matthew 6.33

In the Gospel of the feeding of the five thousand, Christ once again teaches us the need for faith, without anxious worry about food and clothing. Then He stirs us up with a miracle in which He actually demonstrates in deed what He says in words in the Sermon on the Mount, **"Seek first his kingdom and his righteousness, and all these things shall be yours as well"**.

We see here that the people follow Him to hear God's Word and to witness signs. They are seeking God's kingdom. Jesus does not forsake them but provides them richly with food. He shows quite clearly that before those who seek God's kingdom should suffer want, the grass in the wilderness should rather become corn and one piece of bread should rather become a thousand loaves, so that what He declared to the devil at the time of His temptation would stand fast, **"Man shall not live by bread alone, but by every word that proceeds from the mouth of God"**. Matthew 4.4.

So that this principle of God's Word should be confirmed and stand fast, He proceeds to provide for these people what they should eat. He consults Philip about the matter even before they make any complaints and ask for food.

From this we also should learn to let Him do the worrying for us, and we should realize that He thinks about us more and sooner than we think about ourselves.

SL.XI.562,1

PRAYER: You know all our needs, O Lord, even before we think about them ourselves. You have promised never to leave or forsake us. Be with us then, O Lord, at all times, for the sake of your truth and mercy. Amen.

MONDAY

LESSON: JOHN 15.12-17

As the Father has loved me, so have I loved you; abide in my love.   John 15.9

In His feeding of the five thousand our Lord gives us a splendid example of His manifold love for men. In the first place, His miracle in providing so much food is not performed only for the benefit of His godly followers who followed Him for the sake of His works and words. It benefited also those who were concerned only about their bodily welfare, who sought only food, drink and temporal honour from Him.

Soon after this Jesus set some of these people straight at Capernaum when He said, **"You seek me, not because you saw signs, but because you ate your fill of the loaves".** **John 6.26.** They actually wanted to take Jesus by force and make Him their king (John 6.15).

Here, on the other side of the Sea of Galilee, Jesus sends His rain and lets His sun shine on the evil and on the good (Matthew 5.45).

In the second place we should note how Jesus, in a most friendly manner, bears with the crudeness and weak faith of His disciples. His testing question to Philip and his apparent appeal to reason, and Andrew's rather childish contribution to the matter under discussion, are recorded here to bring to light the imperfection of the apostles. Over against all this, His own love and friendly treatment of them shines forth even more beautifully and with greater love.

All this should stimulate our faith and act as an example for us to follow. The members of our body and all creatures also offer us common instruction. For all that God has created is full of love; the one creature bears, helps and rescues the other.

SL.XI.562,2

PRAYER: Lord Jesus, your love for us was truly wonderful and passing knowledge. Let this love always be aglow within us so that we accept it in true faith for our salvation and practise it for the benefit of all our fellowmen, for your love's sake. Amen.

TUESDAY

LESSON: MATTHEW 7.7-12

Jesus then took the loaves, and when he had given thanks, he distributed them to those who were seated; so also the fish, as much as they wanted. And when they had eaten their fill, he told his disciples, "Gather up the fragments left over, that nothing may be lost".   John 6.11,12

In taking the five loaves and blessing them, Jesus gives us to understand that there is never anything so insignificant that it cannot be of some use for His disciples. He can bless even a little for them, so that they eventually have more than enough, whereas those who are rich often do not have enough with all their riches.

"Those who seek the Lord lack no good thing", as the Psalmist declares, but the rich often suffer hunger. **"The young lions suffer want and hunger." Psalm 34.10**. In her *Magnificat* Mary also reminds us that **"He has filled the hungry with good things, and the rich he has sent empty away". Luke 1.53**.

On the other hand, in giving the order that the fragments should be gathered up, Jesus teaches us to be saving, to look after His blessings, to make good use of them so that one never tempts God by the misuse of His blessings.

Just as He wants us to have faith when we have nothing, and to be quite sure that He will provide for us, so also He does not want us to tempt Him by despising the blessing He has given us, or by letting them lie to rot away while awaiting others from heaven by way of a miracle.

What He has provided, we should accept and use. What He has not provided, we should wait for with firm faith.

SL.XI.563,3-4

PRAYER: You have often shown us in your Word, O Lord, that your children will never lack any good thing. We trust you to provide all the "good things" we need as your children. Grant us your grace that we never misuse any of these good things, for Christ's sake. Amen.

WEDNESDAY

LESSON: PSALM 121

My help comes from the Lord, who made heaven and earth.
Psalm 121.2

There are situations in life when God really strips us bare and we suffer want even in regard to such matters as clothing, housing and the like. But before very long, clothing has to be found, otherwise the very leaves would have to be plucked from the trees and become coats and cloaks for us to wear, just as it happened to the children of Israel in the wilderness, whose clothing and shoes remained intact (Deuteronomy 8.2,4). So also the wild deserts became their houses and provided ways for them where there were no ways, and water where there was no water; indeed, stones became water for them.

God's Word stands fast which says, **"He cares about you"**. 1 Peter 5.7. What Paul says to Timothy is only too true: **"God . . . richly furnishes us with everything to enjoy"**. 1 Timothy 6.17.

Christ's own words in His Sermon on the Mount also apply here: **"Seek first his kingdom and his righteousness, and all these things shall be yours as well. Therefore do not be anxious."** Matthew 6.33,34. Such words must remain true and stand fast into all eternity.

It is quite a common sight that poor people and their children are better conditioned, and that their provisions seem to go further and to be more beneficial, than is the case with the wealthy and their rich supplies. In many ways we are reminded that earthly provisions are not the only matter of importance. God's Word nourishes all men.   SL.XI.538,13

PRAYER: Lord Jesus, our Saviour and Redeemer, you have assured us that you will be with us always, even to the end of time. For this reason we now turn to you in the faith and conviction that you will always hear us, for your truth's sake. Amen.

THURSDAY

LESSON: PSALM 36

Thy steadfast love, O Lord, extends to the heavens, thy faithfulness to the clouds.   Psalm 36.5

God's power and might is in the very bread we eat. He is present in this bread and nourishes us through it and under it, but in an invisible manner. We think that it is the bread that does it all! But where no bread is available, He nourishes men without bread by His Word alone. He acts here also as He acts under the bread, invisibly. The bread is His "fellow worker", as Paul says, **"We are fellow workers for God".** 1 Corinthians 3.9.

Through and under our external office of the ministry He gives His grace inwardly, that grace which He could actually give without our office and does give without it. But while the office is there, one should not despise it or tempt God.

So also He nourishes us through bread externally, but inwardly He alone gives the growth and digestion which the bread cannot give. In short, all creatures are God's masks and mummers, whom He wants to work along with Him and help Him to accomplish all sorts of things, which He could certainly accomplish without their co-operation and also does accomplish without them.

This is what He has ordained, so that we should learn to cling to His pure Word alone. If there is bread, do not put all your confidence in it; if there is no bread, there are still no grounds for despair. Use the bread when it is available, and do without it when it is not available.

But at all times we should be certain that we are nourished by the Word of God, whether bread is available or not. With this faith one conquers greed, bodily indulgence and temporal concern for our nourishment.

SL.XI.539,16

PRAYER: Keep us ever alert, heavenly Father, to the fact that we continually need the blessing of your Word in all that we do in our daily lives, even in our eating and drinking, through Jesus Christ our Lord. Amen.

FRIDAY

LESSON: ROMANS 6.1-11

Truly, truly, I say to you, he who hears my word and believes him who sent me, has eternal life; he does not come into judgement, but has passed from death to life.

John 5.24

The meaning of Jesus is that he who clings to the Word will not feel or see death, even in the midst of death as He also declares later on: "**He who believes in me, though he die, yet shall he live**", for I am the life, **John 11.25.**

Here we see what a wonderful thing the Christian faith really is for it already saves us from death eternally and brings it to pass that we never die. The death and dying of a Christian is just like that of an unbeliever externally; but inwardly there is as much difference here as the difference between heaven and earth. For the Christian sleeps in death and passes through it to life, but the unbeliever passes from life to experience death eternally.

We also see this from the way in which some shake in terror, are full of doubt and even despair, and completely lose all reason and sense in the throes of death.

This is why Scripture also calls death a sleep. For just as the one who falls asleep does not really know what is happening to him, and recovers consciousness quite suddenly in the morning when he wakes up, so we, too, will arise on the last day without any knowledge how we died and passed through death.

SL.XI.571,11

PRAYER: Lord Jesus, draw us ever closer to you in true and living faith so that we firmly believe that, whether we live or die, we are yours and the heirs of eternal life and blessedness with you, the Father, and the Holy Spirit. Amen.

SATURDAY

LESSON: JOHN 7.14-24

If I cast out demons by Be-elzebul, by whom do your sons cast them out?   Luke 11.19

Jesus certainly confronts his enemies here with a telling and crushing question, when He asks them: **"If I cast out demons by Be-elzebul, by whom do your sons cast them out?"** "Is it not rabid hatred to condemn in me what you praise in your own children?" He means to ask them, "When your children do something, it is from God; but because I do a thing, it must be from the devil." That is how the world must react to Christ. What Christ does is of the devil; if someone else did it it would be right.

This is also the reasoning of the tyrants and enemies of the Gospel today. They condemn in us what they praise in themselves, and they confess it and teach it. This is how they must act, so that the judgement passed on them is publicly approved, namely, that their condemnation is correct. The **"sons"** who cast out devils, whom Christ mentions here, were, I believe, exorcists who functioned among the people. God bestowed many spiritual gifts on His people from of old. He calls them their **"sons"** as though He meant them to understand: "I am God's son and yet I must belong to the devil; but those who are your 'sons' born from you do the same as I do but must not be regarded as belonging to the devil".

SL.XI.554,6

PRAYER: Lord Jesus, you suffered scorn, mockery, contempt and blasphemy for us, and men turned a deaf ear to your testimony and proclamation. In all this we know, O Lord, that you have set a pattern for us to follow in your name. Amen.

SUNDAY

LESSON: JOHN 8.46-59

Which of you convicts me of sin? If I tell the truth, why do you not believe me?   John 8.46

This Gospel teaches us how hardened sinners become even more furious when one instructs them and encourages them in a friendly manner. Christ here asks them in a really friendly manner to supply a reason why they do not believe in Him, when they are in no position at all to find fault either with His life or His doctrine.

His life is quite blameless. He can boldly confront the Jews with the challenge, **"Which of you convicts me of sin?"** His doctrine, too, is irreproachable for He says, **"If I tell the truth, why do you not believe me?"** Christ is one whose walk of life squared in every way with what He taught.

Every preacher should always be quite confident about two factors. In the first place, he should lead a blameless life so that he may always have a courageous approach to his work, and that he may not provide anyone with an easy excuse to blaspheme his doctrine. Secondly, his doctrine must also be blameless so that he never misleads anyone who follows him.

In both respects, then, he will be doing what is right. With his good life he will be gaining the advantage over his enemies, who are more concerned with his life than his doctrine, and may despise his doctrine because of his life. With his doctrine he is serving his friends, who are more concerned with his doctrine than with his life, and will put up with his life for the sake of his doctrine.   SL.XI.566,1-2

PRAYER: Provide your Church with faithful pastors, O God, who practise what they preach and whose proclamation is always sure and certain, following the example of our Lord Jesus Christ. Amen.

MONDAY

LESSON: JOHN 8.45

Because I tell the truth, you do not believe me.

John 8.45

It is true that no pastor's life is ever so good that it is without sin before God. And so it is enough if he is blameless in the eyes of his people. But his doctrine must be so good and pure that it stands up not only before men but also before God.

A godly preacher may well find himself in a position to ask his hearers, "Who from among you is going to find fault with me? From among you, I say, my fellow human beings! But before God I am a sinner."

Moses does the same thing when he claims that he had not taken anything from them or harmed any one of them (Numbers 16.15).

Samuel, Jeremiah and Hezekiah could also appeal to their blameless lives before the people to stop the mouths of slanderers.

Christ does not speak about His doctrine here. He does not say, "Who among you can fault my doctrine". He says, **"Because I tell the truth"**.

One must be sure that one's doctrine is the truth and right before God, and not be concerned only how it is regarded by men.

SL.XI.568,3

PRAYER: Grant us at all times such conviction of faith, heavenly Father, that we never have the slightest doubt that the whole truth of salvation has been revealed to us in and through Jesus Christ our Saviour. Amen.

TUESDAY

LESSON: ROMANS 12.14-21

I do not seek my own glory; there is One who seeks it and he will be the judge.   John 8.50

Why does Jesus not say in John 8.49, "I honour my Father and you dishonour Him"? He says, "**You dishonour me**".

In a veiled manner He indicates that His Father's honour and His own honour are identical, one and the same thing, just as He is one God together with His Father. At the same time, however, He wants to remind us that if our ministry in praise of God is to obtain its due honour, it must also suffer shame.

We should also keep this in mind in our dealings with rulers and priests. When they question our lives, we will put up with it, and repay them with love for hate and good for evil; but when they attack our doctrine they are attacking God's honour.

Here there must be a limit to love and patience. We must not remain silent but say, "I honour my Father, and so you dishonour me. It does not matter much that you dishonour me, for I am not seeking my own honour. But at the same time take warning! There is one who is seeking my honour and judging it. The Father will demand it from you and not leave you unpunished. He does not only seek His honour, but mine as well, for He has declared:"**Those who honour me I will honour**'." 1 Samuel 2.30.

This is our consolation, so we can be quite joyful. Even though all the world casts shame on us and dishonours us, we are certain that God requires our honour and will punish, judge and avenge. O that we would only believe it and wait upon Him! He is certainly coming!

SL.XI.569,7

PRAYER: You have assured us, both by much instruction and many examples, O Lord, that you will adequately defend the honour of your Word and those who proclaim it. Fill our hearts with courage and confidence so that we never lose heart, in and through Jesus Christ our Saviour. Amen.

WEDNESDAY

LESSON: JOHN 17.1-5

Truly, truly, I say to you, if any one keeps my word, he will never see death.   John 8.51

Jesus really spoils things for His enemies when He not only offers a good and stout defence of His doctrine, but ascribes such might to it that it holds full sway over the devil, death and sin, imparting eternal life and preserving men therein.

See here how divine wisdom and human reason come into conflict! How can any man comprehend that a word spoken physically from a human mouth can save from death eternally?

But away with blindness! We want to deal with this beautiful passage. He speaks here not concerning the word of the Law but concerning the word of the Gospel which is a discourse concerning Christ who died for our sins. God did not want to impart Christ to the world in any other way but by including Him in His Word and thus spreading Him out and setting Him forth. Otherwise Christ would have remained completely isolated by Himself and would never have become known. And thus He would have died for Himself alone.

Because the Word portrays Christ for us, it portrays for us Him who conquered sin, death and the devil. Hence, anyone who grasps and holds the Word, grasps and holds Christ, and through the Word he also becomes freed from death eternally. Thus it is a Word of life. It is true that he who keeps this Word will never see death eternally.

SL.XI. 570,8

PRAYER: Thanks and praise be to you, O God, for the riches of your grace and mercy revealed to us in your holy Gospel, culminating in the assurance of eternal life and salvation in and through Jesus Christ our Saviour. Amen.

THURSDAY

LESSON: 1 CORINTHIANS 15.51-56

I shall not die, but I shall live, and recount the deeds of the Lord.   Psalm 118.17

How does it come to pass that one does not see death or taste it, when Abraham and all the prophets died, who certainly had the Word of God, as the Jews also maintained? Here we must pay close attention to what Christ actually says, and note that He makes a distinction between death in the ordinary common sense, and not seeing death or tasting death.

We must all pass through death and die. But a Christian does not taste death or see death, that is, he does not feel death. He is not terrified in the face of death. He enters it quietly and softly, as though he is falling asleep and not dying at all. But the godless man must feel death and be terrified by it eternally.

To taste death means to experience the power and might or the bitterness of death, and, indeed, eternal death and hell. God's Word makes this distinction. The Christian knows this, and it helps him in the hour of death. He does not see death. He sees nothing but life and Christ in the Word, and so he does not feel death. But the godless man does not have this Word; he has no life, but sheer death. So he feels death, and eventually this is also the bitterness of eternal death.

With the believer it is all so very different. He knows the Word of Christ: **"I am the resurrection and the life; he who believes in me, though he die, yet shall he live, and whoever lives and believes in me shall never die".** John 11.25,26.

SL.XI.571,10

PRAYER: Be with us, dear Lord Jesus, especially in the hour of our death, that, firmly relying on your promises, we may not taste death, but pass through death into life eternal, as you have assured us. Amen.

THE WEEK OF JUDICA

FRIDAY

LESSON: GALATIANS 3.15-18

Your father Abraham rejoiced that he was to see my day; he saw it and was glad.   John 8.56

Christ here declares in opposition to the Jews that Abraham and the prophets still live and never died, but that in the midst of death they have life. But they lie and sleep in death. **"Your father Abraham"**, He says, **"rejoiced that he was to see my day; he saw it and was glad"**. The prophets also saw Him.

Where and when did they see Him? Not with bodily eyes, as the Jews understood Him to say, but with the vision of the faith which they had in their hearts. Abraham recognized Christ when He said to him, **"By your descendants shall all the nations of the earth bless themselves"**. **Genesis 22.18**. At that time he saw and understood that Christ was to be born from his seed through a pure virgin and suffer for the whole world. He would not be cursed along with Adam's children, but remain blessed. He knew that this message would be proclaimed in all the world, and bestow a blessing on the whole of mankind.

Christ's **"day"** is the time of the Gospel which is the light of this day which shines with Christ, the sun of righteousness, and lights up all the world.

This is a spiritual **"day"**, but it had an historical beginning in Christ's time which Abraham also **"saw"**.

SL.XI.572,13

PRAYER: Open the eyes of our faith and understanding by your Holy Spirit, O Lord, that with Abraham of old we always rejoice to have seen Christ's day, the day of salvation, and are really happy and joyful in our knowledge of Christ. Amen.

SATURDAY

LESSON: HEBREWS 1.1-13

Jesus said to them, "Truly, truly, I say to you, before Abraham was, I am".   John 8.58

Jesus gives the basis and reason why it is just His Word and not that of anyone else which makes men live. It is simply this: that He **"was"** even before Abraham. **"Before Abraham was, I am."** Jesus is the one true God.

If the person who offered Himself for us were not God, it would help and avail nothing before God that He was born of a virgin, or had suffered a thousand deaths. But the fact that the seed of Abraham who gives Himself for us is also true God makes His sacrifice such a blessing for us, and conquers sin and death for us.

Jesus is not speaking here of His human nature which could be seen and felt. From His human aspect it could be seen that He was not yet fifty years old, and hence could not have seen Abraham. But with the nature by which He infinitely antedated Abraham, He also antedated all other creatures and the whole world.

According to His spiritual essence He was also man before Abraham, that is, in the word and knowledge of faith He was in the saints who all knew and believed that Christ, God and man, would suffer for us. The writer of Hebrews says, **"Jesus Christ is the same yesterday and today and for ever".** **Hebrews 13.8.** In the Revelation of John we read of the Lamb slain from the foundation of the world (Revelation 13.8). Here Jesus is speaking of His divine nature.

SL.XI.573,14

PRAYER: Lord God, heavenly Father, fill our hearts with such faith and knowledge that we always fully appreciate the precious gift of your only begotten Son, and all the blessings of salvation you have so richly bestowed on us in and through Jesus Christ our Saviour. Amen.

SUNDAY

LESSON: MATTHEW 13.45,46

If any one keeps my word.   John 8.51

It is quite clear from the context in which these words stand what Jesus means here by "keeping" His Word. He does not mean "keeping" in the sense that "keep" has when one speaks about "keeping" the Law. One "keeps" the Law by means of works. When Christ speaks here of "keeping" His Word, He means "keeping" it in one's heart by faith, not keeping it with the fist or with works.

This is the wrong idea that the Jews have when they rage in such a horrible fashion against Christ and say to Him, **"Now we know that you have a demon. Abraham died, as did the prophets; and you say, 'If any one keeps my word, he will never taste death'."** John 8.52. They do not know what "keep", "dying" and "living" mean in this context.

It is not without good reason that Jesus employs the word "keep" here, because keeping His Word involves a struggle and a battle, for sin bites, death exerts its presence, and hell threatens. Under such conditions we must "keep" Christ's Word, cling to it firmly and not let ourselves be parted from it.

Note how Christ replies to the Jews in praise of His doctrine. "You claim", He says, "that my Word is from the devil and you want to suppress it even beneath hell. But I say that it has divine power within it, and exalt it above all the heavens and all creatures."

SL.XI.570,9

PRAYER: Lord Jesus, you have clearly shown us in your Gospel that your teaching is the most precious thing we can ever learn in our earthly lives. Grant us your grace to appreciate this fact fully at all times so that we keep your Word, for your truth's sake. Amen.

MONDAY

LESSON: MATTHEW 16.21-23

Christ also suffered for you, leaving you an example, that you should follow in his steps.   1 Peter 2.21

Jesus spoke the words of Matthew 16.21-23 before He entered upon His suffering, as He was on His way to Jerusalem. His immediate purpose was to celebrate Easter at Jerusalem. In all probability the disciples had not the slightest idea of His impending sufferings at this time. They thought that they would have a joyful time at the festival.

Christ mentions His sufferings on this journey so that the faith of His disciples might be strengthened later on when they recalled His words in which He had told them of His sufferings. He had submitted to these sufferings willingly and was not simply crucified through the power and cunning of the Jews.

Isaiah had long foretold that He would willingly and gladly offer Himself (Isaiah 53.7). The angel, on Easter morning, also reminded the women to remember the words He had spoken to them (Luke 24.6) that they might know and more firmly believe that He suffered all this willingly and for our good.   SL.XI.526,2

PRAYER: Lord Jesus Christ, thanks and praise to you for your willingness and readiness to suffer and die on our behalf and for our good, for your mercy's sake. Amen.

TUESDAY

LESSON: HEBREWS 10.1-7

[Christ said,] " 'Lo, I have come to do thy will, O God', as it is written of me in the roll of the book".   Hebrews 10.7

Christ's sufferings are understood correctly when we do not simply regard the sufferings as such, but recognize and grasp His heart and will to suffer. For if one regards His sufferings in isolation, without recognizing His heart and will therein, one will be shocked by Christ's sufferings rather than rejoice in them. But if one sees that Christ's heart and will are in these sufferings, it produces real comfort, confidence and pleasure in Christ.

The psalmist praises this will of God and Christ in suffering when he says, "In the roll of the book it is written of me; I delight to do thy will, O my God; thy law is within my heart". Psalm 40.7,8. The epistle to the Hebrews also refers to this when it says, "By that will we have been sanctified". Hebrews 10.10. It does not say through the suffering and blood of Christ, which is pure enough, but through the will of God and of Christ, that they were both of one will to sanctify us through Christ's blood.

This will to suffer He also manifests in the Gospel (Matthew 16.21-23), where He proclaims beforehand that He is going up to Jerusalem to suffer Himself to be crucified. It is as though He were saying, "Look into my heart to see that I am doing this willingly, without compulsion, and gladly, so that you may not be shocked or dismayed thereby when you see it come to pass, and begin to think that I am doing it unwillingly, that I must do it, that I am forsaken and that the Jews are doing it by their authority.

SL.XI.526,3

PRAYER: Thanks be to you, loving Father, for sending us such a ready and willing Saviour, whose love for us has been manifested in His readiness and willingness to suffer and die for us and in our stead. Mercy and love are all your ways, and those of your Son, Jesus Christ our Lord. Amen.

WEDNESDAY

LESSON: PSALM 19.7-14

They understood none of these things; this saying was hid from them, and they did not grasp what was said.
Luke 18.34

What Jesus said to the disciples had no meaning for them at this time. **"This saying was hid from them."** This amounts to saying, "Reason, flesh and blood cannot understand or grasp that Scripture should declare how the Son of Man must be crucified". Still less can it understand that such is His will, and that He does this gladly.

Reason does not believe that this is necessary for us, it wants to take care of itself before God with works. God must reveal this in our hearts by His Spirit, after proclaiming it outwardly into our ears by His Word.

Even those to whom the Spirit reveals it inwardly find it hard to believe this and have to struggle with this.

So great and wonderful a thing it is that the Son of man is crucified willingly and gladly to fulfil the Scriptures, that is, for our good. It is a mystery and remains a mystery.

SL.XI.527,4

PRAYER: O Lord, we are always in need of the enlightenment of your Holy Spirit through your Word. We thank you that through the Spirit we can understand the treasures of your Word and make them our own. Amen.

MAUNDY THURSDAY

LESSON: ROMANS 15.1-6

Bear one another's burdens, and so fulfil the law of Christ.
Galatians 6.2

Not the least part of love or self-surrender is for me to be able to give away my self-conceit or arrogance. I can no doubt give my neighbour temporal good and bodily service with my painstaking toil. I can also serve him with instruction and intercession, for example, by visiting him and consoling him when he is sick or sad. I can feed him when he is hungry, free him from imprisonment, and such like. But the greatest of all the services I can render my neighbour is bearing his weakness.

We will always fall short of the mark here. We will never attain to the perfection of Christ in this regard. He is the pure, bright Sun in which there is no mist. Our light is just like a glimmering stalk of straw in comparison with this Sun. Christ is a glowing oven full of fire and perfect love. But He is still satisfied with our little candle, if we provide some sort of evidence of letting our love shine forth.

Take a look at the Gospel record and see how Christ dealt with His disciples. He bore with them when they were guilty of foolish conduct, and even when they, at times, went astray. In their service, His wisdom yielded to their folly. He did not condemn them, but bore their weakness with long-suffering patience. **"What I am doing you do not know now, but afterward you will understand"**, He tells them on one occasion. **John 13.7.** Through such love He gives up His righteousness, judgement, might, wrath, punishment, and the rights he has over us and our sins. He could condemn us because of our folly. But He does no more than to say, "You are in the wrong; you do not know anything; do not, however, reject me, but trust me".

And so I say that it is no small example of love to be able to bear with our neighbour when he is weak in faith and love.

SL.XI.597,26

PRAYER: Dear Lord Jesus, fill our hearts at all times with such love for our neighbour that we understand his weaknesses and needs and continue to bear with him, for your name's sake. Amen.

GOOD FRIDAY

LESSON: 2 CORINTHIANS 5,14,15

Christ died for sins once for all, the righteous for the unrighteous, that he might bring us to God.   1 Peter 3.18

Thorns pricked the sacred head of Christ, but you have actually deserved the pricks of more than a hundred thousand thorns. To be sure, you have deserved to be pricked by such thorns in all eternity, and much worse than He was pricked. Christ had to suffer the agony of having His hands and feet pierced with nails; you have deserved to suffer from much worse nails in eternity.

This is what will indeed befall those who disregard Christ's sufferings on their behalf. In this grim reflection, Christ does not lie or scold; what He indicates must surely follow. St. Bernard says, "I thought I was secure and knew nothing of the eternal sentence passed upon me in heaven until I saw that the only-begotten Son of God had mercy on me, stepped forth and submitted to the sentence of condemnation on my behalf. If there is such seriousness here it is not for me to play around any longer and to be secure."

This also explains Christ's words to the women of Jerusalem: **"Do not weep for me, but weep for yourselves and for your children . . . If they do this when the wood is green, what will happen when it is dry?"** Luke 23.28,31. Jesus means to say: "From my sufferings learn what you have deserved and what will befall you".

Christ's sufferings should always be pondered with the greatest of seriousness on our part. They are written for our warning to teach us the awful and horrible nature of sin.

SL.XI.577,6-7

PRAYER: Lord God, our heavenly Father, let the awful sufferings and death of our Lord Jesus Christ be for us a continual reminder of the horrible nature of all sin in your sight. Move us at all times to a serious consideration of our Saviour's passion and death on our behalf. Amen.

SATURDAY

LESSON: 1 JOHN 5.6-12

The God and Father of our Lord Jesus Christ . . . destined us in love to be his sons through Jesus Christ, according to the purpose of his will, to the praise of his glorious grace which he freely bestowed on us in the Beloved. In him we have redemption through his blood, the forgiveness of our trespasses, according to the riches of his grace which he lavished upon us.   Ephesians 1.3,5-8

When we discover what the Gospel of God's free and unmerited love really is, we see how foolish it is to teach that people should bear suffering and death patiently to atone for their sins and to obtain grace. Some claim that if one bears all this patiently and willingly, all one's sins will be forgiven accordingly. These people are seducers, because they conceal Christ with His death upon which our comfort depends. They induce people to rely on their own suffering and death.

This is the very worst thing that can befall anyone in the end, because it is a way that leads straight into hell. You must learn to say, "What is my death and patience? Nothing at all! I will have nothing at all to do with it and will close my ears to it as far as any consolation is concerned. Christ's suffering and death is my one consolation. On this I place my reliance, and trust that through it my sins are forgiven. I will gladly suffer death for my God's praise and honour freely, gratuitously and in my neighbour's service, but place no reliance on it for myself."

SL.XI.527,5

PRAYER: Lord Jesus Christ, thanks and praise be to you for the completeness of your work of salvation for us, and for making this known to us in your holy Gospel for our eternal comfort and consolation. Amen.

SUNDAY

LESSON: MARK 16.1-8

Then Jesus said to them, "Do not be afraid; go and tell my brethren to go to Galilee, and there they will see me.
Matthew 28.10

Jesus Himself pointed out the benefit of His suffering, death, and resurrection when He said to the women, **"Do not be afraid; go and tell my brethren to go to Galilee, and there they will see me"**.

This is the first word that they heard from Jesus after His resurrection from the dead. He hereby confirms all His former teachings, as well as the blessings He had already conferred on them. They are reminded here that they will now indeed be the recipients of all these blessings. Not only this; He also intimates that the Christians who believe His words are His **"brethren"** even though they do not see like the apostles did.

He does not wait until we beg or beseech Him that we may become His brethren. All ideas of meritorious services are completely ruled out here.

What did the apostles merit? Peter denied the Lord three times; the other disciples all fled from Him; they stayed with Him like a hare stays with its young. He should have called them deserters, traitors and scoundrels rather than brethren. So this word was sent to them through these women by sheer mercy and grace.

The apostles could not help feeling this. We feel it, too, when we are held fast in sins, temptations and damnation.

SL.XI.603,2-3

PRAYER: We thank and praise you, dear Lord Jesus, for the wonderful grace and mercy which you have so richly bestowed upon us unworthy sinners in demonstrating by your resurrection that we are your brethren, with all the privileges of brethren. Amen.

MONDAY

LESSON: REVELATION 1.4-8

He is not ashamed to call them brethren.   Hebrews 2.11

The fact that Christ receives such abandoned wretches as you and me, and calls us brethren, is a fact full of all consolation for us. If Christ is our brother, I would like to know what we still lack?

The situation in which we find ourselves is very much like that which exists among earthly brothers. Earthly brothers have common possessions, as well as one father and one inheritance, otherwise they would not be brothers.

In Christ we also share common possessions and have one Father and one inheritance. But this inheritance never becomes less by being shared like an earthly inheritance. It becomes ever greater and greater. For it is a spiritual inheritance.

The earthly inheritance is dissipated when it is divided into many parts, but in the spiritual inheritance which is ours in Christ, he who has a part of it has all of it.

What is this inheritance which makes us Christ's brothers? In His hands are all times of life and death, sin and grace, and all that is in heaven and on earth, eternal truth, might, wisdom and righteousness. He rules and reigns over everything: hunger, thirst, good fortune, misfortune, over everything that is conceivable, whether it be in heaven or on earth, not only spiritual matters, but also earthly matters.

In short, He has all things in His hands, whether they are eternal or temporal. My faith in Christ, then, fully covers all my needs.

SL.XI.604,4-5

PRAYER: Keep us ever mindful, O Lord, of all that we have for time and eternity in our relationships with you, the beginning and ending of all our faith and hope, as your privileged brethren, for your love's sake. Amen.

TUESDAY

LESSON: ROMANS 8.14-17

[Let your adorning] . . . **be the hidden person of the heart with the imperishable jewel of a gentle and quiet spirit, which in God's sight is very precious. 1 Peter 3.4**

The title that we are Christ's brethren is so exalted that no human heart can really comprehend it. Unless the Holy Spirit confers this grace, no one can say, "Christ is my brother". No man's reason would be bold enough to make such a claim, even though it may occasionally be made with the tongue, as in the case of our modern charismatics. Nor is it enough just to make such claims — this must be a matter of the heart — otherwise it is pure hypocrisy.

If you really know this in your heart, it will become something so great and important for you, that you will keep quiet about it rather than chatter about it to all and sundry. To be sure, face to face with the magnitude of this blessing you may even have your doubts and uncertainties whether it is really true or not. Those who are always crying out, "Christ is my brother, Christ is my brother!" are not necessarily Christ's true brethren.

With a true Christian it is very different. For a true Christian it is a wonderful thing to hear that he is Christ's brother. The flesh is dismayed at this and not so very much will be said and openly acknowledged about it all.

SL.XI.605,7

PRAYER: Give us at all times a quiet, confident faith, O Lord, not given to empty and foolish boasting, but fully trusting in your assurance that we are your brethren in and through your glorious resurrection from the dead. Amen.

WEDNESDAY

LESSON: ISAIAH 55.6-9

Now we see in a mirror dimly, but then face to face. Now I know in part; then I shall understand fully, even as I have been fully understood.   1 Corinthians 13.12

We should always be very careful not only to hear the truth that we are Christ's brethren with our bodily ears. We should feel and experience this truth in our very hearts. Then we shall never become over-weening and conceited, but this fact will fill our hearts with wonder.

True, pious and godly Christians are always deeply conscious of their very serious limitations. In humility and modesty they will begin to wonder how such miserable sinners as they are, drowned in sins, could ever become worthy enough to have God's Son as their brother. How does it come to pass that such a wretched creature as I am enjoys such a privilege?

At the same time, such a Christian is amazed at this fact and meditates upon it. It certainly requires great effort to believe it. Indeed, if one actually experienced this fact for what it really is and involves, one would perforce have to die in that very instant. For man who is flesh and blood cannot comprehend this fact.

As long as we live in this life, our heart is far too restricted to be able to grasp such a fact. After death, when our heart is enlarged, we shall be able to comprehend fully what we have heard through the Word.

SL.XI.606,8

PRAYER: Your ways are not our ways, and your thoughts are not our thoughts, heavenly Father. Enlighten us by your Holy Spirit in such a way that we believe your Word, even where we may not fully understand it, for Christ, our Saviour's sake. Amen.

THURSDAY

LESSON: 2 CORINTHIANS 4.13-15

Jesus said to her, "Do not hold me, for I have not yet ascended to the Father; but go to my brethren and say to them, I am ascending to my Father and your Father, to my God and your God".   John 20.17

In these words of Jesus to Mary Magdalene, as reported in John's Gospel, Jesus sets forth a very clear explanation of the benefit and profit of His death and resurrection. **"Go to my brethren and say to them, I am ascending to my Father and your Father, to my God and your God."**

This is one of the great consolatory passages of the Gospel at which we can knock with all boldness and confidence. It is as though Christ is saying here, "Go, Mary, and tell my disciples, those deserters, who really merited punishment and eternal damnation, that my resurrection will redound to their great advantage. Through my resurrection I have brought it about that my Father is your Father and my God your God."

A few brief words! But they contain a very important truth, namely, that we have a trust and confidence in God which is the equal of that which Christ, the very Son of God Himself has.

Who can grasp such boundless joy? Who can explain how a poor, miserable sinner can call God his Father and God, even as Christ Himself does?

SL.XI.606,9

PRAYER: Dear heavenly Father, your ways in Jesus Christ our Lord are beyond all our powers of understanding and telling. Grant us the faith to cling with all our hearts to the benefits and profits of our Lord's resurrection, that with Him you are our Father and our God in and through Jesus our Saviour. Amen.

THE WEEK OF EASTER

FRIDAY

LESSON: MATTHEW 26.69-75

Jesus our Lord . . . was put to death for our trespasses and raised for our justification. Romans 4.25

You cast your sins from yourself on to Christ when you firmly believe that His wounds and sufferings are your sins, that He bore them and paid for them as Isaiah declared: **"The Lord has laid on him the iniquity of us all"**. **Isaiah 53.6.** Peter also says: **"He himself bore our sins in his body on the tree"**, that is, the cross, **1 Peter 2.24**, and St. Paul wrote to the Corinthians: **"He hath made him to be sin for us, who knew no sin; that we might be made the righteousness of God in him". 2 Corinthians 5.21 A.V.**

On this and similar passages you must stake everything in full reliance, and the more so if your conscience is giving you serious trouble. If you do not do this, but presume to quieten your conscience by way of your own penitence and satisfaction, you will never find peace and end up in despair. It does not matter how much penitence and satisfaction we have to offer, our sins keep on piling up and gaining the upper hand. But when we see them borne by Christ, and conquered by His glorious resurrection from the dead and we have boldness of faith, our sins are dead and blotted out. For they could not remain on Christ. They have been swallowed up by His resurrection. Now you see no wounds, no pains in Him, that is, no signs of sin.

SL.XI.580,13

PRAYER: Thanks and praise be to you, Lord Jesus, for the complete victory over sin which you gained for us when you bore our sins on the cross and destroyed them in your glorious resurrection from the dead. Amen.

166

SATURDAY

LESSON: MATTHEW 27.1-14

In this is love, not that we loved God but that he loved us and sent his Son to be the expiation for our sins.

1 John 4.10

You must learn to look right through the sufferings of Christ and see His friendly heart, how it is filled with love for you, and how it moved Him to assume the heavy load which your conscience and sins laid on Him. In this way your heart will be warmed towards Him, and your confidence and faith will be strengthened. Thereupon you should mount even higher through Christ's heart to God's heart, and see that Christ would never have manifested His love for you if God in His eternal love had not willed it. Christ rendered obedience to God's love in His love for you.

In this way you will discover the fatherly heart of God in its wonderful goodness, and, as Christ Himself declares, you will be drawn to the Father through Him. Then you will also understand Christ's saying that **"God so loved the world that he gave his only Son, that whoever believes in him should not perish but have eternal life". John 3.16.**

To come to a true knowledge of God, we must not try to find Him simply in His power or wisdom, which can be bewildering, but we must grasp Him in His goodness and love. In this respect, faith and confidence has something to cling to, and man becomes truly born anew in God.

SL.XI.581,14

PRAYER: Make it ever more clear and certain for us, heavenly Father, that in all that Christ, our Saviour, bore and suffered for us sinners, love was operating, and that in this manifestation of love you have clearly revealed your inner and true nature to us, for Christ's sake. Amen.

SUNDAY

LESSON: JOHN 20.19-31

On the evening of that day, the first day of the week, the doors being shut where the disciples were, for fear of the Jews, Jesus came and stood among them and said to them, "Peace be with you".   John 20.19

As Christians, we must apply the resurrection of the Lord Jesus Christ to ourselves individually. It is not enough simply to believe that He rose from the dead, for such a faith in itself will not mean peace and joy for us, nor power and might. You must also believe that He rose for **your** sake and for **your** benefit. He was not raised into glory for His own sake alone, but that He might help you and all who believe in Him, and that through His resurrection He might overcome sin, death and hell.

This is also indicated by the way in which Christ enters through the locked doors, and steps forth and stands in the midst of His disciples. The manner in which He stood here in the midst of the disciples resembles the manner in which He also stands in our hearts. In this way He is also in our midst, just as He was standing there among the disciples.

When He stands in our hearts in this manner, we hear His loving voice speaking to our conscience, "Be at your ease: there is no need at all for any anxiety. Your sins are forgiven you and removed from you and nothing can henceforth harm you."

SL.XI.725,2-3

PRAYER: Lord God, heavenly Father, in your great love for us you gave your Son to suffer and die for our sins. By His glorious resurrection from the dead you have demonstrated that the sacrifice of your Son has been accepted and that now all is well with us in time and eternity, in and through our Saviour Jesus Christ. Amen.

MONDAY

LESSON: ROMANS 10.14-17

He who hears you hears me, and he who rejects you rejects me, and he who rejects me rejects him who sent me.

Luke 10.16

Christ enters our hearts and takes His stand there through the office of the ministry. Since God has given orders that His Word should be preached, we should never in any manner despise the mortal man in whose mouth that Word has been placed, so that we do not form the opinion that each individual must wait for a special sermon from heaven which God Himself preaches to him verbally.

Therefore, if God grants faith to anyone, He employs the regular means which He has appointed for this purpose. He accomplishes His end through the preaching of men, through an external, human word.

He enters through a closed door when He enters a human heart by means of the Word without smashing or disturbing anything. When God's Word comes, it does not injure the conscience, disturb the understanding of the heart, or upset the external senses as those false teachers do who smash all doors and windows, break in like thieves and leave nothing whole and undisturbed, and bring it to pass that the whole of life, conscience, understanding and the senses become completely unhinged and lose all rhyme or reason. Christ does not do this.

God's Word proclaimed by men converts sinners. There are two factors involved: preaching and faith. His coming to us is the preaching or proclamation. His standing in our hearts is faith. It is not enough for Him to stand simply before our eyes and ears; He must stand in our midst, in our hearts, with His gift of peace.

SL.XI.726,4

PRAYER: Heavenly Father, awaken and increase in us a true reverence for your saving Word proclaimed to us by the ministers of your Word, so that in this manner Christ, our Saviour, may take His stand in our hearts with His message of peace and joy as a result of His glorious resurrection from the dead. Amen.

TUESDAY

LESSON: PSALM 27

The peace of God, which passes all understanding, will keep your hearts and your minds in Christ Jesus.
Philippians 4.7

The fruit of Christian faith is peace; not merely the outward peace which we sometimes enjoy here on earth, but the peace which Paul mentions in the Epistle to the Philippians, the peace **"which passes all understanding"**. Where this peace reigns, one should not and cannot apply the standards of human reason. This is also clear from the Gospel under consideration (John 20.19-21). At first the disciples sit behind locked doors in great fear of the Jews. They cannot go abroad; death stares them in the face on all sides. There is external peace here. No one is really harming them. But inwardly their hearts are floundering and have no peace or rest.

The Lord comes to them in the midst of their fear and terror, calms their hearts, and makes them joyful. He takes away their fear.

He does not do this by removing the danger, but by changing their hearts so that they cease fearing. This does not change or remove the animosity of the Jews, because they are angry and wrathful, just as much as before. Outwardly, everything remains as it was. But the disciples are changed inwardly; they gain so much boldness and confidence that they joyfully declare, **"We have seen the Lord"**. Christ calms their hearts so that they become courageous and bold. They are no longer concerned how much the Jews may rage against them.

SL.XI.726,5-6

PRAYER: Heavenly Father, fill our hearts at all times with such boldness and confidence that we never compromise our faith because of the fear of men, but speak out clearly, loudly and joyfully, for Christ's sake. Amen.

WEDNESDAY

LESSON: ACTS 14.19-22

We rejoice in our sufferings, knowing that suffering produces endurance, and endurance produces character.
Romans 5.3,4

True Christian peace which calms the heart and brings contentment to the soul is not necessarily the accompaniment of a time when no misfortune is at hand, but it can come to men in the midst of misfortune, when all without is anything but peace. This is the difference between earthly peace and the peace of Christ.

Earthly peace arises from the removal of the external evils that have destroyed peace. When foes assemble before a city, there is no peace; but if the foes are removed peace is restored. The same holds for poverty and sickness; when they press upon you, you are discontented. But when they are removed and you are rid of your misfortune, you once again enjoy external peace and quiet. Such an alteration of fortune does not necessarily change a man; after his troubles are gone, he can remain just as dejected as he was before their removal. The only difference is that he felt them and was disturbed by them when they were present.

Christian or spiritual peace brings about a change. Outwardly, misfortunes in the shape of enemies, sickness, poverty, sin, the devil and death, can certainly continue to press upon you without intermission. In spite of all that, as a Christian you have peace, strength and consolation inwardly in your heart. A Christian heart is never unduly disturbed by misfortune, and, indeed, it is even more courageous and joyful in the face of misfortune than when the latter is absent. That is why it is called by St. Paul a peace which passes all understanding (Philippians 4.7).

SL.XI.726,7-8

PRAYER: Grant us your grace, heavenly Father, so that we may never waver in our faith but ever stand fast in the peace and hope secured for us and assigned to us in and through the resurrection of our Lord Jesus Christ. Amen.

THURSDAY

LESSON: 2 CORINTHIANS 2.14-17

I can do all things in him /Christ/ who strengthens me.
Philippians 4.13

If I really believe from the bottom of my heart that my Lord Jesus Christ by His resurrection from the dead has gained the victory over all that can distress me, sin, death and all evil, that He wants to be close to me and with me so that there is nothing lacking to me in body and soul, that in Him I have enough of everything and that no misfortune can harm me, if I really believe all this, it becomes impossible for me to become faint-hearted and weak, no matter how heavily sin or even death press upon me.

Faith is an ever-present reality telling me, "If sins oppress you and death terrifies you, fix your whole attention on Christ. He died and rose again for your sake; He has overcome all misfortune; what can really harm you?"

If any other misfortune such as sickness or poverty presses heavily upon you, close your eyes to it and do not let your reason gain the upper hand. Cast yourself upon Christ and cling to Him; in this way you will be strengthened and comforted. If you look to Christ and rest your faith in Him, no evil that you may encounter is so great that it can really harm you and make you despondent. Where true faith exists, peace must also follow. It cannot be otherwise.

SL.XI.728,9

PRAYER: Thanks and praise be to you, heavenly Father, for the riches of all the blessings available to us in and through the resurrection of our Lord Jesus Christ, especially the wonderful peace of heart and mind which is ours even in the midst of trial and tribulation. Keep us ever in your love and grace, in and through Jesus our Saviour. Amen.

FRIDAY

LESSON: EPHESIANS 4.9-16

As the Father has sent me, even so I send you. John 20.21

The most important work of love that any Christian can perform after coming to faith in Christ is to bring others to faith in the way he was brought to faith. In this connection Christ lays an obligation upon every individual Christian and sets up the office of ministering the external Word. He Himself came to the disciples with this office and the external Word.

Let us grasp this clearly, for we must be told about it and the Lord wants to tell us here, "You have enough from me: peace and joy, and all that you should have. For your own persons you need no more. Hence, get busy; take a close look at the picture and do as I have done to you! My father sent me into the world for your sakes alone, to help you, not to benefit myself. I have carried out His will, died for you and given you all that I am and have. Think of this and do likewise. From now on serve and help everyone else. Otherwise there is nothing here on earth for you to do. Through faith you already have enough of everything. And so I send you out into the world as my Father has sent me. Every single Christian should instruct and teach his neighbour in order to bring him to faith."

This authority has not only been given to the pope and his bishops; it has been entrusted to all Christians. They should openly confess their faith to bring others to that faith as well.

SL.XI.730,13

PRAYER: Heavenly Father, give us at all times a joyous faith and a ready tongue to confess you before men and lead them to the joy of the salvation which is ours in and through Jesus Christ our Saviour. Amen.

SATURDAY

LESSON: COLOSSIANS 3.12-17

Receive the Holy Spirit. If you forgive the sins of any, they are forgiven; if you retain the sins of any, they are retained.   John 20.22,23

This is a great and powerful authority which no one can adequately praise, bestowed upon poor mortal man and valid over sin, death, hell and all things. The pope boasts that Christ has given him authority over all earthly and heavenly matters in the spiritual domain. This could be quite right, correctly understood. But he applies all this to the earthly sphere and government. This is not what Christ means.

He is here conferring spiritual authority and government and He means to say: "When you speak a word over a sinner, this word has also been spoken in heaven, and it avails as much as if God Himself had spoken it in heaven. For when you speak this word, God is in your mouth and hence this work is as powerful as a word spoken by God Himself."

It follows, therefore, that when Christ speaks a word because He is Lord over sin and death, and says to you, "Your sins are forgiven you", then your sins must be gone and nothing can gainsay it. On the other hand, if He declares, "Your sins are not forgiven you", then they must remain unforgiven, and in this case not even an angel, or a saint, or any creature can forgive you those sins, even if you martyr yourself to death over them.

It is this power to forgive sins that Christ confers on every individual Christian inasmuch as Christ has made all authority in heaven and on earth available to us (Matthew 28.18). Here Christ rules not in any material manner, but spiritually, and He also rules His Christians spiritually.

SL.XI.731,15-16

PRAYER: Grant us your Holy Spirit, heavenly Father, the Spirit of truth and understanding so that we may fully appreciate the very great authority which we enjoy to proclaim forgiveness to our neighbour, in and through our Saviour Jesus Christ. Amen.

SUNDAY

LESSON: JOHN 10.11-16

I am the good shepherd. The good shepherd lays down his life for the sheep.   John 10.11

Pastors can never become any more than the mouth of our Lord Jesus Christ and the instruments whereby He continues to proclaim His Word visibly here on earth. He permits His Word to go out into public so that all may hear it; but the inward acceptance of the Word in the heart is a spiritual experience that takes place through faith. It is a hidden work of Christ. Christ accomplishes this work where He recognizes that it must be accomplished in accordance with His divine discernment and pleasure. That is why He also calls Himself "**the good shepherd**".

What is a "**good shepherd**"? "**The good shepherd**", says Christ, "**lays down his life for the sheep . . . And I lay down my life for the sheep.**"

This one great act really covers everything. To impress all this upon us Christ uses a very pleasing illustration. A sheep is really a very foolish creature and usually regarded as a very simple creature. It is proverbial to say of a simple man, "He is a real sheep". But the sheep possesses one very outstanding quality. It quickly learns to obey the voice of its shepherd, and normally follows no one but its shepherd. It is so constituted that it clings to its shepherd and looks to him for all help and assistance. It cannot help itself, provide pasture or any healing. It is powerless against wolves and is dependent entirely on the help of others.

In this respect the members of Christ's kingdom are His sheep. In all their needs they are dependent on Him and look to Him alone for needed help, support, protection and their whole welfare.

SL.XI.781,8-9

PRAYER: We know very well what rich blessedness is ours, Lord God, in being sheep of the good shepherd. Preserve us amidst all trials and difficulties here on earth by keeping us ever close to our good shepherd, Jesus our Saviour. Amen.

MONDAY

LESSON: LUKE 5.27-32

Those who are well have no need of a physician, but those who are sick.   Matthew 9.12

Even though we are weak and sickly, we should still not lose heart and begin to think that we do not belong to the kingdom of Christ. The more we become aware of our infirmities, the closer we should walk with Christ. For it is His office to heal us and to make us well.

If you are sick and a sinner and feel your need, you have all the more reason to come to Him and say, "I come to you just because I am a sinner so that you may help me and rescue me from my sins". In this way your need drives you to Christ. For the greater your weakness, the more necessary it is for you to seek help and healing. That is also what He desires and hence He coaxes us so that we joyfully approach Him.

Those who are not such shepherds suppose that they can lick people into a godly shape by shouting at them clamorously in hostile fashion and bringing force to bear on them. They succeed only in making matters worse.

One sees the result of this on all sides in today's conditions. Matters have reached such a pass through the activity of hirelings in the Church that utter confusion prevails everywhere. **"He who is a hireling and not a shepherd, whose own the sheep are not, sees the wolf coming and leaves the sheep and flees; and the wolf snatches them and scatters them." John 10.12.**

SL.XI.784,15

PRAYER: Lord God, our heavenly Father, give us shepherds who really care for your sheep and protect them from all hirelings, for Christ's sake. Amen.

TUESDAY

LESSON: 1 TIMOTHY 2.1-6

A bruised reed he will not break, and a dimly burning wick he will not quench.   Isaiah 42.3

Matthew declares that these words of Isaiah were fulfilled in Christ (Matthew 12.20). A bruised reed is a reed very close to breaking point. One who has received a very serious injury, or is carrying a very heavy wound, that is, a Christian who is not only weak and stumbling, but who is overwhelmed in temptation, actually breaking a leg, so to say. It may be that he has fallen so deeply that he denies the Gospel, as Peter did when he denied Christ.

Even if such a man has stumbled, suffering a reverse and a complete upset, you should not reject him as though he never belonged to Christ's kingdom. You must allow Christ to retain His peculiar characteristic, that in His kingdom there is nothing but grace and mercy, pure and abounding. He is ever ready to help those who realize their wretchedness and misery, and who would be glad to get rid of it.

Christ's kingdom is a kingdom where men find true comfort and consolation. He is a consoling, friendly shepherd, coaxing and encouraging every man to draw close to Him. Christ alone is the one true, good shepherd who heals all ills and helps the fallen to rise again. He who does not do that is no shepherd.

SL.XI.785,16-17

PRAYER: It is your declared will, heavenly Father, that all men should learn to know your mercy, grace and salvation. Grant that we, too, may become enthused to help fallen sinners to find real help and consolation, for Christ, our Saviour's sake. Amen.

WEDNESDAY

LESSON: PSALM 85

The Lord is merciful and gracious, slow to anger and abounding in steadfast love.   Psalm 103.8

In preaching Christ it should be made quite clear that Christ rejects no one, no matter how weak he may be, but readily accepts everyone. He comforts and strengthens His sheep, like the good shepherd that He always is.

If Christ is proclaimed in this way, as He really is, the hearts of men will incline to Him of their own accord. There will be no need to use compulsion or force in bringing men to Christ. The Gospel coaxes men and makes them willing so that they get real pleasure and satisfaction in serving Christ.

A confident attitude also results from all this. Men begin to love Christ so that they gladly do all that He wants them to do. Confident obedience supplements all force and compulsion. When we come under compulsion, we render obedience only with ill-will and reluctance. God does not want this. It is all wasted effort.

When I begin to realize that the Lord is dealing with me in such a friendly manner, He takes hold of my heart so that I render Him ready obedience. Pleasure and real joy of heart follow.

SL.XI.786,20

PRAYER: Heavenly Father, you are always ready to pardon and forgive us our sins, rather than bring us to the judgement we so richly deserve. All this you have made very clear to us in the salvation which your own Son, Jesus Christ our Saviour, accomplished for us. Amen.

THURSDAY

LESSON: ROMANS 2.19-26

The law was given through Moses; grace and truth came through Jesus Christ. John 1.17

You have often heard how God sent a twofold proclamation into the world. The one is to proclaim God's Word as Law and tell men: "**You shall have no other gods before me**". "**You shall not kill, commit adultery, steal.**" **Exodus 20.3,13-15**. In this proclamation men also hear the threat that if they do not keep this Law they will die. This proclamation never succeeds in making a man truly righteous in his heart. For although a man is compelled by this proclamation to live a pious life outwardly before his fellowmen, in his heart of hearts he is hostile to this Law and would prefer that it did not really exist.

The other form in which God's Word is proclaimed is the Gospel. This tells us where a man must look for the ability to do what the Law demands. The Gospel does not drive a man on with threats; it coaxes men in all friendliness. The Gospel does not say: "Do this; do that!" but, "Come, I will instruct you where you can receive and obtain the wherewithal to become truly acceptable to God. See, here is the Lord Jesus Christ. He will give you all this."

These two forms of proclamation are in opposition to each other, like taking and giving, demanding and donating, and one must get a good grasp of this distinction. This distinction has always played a very important role in God's government of the world and still does. The Law must be preached to rough, uncouth men who have no knowledge at all of the Gospel. These men must come under the compulsion of the Law until they are mellowed and acknowledge their weaknesses. When they reach this stage, they are ready for the Gospel. SL.XI.778,2-3

PRAYER: Lord God, our heavenly Father, continue to show us by your holy Law that we are poor, lost and condemned sinners when judged by our works, but above all continue to let the light of your wonderful Gospel shine into our hearts with its message of salvation, for Christ's sake. Amen.

179

FRIDAY

LESSON: PSALM 23

He who descended is he who also ascended far above all the heavens, that he might fill all things.   Ephesians 4.10

You have heard how our Lord Jesus Christ, after His suffering and death was translated and entered an immortal existence. We must not understand this to mean that Christ is now sitting idly up in heaven and that He is nothing but an object of continual joy to Himself alone. He has taken over the full kingship of His kingdom and is exercising full rule over His kingdom. He is the King of whom all the prophets and the whole of Scripture has so much to tell us. St. Paul says that he now fills all things. And so we must ever regard Christ as being continually present in His kingdom and exercising the government of His kingdom.

We must not hold the view that He is sitting up in heaven in a state of idleness, but that from heaven above He now rules and fills all things, as St. Paul reminds us. He is especially concerned with His kingdom, which exists wherever the Christian faith exists. Therefore His kingdom is present in our midst here on earth. In regard to this kingdom, matters have been so ordained, that it should improve and become purer from day to day. This kingdom is not ruled by any forms of outward authority and might, but by the oral preaching of the Word of God, and more especially by the preaching of the Gospel.

SL.XI.780,6

PRAYER: Your presence in our midst, Lord Jesus, is a source of great consolation and joy to us at all times. Continue to bless us, especially in the proclamation of your Word of salvation. Let it always have free course in our midst, for your mercy's sake. Amen.

SATURDAY

LESSON: MATTHEW 5.13-16

I am not ashamed of the gospel: it is the power of God for salvation to every one who has faith, to the Jew first and also to the Greek.   Romans 1.16

The source of all power in Christ's kingdom rests in God's Word of truth and salvation. Those who hear that Word and believe it are members of God's kingdom.

Among the members of God's kingdom the Word becomes so powerful that it provides them with all that they need, and brings them all the blessings they desire. For it is the power of God which both can and does save all who believe it, as Paul reminds the Romans.

If you believe that Christ died to rescue you from every misfortune, and cling to the Word on this basis, it becomes so sure and firm that no creature can overturn it. Even as no one can overthrow this Word, no one can really harm you, inasmuch as you believe in it. With this Word, then, you overcome sin, death, the devil and hell, and eventually you will also find your refuge with the Word in eternal peace, joy and life. In short, you will become a partaker of all the power and might which the Word contains.

God's kingdom is really a wonderful kingdom. The Word is in this kingdom, and is orally proclaimed before the whole world. But the power of the Word is quite hidden; none become aware of the activity and great importance of the Word except those who believe. This must be experienced and tasted in the heart.

SL.XI.781,7

PRAYER: Open our hearts by your Holy Spirit, Lord God, that we always receive your saving Word for what it is, the source of all our knowledge and power as your children. Help us through your means of grace to grow and increase as your children, in and through Christ Jesus our Saviour. Amen.

SUNDAY

LESSON: JOHN 16.16-23

Truly, truly, I say to you, you will weep and lament, but the world will rejoice; you will be sorrowful, but your sorrow will turn into joy.   John 16.20

You see here how Christ announces to His disciples that they will become sad because He is about to leave them. They are still quite simple and unlearned, considerably disturbed by what Jesus said when He instituted His Holy Supper. They cannot understand what He is talking about. Indeed, the subject of Christ's discussion here is too profound and incomprehensible for our weak, fallen nature. It was necessary for the disciples to be sorrowful before they experienced joy.

Christ Himself is an example for us, to show us that we cannot enter glory without a cross. That is also why He said to the two disciples on the way to Emmaus, **"Was it not necessary that the Christ should suffer these things and enter into his glory?"** Luke 24.26.

If the beloved disciples were about to experience great joy, it was necessary for them to have previously experienced great sadness. This joy, however, came to them from the Lord Jesus, for in the Gospel it is established that outside of Christ there is no joy. On the other hand, where Christ is, there is no sorrow, as we are clearly reminded in the text.

SL.XI.830,2

PRAYER: In you alone, Lord Jesus, there is the true joy of salvation. Implant this in our hearts in full measure as our greatest treasure, for your love's sake. Amen.

MONDAY

LESSON: PSALM 30.1-5

A little while, and you will see me no more; again a little while, and you will see me.   John 16.16

"A little while", Jesus says, "**and you will see me no more**". He is about to be taken captive and put to death on the cross. But this will not be for long. During this "**little while**" they will certainly be sad. "But cling firmly to Me and follow Me", the Lord means to say to His disciples, "matters will soon take a turn for the better". He would be in the grave for only three days, during which the world would rejoice as though it had triumphed over Him. And His disciples would mourn and weep.

"**Again a little while, and you will see me**", says Jesus to His disciples, "**because I go to the Father**". cf. John 16.10. He would rise again on the third day and they would rejoice, and their joy no man would take from them. It would not be a joy just for three days like the joy of the world, but eternal joy. In these words the evangelist John has set forth an excellent summary of the death and resurrection of Christ: "**A little while, and you will see me no more; again a little while, and you will see me**".

The "little while" has special significance for us. Grief is but for a moment, a "little while", as the Lord also reminds His children through Isaiah, "**For a brief moment I forsook you, but with great compassion I will gather you. In overflowing wrath for a moment I hid my face from you, but with everlasting love I will have compassion on you, says the Lord, your Redeemer.**" Isaiah 54.7,8.

SL.XI.831,4-6

PRAYER: You have assured us, heavenly Father, that you will never lay a cross on us without supplying us with the strength to bear it, and that joy will always follow our sorrows. Fix this firmly in our hearts by faith so that we boldly endure unto the end, in and through Jesus and His love. Amen.

TUESDAY

LESSON: HABAKKUK 2.2-4

You have need of endurance, so that you may do the will of God and receive what is promised. "For yet a little while, and the coming one shall come and shall not tarry."
Hebrews 10.36,37

The first "**little while**" which Jesus mentioned when He said, "**A little while, and you will see me no more**", the disciples understood very soon after this when they saw Him taken captive and put to death. But the second "**little while**" when He said, "**Again a little while, and you will see me**", they could not comprehend. We cannot comprehend this either. Moreover, the explanation He offered, "**Because I go to the Father**" (v.10), was even less intelligible to them.

This is also our experience. Although we know and hear that trials, misfortune, and sorrow are to endure only for "**a little while**", existing circumstances always present a different picture from what we believe. We begin to have doubts and waver, and find it difficult to resign ourselves to our allotted obligations. We hear well enough, and we know quite well that it will be only "**a little while**"; but just how things will turn out we do not know, as was the case with the disciples.

If they cannot comprehend this, why does Jesus mention it to them? He says it so that we should not lose heart, but cling firmly to the Word, as He says, believing that it is quite sure and certain. We should be sure that matters cannot be otherwise than set forth in the Word, however much appearances may be to the contrary. Even if a man cannot at once believe the Word, God comes to his assistance. God does this without assistance from human reason, man's free will or any contribution by man.

SL.XI.832,7-8

PRAYER: Lord God, heavenly Father, to you we look for mercy, grace and faith, so that we may confidently accept the promises and assurances of your Word, for the sake of Him who is the Word, your Son, Jesus Christ. Amen.

WEDNESDAY

LESSON: 1 CORINTHIANS 15.12-19

If Christ has not been raised, then our preaching is in vain and your faith is in vain.   1 Corinthians 15.14

Like the disciples of old we are not slow in choosing crosses and sufferings for ourselves in the belief that we shall endure them without much difficulty. Peter declared boldly that he would rather die than deny Christ and all the other disciples concurred with him (Matthew 26.35). But when the particular hour arrives contrary to your expectation, you will hardly stand your ground unless you have become a new man. The Old Adam gives up very quickly and cannot stand up to any great pressure. To do that is quite contrary to his inclinations, purposes and aims.

So you must have your own little hour in which you suffer for a time. Christ withdraws Himself from you, and allows you to become enmeshed in the power of sin, death and hell. Your heart will become powerless to devise a way of bringing peace to your conscience, do whatever it may. Christ goes on His way and dies. Then you will hear the little refrain: **"A little while, and you will see me no more"**.

Where will you turn? There is no consolation, no help anywhere. You are held fast in the midst of sin, in the midst of death, in the midst of hell. If Christ did not come to you in this situation, without any merit on your part, you would have to remain for ever in such fear and terror. This would also have been the situation of the disciples had Christ not risen and become alive again. Therefore it was necessary for Him to rise again from the dead.

SL.XI.834,12

PRAYER: In the resurrection of your Son, our Lord, heavenly Father, you have given us sure and certain proof of the validity of His death for the forgiveness of our sins, life and salvation. Grant us the full joy of believing this with our whole hearts, in and through our Saviour Jesus Christ. Amen.

THURSDAY

LESSON: PSALM 33.13-22

You have sorrow now, but I will see you again and your hearts will rejoice, and no one will take your joy from you.
John 16.22

These words are spoken to all Christians. A Christian must face temptation, fear, distress, opposition and sorrow in whatever manner they may arise. Jesus makes no mention here of suffering on a cross; He simply mentions **"sorrow"**, and that they will have reason to "weep and lament".

In the world, Christians always experience persecutions of many kinds. Some suffer the loss of goods; others come under disgrace and contempt as the result of evil rumours. Some are drowned; others burnt. Some even lose their head. One meets his end in this way; another in that way. It is the invariable experience of the Christian to suffer misfortune and persecution. Only rarely is he quite free from distress and opposition. He is always being belaboured and flogged in some way or other, and he can look for nothing better as long as he is here on earth. This is the badge by which he is known. He who is a Christian must not be ashamed of this badge.

Why does God act in this way? Why does He allow His children to be persecuted and hounded in this manner? He does it to subdue and suppress man's free will so that man does not seek help and assistance from his own efforts but, as far as free will is concerned, he becomes a fool in regard to the works of God and learns to trust and rely on God alone and not on himself.

SL.XI.835,16-17

PRAYER: It is your will, heavenly Father, that we must experience trials and tribulations as your children in the midst of a hostile world. Strengthen our faith and endue us with the grace to squarely meet all our commitments, for the love of our Saviour. Amen.

FRIDAY

LESSON: EPHESIANS 1.3-11

There is no other name under heaven given among men by which we must be saved.   Acts 4.12

We can never form a correct estimate of persecutions, trials, and other troubles, or understand them correctly, unless Christ Himself awakens and enlightens us, and His resurrection becomes a power in us. All our own pretentious doings must be shattered and accounted as nothing.

In the Gospel for this week (John 16.16-23), we are given a powerful reminder that man with all his own powers is nothing. Here we have a condemnation and refutation of all that was formerly proclaimed about good works and all that may be claimed for good works in a similar way in the future. This much is quite clear: where Christ is absent, there is nothing significant for any Christian.

Ask St. Peter how he was minded when Christ was not with him and what kind of good works he performed? He denied Christ and confirmed his denial with cursing and swearing (Matthew 26.74). Those are the kind of good works we perform when Christ is not with us.

All this should help us to build on Christ alone, and to rely on no other creature in heaven or on earth. In His name alone and in no other there is preservation and salvation for us (Acts 4.12;10.43).

SL.XI.836,18-19

PRAYER: Dear Lord Jesus, enlighten us in such a way by your Holy Spirit that we learn to trust with our whole hearts in the salvation that you alone have provided for us as the beginning and the ending of our Christian faith. Amen.

SATURDAY

LESSON: PSALM 145.1-13

I go to the Father.   John 16.10

Christ wanted His disciples to come to a clear understanding of His statement, **"I go to the Father"**. The meaning of this statement was hidden; not even the disciples knew what Jesus meant. Put into other words Christ, instead of speaking about going to the Father, could simply have stated, "I must die and you must also die".

According to his Old Adam, Peter wanted to die with the Lord; this was a kind of vision of grandeur for Peter. All of us, no doubt, would also volunteer to die with Christ as all the other disciples offered to do (Matthew 26.35). But all such ideas must disappear from our view of things; an hour must come for us when Christ is not at our side, not dying with us, when we know not where to look for help, like a woman in childbirth.

When that hour arrives, you will come to the Father, that is, God fills you with power from on high, makes of you a new man who no longer has any fears, with a heavenly nature which raises itself in faith. Then you will become courageous and bold. Why? Because you have come to the Father.

Who can ever overthrow the almighty power of God? No one! There is no one who can do anything to you that can really harm you.

SL.XI.840,29

PRAYER: Bring us to the Father, Lord Jesus, that with the help of His almighty power we may overcome all our fears and difficulties and do our full duty as your disciples, for your love's sake. Amen.

SUNDAY

LESSON: JOHN 16.5-15

When he comes, he will convince the world of sin and of righteousness and of judgement.   John 16.8

When the Counsellor, the Holy Spirit, comes He will convince the world of blindness and ignorance. All men who have not been enlightened by the Holy Spirit, no matter how clever they may be thought to be by prevailing external circumstances, rule or dealings, are fools and blind before God. They do not like being reminded of this. In fact, they become very cross and angry if you tell them that all their achievements count for nothing at all before God. They are quite sure that the reason and natural light that God has created in them, must at least count for something.

What can we reply?

There stands the Scripture, the Word of God, plain and clear, telling us that the Holy Spirit will come and convince the world of ignorance in regard to sin, righteousness and judgement.

This is a fixed determination; it cannot be modified or changed. Let him who will, be angry; this is no concern of Christ here.

SL.XI.865,2

PRAYER: Heavenly Father, pour your Holy Spirit upon us in rich measure, that we are not ignorant of your Word and salvation like the world in its blindness, but may at all times cling in firm faith to your saving Word, the vehicle of your enlightening Spirit. Amen.

MONDAY

LESSON: JOHN 14.12-24

When he *[the Holy Spirit]* **comes, he will convince the world of sin . . . because they do not believe in me.**

John 16.8,9

The world is in a wretched plight. Not only is it ignorant of sin, of righteousness and of judgement, but it cannot recognize this fact, not to mention the utter impossibility of getting rid of this ignorance.

Here you see also how all credibility is taken from those who want to train others in the ways of godliness when they do not even know what sin is. It would be both interesting and instructive to examine our theological schools and learned theologians on the meaning of the one little word "**sin**". Have you ever heard it said or taught that "**sin**" is not believing in Christ? They tell us that "**sin**" is to speak, desire, or do something contrary to God's will and commandment.

How does this agree with Christ's statement here that the Holy Spirit will convict the world of sin "**because they do not believe in me**"? It is not so difficult to convict the world of being ignorant of sin, even though it is a very learned world. The world will not find it easy to explain this text.

SL.XI.866,3

PRAYER: Lord God, heavenly Father, keep us ever mindful of the seriousness of the sin of rejecting your salvation in Christ. Open our hearts by your Holy Spirit so that we may cling firmly in true faith to Christ and all His blessings for us, for your mercy's sake. Amen.

TUESDAY

LESSON: HEBREWS 10.26-31

Jesus spoke to them, saying, "I am the light of the world; he who follows me will not walk in darkness, but will have the light of life".   John 8.12

Christ has come and proclaimed the truth that everything we do apart from the Holy Spirit, no matter how great it is and how lovely it appears to be, is sin. We cannot do anything good gladly and willingly without the Holy Spirit. Christ came on earth to take our place. He has taken away all our sins. As a result of this we have received the Holy Spirit through whom we have also obtained love and the desire to do what God wants us to do.

This entire work of Christ is God's free gift to us, so that we should never presume to come before God with our own works, but solely and only through Christ and His merits. Through the work of Christ it also comes to pass that sin for us is no longer what we have done contrary to God's Law. The Law played no part at all in making us righteous and acceptable before God, because by nature we cannot do this.

What then is "sin" in view of the work of Christ? It is nothing else but the rejection of the Saviour and the refusal to accept Him who can remove our sins from us. Where Christ is present, there is no sin. He brings with Him the Holy Spirit, who enkindles faith in our hearts and the desire to do what is good.

The world is no longer convicted or condemned because of any other sin, for Christ has destroyed all sin. In the New Covenant, however, the only thing that is sin is failure to recognize Christ and to accept Him.

SL.XI.868,8-9

PRAYER: Of your mercy and grace, O God, imbue us with such knowledge and understanding of your wonderful love in Christ that we never allow ourselves by any deception of self-love or the devil to be withdrawn from the circle of your grace and mercy, in Christ Jesus our Saviour. Amen.

WEDNESDAY

LESSON: 1 CORINTHIANS 1.18-25

What no eye has seen, nor ear heard, nor the heart of man conceived, what God has prepared for those who love him, God has revealed to us through the Spirit.
1 Corinthians 2.9,10

Putting it in other words, Christ says, "If they had believed in me, everything would have been bestowed upon them as a free gift; for I know that there is no other alternative available to them by nature. But that they refuse to accept me or believe that I cannot help them will mean condemnation for them."

On judgement day, God's judgement upon them will run something like this: "You found yourselves in sins and were unable to rescue yourselves. But for all that, it was not my will that you should be condemned. I sent my only Son to you and wanted to give Him to you as a gift so that He might take away your sins. But you refused to accept Him. And so you are now being condemned solely and only because you do not have Christ as your Saviour."

The words of the Gospel are spoken in honour and praise of the high grace that has been given to us in our Lord Jesus Christ. The conception of such a plan of salvation is absolutely above man's reason.

Reason can only think as follows, "I sinned in works and so I must make restitution with works, blot out my sins and pay for them with works, so that I may obtain the assurance of a gracious God". This is the highest point that reason can reach. In actual fact it is nothing but folly and blindness.

SL.XI.868,10-11

PRAYER: Honour and praise be to you, Lord God, heavenly Father, for the wonderful grace and mercy bestowed on us in Christ. Your love for us is beyond all powers of reason and understanding. Thanks be to you for your inexpressible love! Amen.

THURSDAY

LESSON: PSALM 32

[Christ] is able for all time to save those who draw near to God through him, since he always lives to make intercession for them.   Hebrews 7.25

God makes it quite clear to us that if we want to get rid of our sins we must be able to pay the price with quite different works from those which we perform for ourselves. For even our very best works are still marred by sin, even the works by which we imagine that we are reconciling ourselves to God and atoning for our sins.

Is it not foolish to try to blot out sins with sins? Even in the very best works that you can perform you are sinning, for the simple reason that you cannot perform these works gladly and readily with all your heart. If you were not motivated by fear of some sort of punishment, you would probably prefer to postpone these works.

With these works of yours you actually try to atone for little sins with big sins, or you commit sins just as great as the ones of which you are trying to rid yourselves. It is really great blindness for a man not to see what sin is, or to know what good works are, and to confuse sins with good works. The Holy Spirit therefore comes and convinces the world of sin by showing men that it is sin to reject Christ and not to believe in Him.

What is the solution? Believe that the Lord Jesus Christ has taken your sin away and your sins will be gone. If you do not get rid of your sins in this way you will fall deeper and deeper into sin and its clutches.

SL.XI.869,12-13

PRAYER: Lord Jesus, the lamb of God who takes away the sin of the world, may our faith in the sufficiency of your work of salvation never weaken but ever increase in and through the consolation of your Gospel of grace and love. Amen.

FRIDAY

LESSON: 1 CORINTHIANS 1.26-31

[The Holy Spirit] will convince the world . . . of **righteousness, because I go to the Father, and you will see me no more.** John 16.8-10

Righteousness means piety, a good and honest life before God. Jesus says here that He will convince the world of righteousness, **"because I go to the Father"**.

We have often stated that Christ's resurrection did not take place for His benefit but for our sakes; hence we should make it our very own possession. He rose from the dead and ascended into heaven to establish a spiritual kingdom in which He reigns in us by means of righteousness and truth. He is not just sleeping and resting in heaven or amusing Himself there in idleness but, as Paul reminds us, He is continually active and busy here on earth in His Church, ruling consciences and souls by the Gospel (cf. Ephesians 1.22).

Wherever Christ is preached and acknowledged, He now rules in us from God's right hand, and He Himself is present with us here in our hearts. He rules in His kingdom here on earth in such a way that he exercises power, might and authority over us and all our foes, and helps to free us from sin, death, the devil and hell. His resurrection and ascension is our consolation, life, salvation and righteousness.

This is what Christ means here when He states that men become righteous before God because He goes to His Father and we see Him no more. This the world cannot understand. The Holy Spirit must come to convince the world of its ignorance in this respect.

SL.XI.870,15-16

PRAYER: Continue to abide with us, Lord Jesus, as our consolation, life, salvation and righteousness in your kingdom of truth and salvation, for your love's sake. Amen.

SATURDAY

LESSON: EPHESIANS 1.11-14

It is God who establishes us with you in Christ, and has commissioned us; he has put his seal upon us and given us his Spirit in our hearts as a guarantee.

2 Corinthians 1.21,22

If I am to be accounted righteous before God, it is not enough for me to do good works externally; I must do them from the bottom of my heart with delight and in love, so that I stand unafraid before sin, death and the devil, free and joyful, with a good conscience and all confidence before God, knowing how I stand with Him.

No work and no creature can give me any assurance here. When it comes to righteousness before God I must look to Christ alone, to Him who has gone to the Father in heaven where I cannot see Him but must believe that He is up above and will help me. This faith makes me acceptable to God, for Christ gives me the Holy Spirit in my heart. It is He who makes me ready and glad to perform all good works. In this way I am accounted righteous before God, and in no other way.

As long as you operate with works, you will become more and more wretched and disconsolate the more that you devote yourself to them. The more you rest your faith on Christ alone as your one and only hope and source of righteousness and salvation, the more you will experience the real joy of salvation in Christ.

Where Christ is really acknowledged for what He is, the Holy Spirit cannot remain absent.

SL.XI.871,17-18

PRAYER: Thanks be to you, heavenly Father, for the riches of your grace and mercy in Christ Jesus, and also for the seal and guarantee that you have given us in our hearts through the Holy Spirit, that we are your beloved children in and through Jesus Christ our Saviour. Amen.

SUNDAY

LESSON: JOHN 16.23-30

Truly, truly, I say to you, if you ask anything of the Father, he will give it to you in my name.   John 16.23

The Gospel for *Rogate* speaks to us about Christian prayer and what makes a prayer truly Christian.

The first thing of importance here is God's promise. This is the real basis of Christian prayer, and the source from which it derives its power. Christ here assures us that what we ask will be given to us, and He does this with a solemn pledge when He declares, **"Truly, truly, I say to you, if you ask anything of the Father, He will give it to you in my name"**.

Christ gives us this assurance to make us quite certain that our prayers will be heard. He chides the disciples for having been sluggish in prayer. **"Hitherto you have asked nothing in my name"**, He says to them. He wants them to understand that God is always prepared to give to them much earlier than they ask, and much more than they ask. He offers His blessings to His disciples; they are available whenever they deign to receive them.

It is truly a great disgrace and a severe punishment upon us Christians that Christ can still reproach us with sluggishness in asking, and that such a rich and excellent promise does not incite us to exercise the privilege of prayer.

Here is a great treasure untapped before us and we make so little effort to exercise the privilege of prayer and to utilize its power in Christian faith and life. God Himself bases prayer on His promise, and on this basis He also urges us to pray.

SL.XI.918,2-3

PRAYER: Heavenly Father, you have invited us to bring all our needs before you in prayer in the name of our Saviour. Hear our prayer which we offer in the name of our Saviour Jesus Christ. Amen.

MONDAY

LESSON: JAMES 1.5-8

Ask, and you will receive, that your joy may be full.

John 16.24

In our prayers we should firmly believe that God's promise to us is always sure and certain, and have no doubt that He will give us what He promises. Words of promise from God always call for faith on our part. Faith is a firm, undoubted confidence in the truth of God's promise. He who prays to God with doubts in his heart is tempting God. He has his doubts about God's will and grace. His prayer must be meaningless. He gropes after God like a blind man for a wall.

St. John writes: **"This is the confidence which we have in him, that if we ask anything according to his will he hears us. And if we know that he hears us in whatever we ask, we know that we have obtained the requests made of him."** 1 John 5.14,15. In these words St. John describes how a truly believing heart prays. It is quite sure and certain that prayer is heard and that it will be answered.

The Holy Spirit must give this faith and absolute certainty. Without the Holy Spirit there can be no real Christian prayer. Try it out now and pray in this way! Then you will also experience the wonderful sweetness of this promise of God. You will also gain courage and the comfort of heart to make a variety of prayers, no matter how great or high the petitions may be.

SL.XI.920,5-6

PRAYER: Heavenly Father, your promises to us are sure and certain. Therefore we take you at your Word and bring all our requests and needs before you in prayer in the confidence that you will hear and answer them, in the name of Jesus. Amen.

TUESDAY

LESSON: LUKE 19.1-6

Likewise the Spirit helps us in our weakness; for we do not know how to pray as we ought, but the Spirit himself intercedes for us with sighs too deep for words.

Romans 8.26

In our prayers we must earnestly desire or wish that what we pray for should come to pass. This is what is meant by the word **"ask"** which Jesus uses in the Gospel. Some have described this as "the ascent of the soul to God". The heart lifts itself up and soars up to God with a burning desire, and on this basis it sighs and says, "O that I had this or that!"

According to St. Paul, prayer can be a yearning that cannot always be put into actual words. The mouth cannot always express what the heart feels; the yearning of the heart can surpass all our speaking and even thinking (Romans 8.26).

When Zacchaeus wanted to see Jesus, the possibility of Jesus speaking to him and coming to his house was beyond all his powers of conception. But after this joyful event he was more than satisfied. His efforts had succeeded beyond his fondest desires.

On one occasion Moses cried out to God and God said to him, **"Why do you cry to me?" Exodus 14.15.** Actually Moses on this occasion did not utter a word, but deep sighs came from his heart in the hour of need. Such sighs God calls cries.

St. Paul also declares that God **"is able to do far more abundantly than all that we ask or think". Ephesians 3.20.** Trials, fear, distress, serve to bring out these sighs. They teach us how to sigh to God in prayer.

SL.XI.922,9

PRAYER: You know the meaning of our sighs, heavenly Father, and your Holy Spirit can also interpret them for us at your throne of grace. Hear us, accordingly, when we sigh to you in Jesus' name. Amen.

WEDNESDAY

LESSON: MATTHEW 7.7-12

If you ask anything in my name, I will do it.   John 14.14

An important factor in our prayers is that we must pray to our heavenly Father in the name of Jesus. This is nothing else but to come to God with faith in Christ, and to console ourselves with the confidence that He is our Mediator through whom all things are given to us.

Without such faith and confidence in Christ and His work of salvation we would merit nothing but wrath and displeasure. St. Paul reminds us of all this when he declares in Romans, **"Through Christ we have obtained access to this grace in which we stand, and we rejoice in our hope of sharing the glory of God". Romans 5.2.**

We are really asking in the name of Jesus when we rely on Jesus and believe that we shall be accepted and heard for His sake, and not for our sakes.

Those who ask in their own name, with the presumptuous idea that God will hear them and regard them because of their many, great, devotional and holy prayers, will merit and receive nothing but God's wrath and disfavour. They do not regard a mediator as necessary. For them Christ has no significance and is of no use.

SL.XI.922,10

PRAYER: Lord God, heavenly Father, never let us forget how much we need the work of our Saviour and Mediator. On this basis may our prayers be always pleasing and acceptable to you, in Jesus' name. Amen.

THURSDAY

LESSON: MARK 16.14-20

Then the Lord Jesus, after he had spoken to them, was taken up into heaven, and sat down at the right hand of God.
Mark 16.19

We must regard the ascension of Christ as an efficacious, powerful act which is in continuous and ceaseless operation. We must not just imagine that Christ has ascended into heaven and left us here on earth to be ruled in other ways. On the contrary, He has ascended into heaven because He can achieve most and rule most effectively by that act.

If He had remained visibly here on earth among men, He could never have achieved as much. Not all people would then have been able to be with Him to hear Him. He had to make a start on having to deal with all men, ruling all men, preaching to all men, so that all might hear Him and that He might be with all men.

Take care, therefore, that you do not form the idea that Christ is now far away from you. The contrary is true. When He was on earth He was far away from us; since His ascension He is very close to us.

Reason, of course, cannot understand this, so the ascension is an article of faith. Here one must close the eyes to reason and grasp matters by faith. God's Word tells us that the man Christ Jesus ascended visibly into heaven where He now sits at God's right hand and governs all things.

SL.XI.940,24-25

PRAYER: Christ our Saviour ascended visibly into heaven from where He now rules and governs all things. Make us aware of the full import of this mighty act of our Saviour, heavenly Father, so that we look more confidently to Jesus as Lord of lords and King of kings. Amen.

FRIDAY

LESSON: COLOSSIANS 3.1-4

When he ascended on high he led a host of captives, and he gave gifts to men. Ephesians 4.8

Christ's ascension is a mighty act which should bring us real comfort and assurance. Those who believe in the ascended Lord should be joyful and courageous, take confidence from this act and say, "My Lord Jesus Christ is Lord over death, the devil, sin, righteousness, body, life, enemies and friends. Of what shall I still be afraid?"

If my enemies beset me with intentions of slaying me, my faith declares, "Christ has ascended into heaven and become the Lord of all creatures. Hence my enemies must also be subject to Him. So it is beyond their power to harm me. I defy them to raise a finger against me and disturb one hair on my head without Christ's will."

If this is how faith looks at this matter and rests on this article of Christ's ascension, all is well. Then faith will also become bold and certain and declare, "If my Lord's will is that my enemies should put me to death, I willingly depart".

You see, then, that Christ ascended into heaven not just to sit up there in His own interests but to rule there; to work out all things for our good, that we may derive comfort and joy from His ascension.

SL.XI.941,27

PRAYER: We thank you, Lord Jesus, for the assurance of abiding help and blessing which we derive from your glorious ascension into heaven, and its significance for our faith and lives as Christians at all times. Continue to be with us and bless us as our ascended Lord, for your name's sake. Amen.

SATURDAY

LESSON: PSALM 47

Thou didst ascend the high mount, leading captives in thy train, and receiving gifts among men, even among the rebellious, that the Lord God may dwell there.   Psalm 68.18

All the prophets were very careful to describe the ascension of Christ and His kingdom. As His dying and death are deeply embedded in Scripture, so also is His kingdom, resurrection and ascension into heaven. One must understand Christ's ascension into heaven correctly; otherwise it is powerless and sapless.

Of what use is it to preach only that He has ascended and now sits up there in idleness? The prophet wants to tell us more here in the psalm. Christ ascended into heaven, he declares, leading captivity in His train. This means that He is not only sitting up there on high, but that He is also down here on earth. He ascended on high to be present here on earth, so that He might be able to fill all things and be present in all places. This He could not do during His earthly sojourn, for all eyes could not then see Him.

He sat down where everyone can see Him, and where He can deal with everyone, fill every creature, be present everywhere. All things are now filled by Him, and there is nothing so great in heaven and earth that He does not exercise authority over it. Everything must do what He wills and no more. He not only rules and governs all creatures (for thereby my faith would not necessarily be helped or my sins taken away) but He has also led captivity captive.

SL.XI.942,30

PRAYER: Help us to realize the wonderful blessings and assurances which are ours, Lord Jesus, as a direct result of your ascension into heaven. You are indeed Lord of lords, and King of kings, present with us everywhere. In us sinners, however, dear Lord, let your ascension be a guarantee that you are sin's conqueror, having led captivity captive. Grant us the full realization of all this, in your name. Amen.

SUNDAY

LESSON: JOHN 15.26-16.4

The genuineness of your faith, more precious than gold which though perishable is tested by fire, may redound to praise and glory and honour at the revelation of Jesus Christ.
1 Peter 1.7

You have heard me say a great deal about faith. Now you will hear about witnessing to the faith and about the cross which accompanies faith. Paul reminded the Romans that a **"man believes with his heart and so is justified".** **Romans 10.10.**

The starting point of Christian piety is faith of the heart. This is the beginning of piety, but it is not enough for salvation. One must also lead a truly Christian life and continue therein. Paul also says to the Romans, **"Man believes with his heart and so is justified, and he confesses with his lips and so is saved". Romans 10.10.**

The two things which save us are faith and the confession of faith. Faith saves from sins, hell, devil, death and all misfortune. When we have faith we have enough. Let us then live for God here on earth by extending a helping hand to our neighbour. In this way God wants His name to be praised and His kingdom extended.

Therefore we must praise God's name here on earth, confess our faith, and encourage others to come to God, so that God's kingdom is enlarged and His name praised. Faith must be practised, worked at, fortified and even refined by fire like gold.

SL.XI.992,1-2

PRAYER: Equip us with grace, heavenly Father, always to bear clear witness to our faith in service to our neighbour, for Christ's sake. Amen.

MONDAY

LESSON: MATTHEW 16.24-28

They will put you out of the synagogues; indeed, the hour is coming when whoever kills you will think he is offering service to God.   John 16.2

The cross is pictured here in its true colours. To lie at home sick in bed is nothing compared to this, even though it is often regarded as suffering a cross. Christ is referring here to a very special cross, that of being persecuted, with the possibility of being put to death in disgrace. Not only so, but our persecutors receive praise and win renown. They seem to have right on their side and are honoured. On our side there is nothing but disgrace, shame and injustice.

The persecuting world actually believes that it is advancing God's honour. The world is also of the opinion that we are receiving our just deserts and that God, the Scriptures and all the angels are against us. In the view of the world, we really have no grounds for complaint. We cannot lay claims to justice, but we are accursed and must be removed from the scene with shame and disgrace.

This is precisely what happened to Christ. He was subjected to a most scornful and disgraceful death, hung between two robbers or murderers and regarded as an arch-criminal. Blasphemous words were hurled at Him. "He called Himself God's Son; let Him help Himself now if He wants things otherwise!" And so Jesus says here to His disciples that they will suffer death — not just simple death, but a disgraceful death — and the world will imagine that it is advancing God's honour thereby.

In the face of such hard and harsh reality one must still hold fast to faith and confess that God is gracious to us and is our Saviour against the whole world, with all its glitter and empty show. We must confess our faith, no matter how hard and harsh the opposition may be, if we are really concerned about our true welfare.   SL.XI.993,4

PRAYER: Grant us the needed grace, faith and power, dear Saviour, to bear whatever cross may come upon us, and to confess our faith boldly before the whole world, for your name's sake. Amen.

TUESDAY

LESSON: MATTHEW 10.24-33

I am weary with my moaning; every night I flood my bed with tears; I drench my couch with my weeping. My eye wastes away because of grief, it grows weak because of all my foes. Psalm 6.6,7

The chief requisite for a consistent confession of faith is a firm faith, and it is almost certain that the cross will follow upon a consistent confession of faith. Another experience that we will have, whether in life or in death, is that all that we have done can be represented in such a light that it seems to be opposed to God and Scripture.

It would be better for us to learn this from men here in this life rather than from the devil in death. For men can never push a matter beyond our ears. But the devil has a very sharp tongue and can push something right into our heart, making it tremble, and filling us with such fear that we imagine ourselves to be lost and ruined, and that heaven and earth, God and all His angels, are opposed to us. This is what the prophet is speaking about in the words quoted above from the psalm. It is hard to stand fast in such a situation.

From all this you also see why so few actually confess their faith in a thoroughly consistent manner. One man is afraid of his wife, another man is afraid of his children. There is also concern for property. There are also those, and they are perhaps a majority, who are afraid of themselves.

SL.XI.994,5

PRAYER: Remove from us all fear of men and other earthly considerations, heavenly Father, and let our confession at all times ring out loud and clear, in Jesus' name. Amen.

WEDNESDAY

LESSON: ROMANS 15.13-21

When the Counsellor comes, whom I shall send to you from the Father . . .   John 15.26

So that we do not become despondent and lose heart, Christ here assures us that He will send us a Counsellor or Comforter, and a very unique one at that, one who is almighty. He here calls the Holy Spirit a Counsellor or Comforter.

Although our sins and the fear of death at times make us feel timid and rather crestfallen, the Spirit comes to us and touches our heart and says, "Wake up, and get into things!" He inspires us with courage, speaking to us in a friendly and comforting manner, so that we do not despair in the face of death, but rush into the fray as though we had ten necks to risk and say, "Although I do have sins, they are no longer of any real account for me; and even if I had still more of them and they made a common assault on me, I still have the confidence that they can no longer harm me".

Not that we should no longer be sensible of our sins, for the flesh must be sensible of them. But the Spirit overcomes and suppresses timidity and fear, and guides us safely through such experiences, as He has the power to do. Jesus also says of the Spirit here, **"I will send Him to you from the Father"**. "The Father is the initial person; I am the Son and the Holy Spirit comes from us."

These three Persons are one entity and essence, of equal power and might, as He explains even better in the words that follow.

SL.XI.995,7-8

PRAYER: Let us always enjoy the comfort, consolation and power of the Comforter, the Holy Spirit, whom you, Lord Jesus, send us from the Father, in your name and for your sake. Amen.

THURSDAY

LESSON: EPHESIANS 1.15-23

Even the Spirit of truth, who proceeds from the Father . . . will bear witness to me.   John 15.26

This amounts to saying: He who will comfort you is almighty and Lord over all things. What can any creature do against us when the Creator is at our side? Behold, how great is the comfort of the Holy Spirit! Let all the enemies come on in full array; if the Holy Spirit is our protector and supporter, no danger threatens us.

In his first epistle John says, **"By this we shall know that we are of the truth, and reassure our hearts before him whenever our hearts condemn us; for God is greater than our hearts, and he knows everything".** 1 John 3.19,20. He also says in the next chapter, **"Little children, you are of God, and have overcome them; for he who is in you is greater than he who is in the world".** 1 John 4.4.

The Lord here says to us, "I will send the Spirit to you so that nothing may harm you". Is this not a great consolation? Who will not be bold and courageous after such an assurance?

And the Lord calls Him **"the Spirit of truth"**. Where the Spirit is and where the Spirit comes there is basic and absolute truth, with no falsehood or hypocrisy. The Spirit never plays the hypocrite. But where the Spirit is absent, you will find utter hypocrisy and falsehood. That is also why men fall away when battle threatens; they do not have the Spirit of truth.

SL.XI.995,9

PRAYER: Thanks and praise be to you, dear Lord, for the precious gift of the Counsellor, the Spirit of truth, and all we are and enjoy by His presence with us. Keep Him ever close to us and us with Him, in your name, Lord Jesus. Amen.

FRIDAY

LESSON: 1 PETER 2.7-10

He will bear witness to me.   John 15.26

If the Holy Spirit is in your hearts, He will speak through you and make you sure and certain that the Gospel is the truth. From this conviction will also flow your witness to the Gospel.

What is the Gospel? It is the testimony concerning Christ, that He is the Son of God and the Saviour, besides whom there is no other Saviour.

This is also what Peter means in his first epistle when he reminds us that we are "**a royal priesthood**". **1 Peter 2.9**. We have been chosen by God to proclaim Christ and to make Him known. Such testimony is certainly necessary, even though it always arouses the wrath of the world. The cross follows such testimony or witness.

There will be insurrections against the Gospel. Princes and lords will rise in anger, and all that is great in the world will oppose the Gospel. The world always finds it hard to listen to the Gospel and to tolerate its proclamation. Hence the Gospel is always a proclamation that arouses hostility.

When Christ and faith in Christ is proclaimed as the one source of salvation, the wisdom of the world is placarded as tomfoolery and nonsense. One of these must give way. So the world rejects the Gospel and remains as it was.

SL.XI.996,10-11

PRAYER: Dear Lord Jesus, grant us the courage and faith to witness clearly and consistently to the faith awakened in our hearts by your gift of the Spirit of truth. If our witness involves us in a cross, your Counsellor is greater than all and every opposition. Keep Him ever at our side, for your name's sake. Amen.

SATURDAY

LESSON: 1 THESSALONIANS 1.2-10

And you also are witnesses, because you have been with me from the beginning.   John 15.27

"When you have become sure and certain through the Holy Spirit who has witnessed to you, then first and foremost you will bear witness to Me."

This is Christ's conviction about His disciples. He had, of course, chosen them as His apostles; they had heard His words and doctrine; they had seen His works and His life. All this would be very important to their proclamation of Christ. But, in addition, they still needed the witness of the Holy Spirit, or else they would achieve nothing.

Conscience is always too weak to offer effective resistance to sin. There is no sin so small that conscience can really stand up against it, even such a matter, for example, as laughing in church. Likewise, conscience can achieve very little when death assails us. We must look elsewhere for help to supply courage to a timid and despondent conscience, so that it never gives up, although it may be heavily laden with sins.

This needed help, like the One who promises it, must be almighty help so that the timid conscience which beforehand was previously terrified by the sound of a driven leaf (Leviticus 26.36) is no longer afraid before all the devils of hell. And the conscience which was previously so sensitive that it could not even endure laughter, is now quite able to stand up against any number of sins.

SL.XI.997,13

PRAYER: Make us strong, bold and brave confessors of our faith, heavenly Father, through the witness of the Counsellor, whom you and your Son have promised to send us, in Jesus' name and for His sake. Amen.

SUNDAY

LESSON: JOHN 14.23-31

The law of the Spirit of life in Christ Jesus has set me free from the law of sin and death.   Romans 8.2

On the day of Pentecost, when the disciples of Christ were all together in one place, the Holy Spirit came upon them and filled them. Before this joyful event they sat in deep gloom, fear and sorrow. The Spirit gave them cloven tongues of fire, enkindled them so that they became bold, preached freely in groups and were afraid of nothing.

From all this you see quite clearly that it is not the office of the Holy Spirit to write books or to set up laws, but to abolish all this in the interests of freedom. The Holy Spirit is a God who does His writing in the heart, making it burn. He supplies a man with new courage so that he becomes joyful before God and begins to love Him, and then serves his fellowman with a joyful heart.

To set forth the Holy Spirit in this light is to preach the Holy Spirit correctly. Do not believe anyone who sets forth the Spirit in a different light. If the Spirit comes in this way you see that He annuls the letter of the Law and wants to free men from sins and the Law. Indeed, He wants to make it quite clear that we have no further use for the Law, and that He rules inwardly in our hearts without the Law.

SL.XI.1023,14

PRAYER: Renew our spirits by your Holy Spirit, heavenly Father, and draw our hearts to yourself in Him. Let us not serve you as slaves, with a spirit of bondage, but with freedom and gladness as your true sons, for Jesus Christ's sake. Amen.

MONDAY

LESSON: EPHESIANS 2.19-22

When the Counsellor comes, whom I shall send to you from the Father, even the Spirit of truth, who proceeds from the Father, he will bear witness to me. John 15.26

In what way does the Holy Spirit change the heart and make it new? What means does He use to take hold of the heart? He does it by proclaiming and preaching the Lord Jesus Christ, as Christ Himself declares in John's Gospel, **"When the Counsellor comes, whom I shall send to you from the Father, even the Spirit of truth, who proceeds from the Father, he will bear witness to me"**.

We have often heard that this Gospel, which God allows to be preached in the world and proclaimed to everyone, teaches that no one can become righteous before God through the Law, but that the Law only makes the situation worse for every man. Therefore God sent His beloved Son into the world to die and shed His blood for the world, and to demonstrate that men cannot destroy their sins and get rid of them by their own strength and works.

For the proclamation of this Gospel something additional is needed. I do not necessarily believe this Gospel simply by hearing it preached. For this purpose God has given us the additional gift of His Holy Spirit who impresses this Gospel upon our hearts, so that it sticks to the heart and lives in the heart. In the work of Christ there is the whole treasure of salvation, but it is not necessarily distributed and applied.

If we are to enjoy this treasure, the Holy Spirit must come to us and put this treasure into our hearts, and awaken faith in this treasure in our hearts so that it becomes our very own possession. This is the special work of the Holy Spirit.

SL.XI.1024,15-16

PRAYER: Almighty and merciful Lord, in the gifts of your Holy Spirit you have given us a sure pledge that Christ's work of salvation belongs to us. May your Holy Spirit always continue to bear witness with our spirit that we are your children and heirs of your kingdom, in and through our Saviour Jesus Christ. Amen.

211

TUESDAY

LESSON: MATTHEW 13.44,45

The Counsellor, the Holy Spirit, whom the Father will send in my name, . . . will teach you all things, and bring to your remembrance all that I have said to you.   John 14.26

You will know who the Holy Spirit is, if you know why He was given and what His office is. He it is who applies the treasure of Christ and all that He has to us — Christ who is given to us and proclaimed to us through the Gospel. It is the office of the Holy Spirit to fix this treasure in our hearts as our very own possession.

When He has done this and you experience this treasure in your heart, it follows that you will have to ask yourself: If the real issue here is that your works count for nothing and that the Holy Spirit must work all this in you, why should you continue to flog yourself with works of the Law?

All human works and the Law are no longer of any significance here, not even the law of Moses, for a man who has the treasure of Christ in his heart is above all law. The Holy Spirit teaches him better than all books, so that he understands the Scripture better than we can explain it to him, and of himself does all that God wants of him. The Law can make no demands on him. The only real use of books is that one can use them to demonstrate in what manner the Holy Spirit teaches men.

Our faith must never become a mere private matter which we keep to ourselves; it must burst forth. To establish and prove our faith, we must have Scripture. Take care, then, that you do not regard the Holy Spirit as a law-giver but as the one who abrogates the Law and sets men free, so that not a letter of it remains in force against you as far as your salvation is concerned.

SL.XI.1025,17-18

PRAYER: Come Holy Spirit, Comforter and Counsellor, with all your gifts of grace in Christ, and dwell in our hearts in such a way that we always have a confident assurance and remain free men, in and through Christ our Saviour. Amen.

WEDNESDAY

LESSON: PHILIPPIANS 3.12-16

Not that I have already obtained this or am already perfect; but I press on to make it my own, because Christ Jesus has made me his own.   Philippians 3.12

We should learn to understand that a man who has received the Holy Spirit does not necessarily become a perfect Christian immediately, experiencing no further trouble from the Law or from sin. Nor is the Spirit's presence always immediately evident from a spotless purity.

We do not teach that the Holy Spirit has already fully performed His office and completed it, but simply that He has begun to carry out His office, that His work is beginning to run its course, and continually developing without ceasing.

You will never find a single person who is without sin and sorrow, full of righteousness and joy, and so perfect that he is completely self-sufficient, serving everyone in perfect freedom. Scripture clearly tells us what the work and office of the Holy Spirit is, to save men from sin and its terrors, but that office is still not fully accomplished. Every Christian will at times feel sin in his heart and experience the terrors of death. He will be subject to all the assaults which assail other sinners.

Unbelievers are held so fast in their sins that they no longer feel them. Believers, however, do feel them but they have a helper, the Holy Spirit, who comforts them and strengthens them. Had the Spirit completed His office, this would not be the case.

SL.XI.1026,19-20

PRAYER: We beseech you, O Lord, to grant us the comforting presence and aid of your Holy Spirit, that, whatever by His teaching we know to be our duty, we may by His grace and mercy be able to perform, through Christ our Lord. Amen.

THURSDAY

LESSON: ROMANS 7.13-20

Likewise the Spirit helps us in our weakness; for we do not know how to pray as we ought, but the Spirit himself intercedes for us with sighs too deep for words.

Romans 8.26

In connection with the Holy Spirit and His work it is always necessary to maintain a certain reserve, so that we do not approach the Holy Spirit with an importunity that amounts to arrogance and a joyfulness that is almost levity.

Some people are so filled with the Spirit that they become secure, and imagine themselves to be on the threshold of perfection. A pious Christian is still flesh and blood like other men, except that he deeply deplores his sin and evil lust. He has experiences which he would rather forget. Unbelievers take little account of sin, and do not allow it to bother them unduly.

The important thing here is not merely the experience of evil lust and fighting against it. We must not allow our feelings and experience to determine the issue. We must not conclude that all is lost because we still feel our sins. We must keep on working at our sins every day of our lives, and permit the Holy Spirit to continue His work in us. We must also have the earnest desire to get rid of our sins. This desire never ceases in believers.

Such sighs penetrate so deeply that they reach a level where they are beyond words (Romans 8.26). But they have a precious auditor, the Holy Spirit Himself. He can fully appreciate all this sighing, and comfort the conscience from which it comes.

SL.XI.1026,21

PRAYER: Hear our sighs, O Holy Spirit, Comforter and Counsellor, and keep working on us with your purposes of grace and salvation, in and through Jesus Christ our Saviour. Amen.

FRIDAY

LESSON: EPHESIANS 4.25-32

If we live by the Spirit, let us also walk by the Spirit.
Galatians 5.25

There must always be a mixture or blending in us: we must feel both the Holy Spirit and our sin and imperfection. If there is to be improvement in us, we must resemble a sick person in the hands of a physician. Therefore let no one conclude as follows: this person has the Holy Spirit; therefore he or she must be quite strong, bring forth the most precious works, and never show any signs of weakness. Not so! The Gospel is not a proclamation for everyone.

It is beyond measure a sweet proclamation, but if it encounters raw and acid hearts it does not achieve its purpose. In this case men become only more insolent and frivolous in the belief that there is really no need for them to struggle against sin. They have no real knowledge of sin or misfortune. Therefore the Holy Spirit is given to no one but to those who are truly sorrowful because of their sins, and who are afraid of the consequences. Among such people, the Gospel can go to work usefully and fruitfully.

The gift of the Gospel is such an exalted and noble gift that God does not throw it to dogs. Even if the latter come by chance upon the Gospel and hear it preached, they simply devour it without knowing what they are devouring. For successful work, the Holy Spirit must encounter hearts which feel and realize their sinful lusts, and which know that by nature they are in a hopeless situation. There must be a struggle in the heart if the Spirit is to come with His help. No one should imagine that things can take another course here.

SL.XI.1027,23

PRAYER: Heavenly Father, you have implanted desires in our hearts so great that only you can bring them to pass. Strengthen us by your Holy Spirit that we may successfully complete all that we have begun in your name, and in the name of Jesus Christ our Saviour. Amen.

SATURDAY

LESSON: LUKE 24.44-49

These things I have spoken to you, while I am still with you. But the Counsellor, the Holy Spirit, whom the Father will send in my name, he will teach you all things, and bring to your remembrance all that I have said to you.

John 14.25,26

If the Holy Spirit is to live up to His name, He cannot carry out His office anywhere else but where there is no counsel or comfort available, and where such counsel and comfort is necessary and also desired. The Holy Spirit cannot comfort hard-headed men with frivolous hearts. Such men have never known any kind of inward struggle, or tasted the bitter fruits of despair. They have never felt any particular need or spiritual distress, so the Holy Spirit has nothing to offer them. His office can be carried out only among the sorrowful, those in need of comfort, in hearts that are despairing.

But what is His work? To teach **"all things"** and bring matters to remembrance that men must know. Some have explained this as meaning that the Scriptures do not contain all that man must believe and do or leave undone. The Holy Spirit's work is to teach many things that Christ did not teach. This is absolutely against the work of the Holy Spirit, and even quite absurd.

Christ says quite clearly here: **"He will teach you all things, and bring to your remembrance all that I have said to you"**, that is, "He will explain clearly what I am now telling you better than I am able to teach you with words. You will need no further words or explanations."

Christ bases His Word on the testimony of the Holy Spirit. It is the Holy Spirit's work to bear witness to Christ, and this testimony of the Spirit lives in our hearts so that we understand it and believe it. Hence, if any one teaches you something different about Christ, do not accept it as coming from the Holy Spirit.

SL.XI.1029,29-30

PRAYER: Holy Spirit of God, give us a new mind to comprehend the loving purposes of our God and Father, a new heart ever to rejoice in them, and the perseverance which keeps us on the paths of your will, in Christ's name. Amen.

216

SUNDAY

LESSON: JOHN 3.1-15

The Word was God . . . And the Word became flesh and dwelt among us. John 1.1,14

The Sunday after Pentecost has come to be regarded in the Church as the festival of the Holy Trinity. The word *Trinity* is not found in Holy Scripture; it has been devised and invented by men. That is also why it always sounds a little cold. It would be far better if we simply said "God" in place of the "Trinity".

This word signifies that God is threefold with respect to persons. This is a heavenly matter which the world cannot understand. That is why I have so often reminded you that this article, as well as others, must not be based on reason or on any human similes or allegories; it must be based and grounded on passages of the Scriptures. God Himself knows well what this article means and how He should speak about Himself.

The theological schools have devised many distinctions, dreams and fictions in their efforts to set forth the holy Trinity, and have made fools of themselves in the effort. In this connection, then, we shall take simple statements of Scripture by which we may grasp and comprehend the deity of Christ.

To begin, there are many passages to be quoted here from the New Testament. One of the best known of these passages forms the beginning of John's Gospel, **"In the beginning was the Word, and the Word was with God, and the Word was God. He was in the beginning with God; all things were made through him, and without him was not anything made that was made".** John 1.1-3. Accordingly, since He was not made but was the Maker Himself, He must be very God. And John says a little later, **"And the Word became flesh".**

SL.XI.1146,1-3

PRAYER: Worthy of praise from every mouth, of confession from every tongue, and worship from every creature is your glorious name, O Triune God, Father, Son, and Holy Spirit. Abide with us, your unworthy servants, with your Word and grace, now and for ever. Amen.

MONDAY

LESSON: PSALM 110.1-4

He /Christ/ reflects the glory of God and bears the very stamp of his nature.   Hebrews 1.3

The Old Testament sets forth many clear testimonies on the deity of our Lord Jesus Christ. David says: **"The Lord says to my lord: 'Sit at my right hand, till I make your enemies your footstool'."** The "right hand" means the royal throne and this passage indicates that David's "Lord", Christ, is a Lord and King over all creatures and that everything is to be subjected to Him. **Psalm 110.1.**

In another psalm we read: **"What is man that thou art mindful of him, and the son of man that thou dost care for him? Yet thou hast made him little less than God, and dost crown him with glory and honour. Thou hast given him dominion over the works of thy hands; thou hast put all things under his feet, all sheep and oxen, and also the beasts of the field, the birds of the air, and the fish of the sea, whatever passes along the paths of the sea." Psalm 8.4-8.** In other words, God has made Him Lord over the whole world.

The apostle Paul refers to this psalm in Ephesians and Colossians and gives a masterly interpretation of it (Ephesians 1.20; Colossians 2.9,10). If God has set Him at His own right hand and made Him Lord of all things in heaven and on earth, He must be God. He could not sit at God's right hand and have authority over all creatures if He were not God. For God will not share His glory with any else, as He states in Isaiah 48.11.

So there are two persons, the Father and the Son, to whom the Father has given as much as He Himself has. To sit at God's right hand means being the equal of God and having authority over all God's creatures. The One to whom this has been assigned must be God.   SL.XI.1148,4

PRAYER: Lord Jesus, as true God together with your heavenly Father, you are fully worthy of all honour and worship. Open our hearts at all times to the majesty of your person and the scope of your authority and power. Grant us this in your mercy and grace, Lord Jesus, you who live and reign with your Father and the Spirit, one God, for evermore. Amen.

TUESDAY

LESSON: EPHESIANS 1.3-14

[Jesus Christ] is the true God and eternal life.

1 John 5.20

God has forbidden us to worship any strange gods. Now we are told in John that it is God's will that His Son should be honoured with the honour with which He Himself is honoured. John reports Christ's words to the Jews.

"Truly, truly, I say to you, the Son can do nothing of his own accord, but only what he sees the Father doing; for whatever he does, that the Son does likewise. For the Father loves the Son, and shows him all that he himself is doing; and greater works than these will he show him, that you may marvel.

"For as the Father raises the dead and gives them life, so also the Son gives life to whom he will. The Father judges no one, but has given all judgement to the Son, that all may honour the Son, even as they honour the Father. He who does not honour the Son does not honour the Father who sent him." John 5.19-23.

These are, I believe, crystal clear words about the deity of Christ. Inasmuch, then, as God commands us to have only one God, and to give to no other creature the honour which belongs to God or is God's due, and nevertheless bestows this honour upon Christ, Christ must be God.

SL.XI.1148,5

PRAYER: You have shown us in many clear statements and testimonies, Lord God, that your Son Jesus Christ is true God and deserving of the full honour of the godhead. Keep us ever mindful of the exalted nature of your Son, that we may also be thereby encouraged to place all our faith and trust in Him as our Saviour and Redeemer, in whose name we also ask this. Amen.

WEDNESDAY

LESSON: PSALM 145

We have seen and testify that the Father has sent his Son as the Saviour of the world. Whosoever confesses that Jesus is the Son of God, God abides in him, and he in God.
1 John 4.14,15

Paul says in Romans that God promised the Gospel beforehand through His prophets in the holy Scriptures, "the gospel concerning his Son, who was descended from David according to the flesh and designated Son of God in power according to the Spirit of holiness by his resurrection from the dead, Jesus Christ our Lord". Romans 1.2-4. According to the flesh, then, He had a beginning, but according to the Spirit He has existed in eternity, although beforehand this was not clearly recognized.

It was not necessary for us to make a God of Him; we simply declare Him to be God's Son and accept Him as such. This is also the concern of the Holy Spirit. John says, "When the Spirit of truth comes . . . He will glorify me". John 16.13,14.

In another context the evangelist John writes that Jesus lifted His eyes to heaven and said, "Father, the hour has come; glorify thy Son that the Son may glorify thee, since thou hast given him power over all flesh, to give eternal life to all whom thou hast given him. And this is eternal life, that they know thee the only true God, and Jesus Christ whom thou hast sent.

"I glorified thee on earth, having accomplished the work which thou gavest me to do; and now, Father, glorify thou me in thy own presence with the glory which I had with thee before the world was made." John 17.1-5.

SL.XI.1149,6

PRAYER: Christ Jesus, Son of the eternal Father, through whom the invisible and most high became visible to mortal men, grant that by your grace and power we may so live on this earth that we never lose the eternal treasure reserved for us in heaven, where you live and reign with the Father and the Spirit, one God, for evermore. Amen.

THURSDAY

LESSON: PSALM 8

He is Lord of lords and King of kings.   Revelation 17.14

In the second psalm God says to His Son: "**Ask of me, and I will make the nations your heritage, and the ends of the earth as your possession**". **Psalm 2.8**. Here He is clearly appointed as the King of all things because He is God's Son. There has never been any ordinary prince or king to whom the whole world has been subjected.

In a similar way David openly calls Him a God when He says, "**Thy throne, O God** (RSV margin), **endures for ever and ever. Your royal sceptre is a sceptre of equity; you love righteousness and hate wickedness. Therefore God, your God, has anointed you with the oil of gladness above your fellows**." **Psalm 45.6,7**.

God appoints no one as such a king who is not Himself God. For He will not release the bridle from His own hands. He wants to remain Lord over heaven and earth, death, hell, the devil and all creatures. Inasmuch, then, as God has made Christ Lord over all that has been created, Christ must certainly be regarded as being Himself true God together with God the Father.

SL.XI.1150,7

PRAYER: Almighty God, so reign in our hearts and souls that Christ may have the sole dominion there. Grant that we may sincerely embrace Him with our whole hearts as King of kings and Lord of lords, and continually glorify Him by our works of faith, together with yourself, O Father, and the blessed Spirit, now and for ever. Amen.

FRIDAY

LESSON: MATTHEW 3.13-17

This is eternal life, that they know thee the only true God, and Jesus Christ whom thou hast sent.   John 17.3

You can have no more sure and certain basis for the deity of Christ than to wrap up your heart in clear passages of Scripture and in this way also lock up this truth in your hearts.

Scripture begins in a very gentle manner and introduces us to Christ as a man. Then it brings Him before us as the Lord of all creatures. Finally, we are shown quite clearly and expressly that Christ is God. In this way fine progress is made and we learn to recognize God.

The philosophers and worldly-wise men begin at the top and make fools of themselves in the process. You must begin at the bottom and make your way up so that Solomon's words are not fulfilled in you: **"It is not good to eat too much honey, and he who investigates difficult matters will find the going too hard". Proverbs 25.27.** (Luther's translation.)

Our faith in the two persons of the Father and the Son has been adequately grounded and established on clear passages of Scripture. On the third person, the Holy Spirit, we may well quote Christ's words on sending out His disciples, **"Go therefore and make disciples of all nations, baptizing them in the name of the Father and of the Son and of the Holy Spirit". Matthew 28.19.**

Here Christ assigns deity also to the Holy Spirit, inasmuch as I can trust or believe in no one else but God alone. I always need one who is mighty over death, hell and the devil. He must also be able to rule over all creatures so that they cannot harm me and so that He can always pull me through. I must have one on whom I can freely build. Christ decides that we should believe and trust in the Holy Spirit. Therefore the Holy Spirit must be God.   SL.XI.1150,8-9

PRAYER: Almighty and everlasting God, in your mercy you have granted us the faith to acknowledge the glory of the eternal Trinity. Keep us steadfast in this faith which leads us to the salvation which you have prepared for us in and through our Saviour Jesus Christ. Amen.

SATURDAY

LESSON: EPHESIANS 6.13-18

Be filled with the Spirit.   Ephesians 5.18

In the very first chapter of the Bible we are told, "**The Spirit of God was moving over the face of the waters**". **Genesis 1.2.** This passage is not quite as clear as Matthew 28.19, because the Jews make it a little shaky for us when they tell us that the word for Spirit in Hebrew can also mean "wind". David's statement is clearer: "**By the word of the Lord the heavens were made, and all their host by the Spirit of his mouth**". **Psalm 33.6.** (RSV has "breath of his mouth".) From this passage it is clear that the Holy Spirit is God because the heavens and their host were created through Him.

David also says, "**Whither shall I go from thy Spirit? Or whither shall I flee from thy presence? If I ascend to heaven, thou art there! If I make my bed in Sheol, thou art there!**" **Psalm 139.7,8.** This is no language for a creature! No creature is to be found in all corners of the world, and no creature fills the whole world. This can only be affirmed of God, the Creator.

Accordingly, we stick to the Scriptures and the statements of Scripture which attest the threefold person of God and say, "I know for sure that God the Father, Son and Holy Spirit are a living reality, but just how they are truly one I do not know and will never know".

SL.XI.1151,10-12

PRAYER: Holy, almighty, eternal, divine Spirit, of one authority and dominion with the Father and the Son, set up your throne in our hearts. You who are pure, purify us! You who are light, enlighten us! You who are Lord and giver of life, grant us the true life which knows no end, through Jesus Christ our Lord. Amen.

SUNDAY

LESSON: LUKE 16.19-31

There was a rich man, who was clothed in purple and fine linen.   Luke 16.19

We must not simply form an opinion on this rich man from his external conduct. He is dressed in sheep's clothing and his life outwardly glitters and seems beautiful, covering the wolf to perfection.

The Gospel does not accuse him of adultery, murder, robbery, or violation of law. It brings no charge against him with which the world or reason could find fault. He was just as honourable in his life as the Pharisee who fasted twice in the week and did not do what other men did, and of whom Luke also writes in his Gospel (18.11,12). Had he committed any gross crime, the Gospel would undoubtedly have mentioned it. It describes this man in such detail that it even mentions his "**purple**" clothing and what kind of table he kept.

These are external matters, and God does not necessarily judge any man according to them. In all probability this rich man led a fine, holy life, outwardly and according to his own thinking and that of other men, keeping the whole law of Moses. He cannot be judged simply by external appearances. One must look into his heart and judge him according to his spirit.

The Gospel has very sharp eyes; it looks into the depths of the heart. The Gospel can fault works of which reason may approve. Nor is the Gospel fooled by the sheep's clothing. It knows how to regard the fruit of a tree whether it is good or bad, as the Lord also says in Matthew's Gospel, "**Every sound tree bears good fruit, but the bad tree bears evil fruit**". **Matthew 7.17.**   SL.XI.1195,2-3

PRAYER: You can read our hearts, O God, and know what we really are. You are never deceived by sheep's clothing. May we always act in love and truth towards all our fellowmen and thereby demonstrate by fruits of faith that we are your true children by faith in Jesus Christ our Saviour. Amen.

MONDAY

LESSON: 2 CORINTHIANS 8.8-15

There was a rich man . . . who feasted sumptuously every day.   Luke 16.19

When we measure this rich man by the fruits of faith we shall find a heart and a tree of unbelief. The Gospel reproaches him for feasting sumptuously daily, and for decking himself out in costly apparel. Reason does not regard such matters as especially great sins. It could even be that a man imbued with the idea of work-righteousness would regard all this as perfectly in order, imagining that he had deserved all this by his holy life, without any real conception of committing sin by such conduct because of his unbelief.

This rich man is not really reproached for his costly food and his splendid attire. Many holy men and women, kings and queens in times past, have worn costly attire like Solomon, Esther, David, Daniel and many others.

The rich man in this Gospel is reproached for setting his heart on these things — seeking, choosing and clinging to them; finding all his joy, pleasure and relish in them, and making idols of these things.

This is what Christ indicates with the expression "**every day**". He lived in this glorious manner "**every day**". He sought and chose this way of life deliberately. He was not forced to accept it by circumstance or because of his office. This way of life could not redound in any way to the welfare of his neighbour. He was simply concerned about fulfilling his own pleasure. He lived for himself and served no one but himself.

Herein we see the secret sin of his heart, his unbelief and lack of true faith manifesting itself in selfish, sinful and wicked fruits. SL.XI.1196,4

PRAYER: Open our eyes and hearts to the needs of our neighbour, heavenly Father, that our lives do not simply become a continuous exercise in self-interest and routines which promote nothing but ourselves, but keep our hearts open to receive your love for service to our neighbour, for Jesus' sake. Amen.

TUESDAY

LESSON: 1 TIMOTHY 6.6-10

If riches increase, set not your heart on them.
Psalm 62.10

Where there is true Christian faith, rich attire and sumptuous food will never be major considerations. Christian faith does not look for earthly good, honour, pleasure, power or anything outside of God Himself. It seeks, desires and clings to nothing but God, who alone is the highest good.

Whether there is costly fare or little to eat, whether there is splendid attire or nothing but very simple clothing, makes very little difference to Christian faith. Even if Christians must wear costly attire and wield great power in a position of honour, they think little of it. It may be that they have been forced into this by circumstances or that they must adopt such procedures in the interests of their neighbour. Queen Esther declared that she wore her royal crown reluctantly, but was compelled to do so for the sake of the king. David would have preferred to remain a common man. He was compelled to become king for God's sake and the sake of the people.

This is the way all believers regard their elevated roles in this world. They are compelled to accept power, honour and glory, but they never allow their roles in life to ensnare their hearts. Basically they continue to serve God and their neighbour however they may find themselves situated in this life.

SL.XI.1196,5

PRAYER: O God, our Father, your Word is better than gold, and your counsels are more precious than anything else in life. Grant us wisdom to seek the true riches, to know and possess you, and to be known and possessed by you, through Jesus Christ our Lord. Amen.

WEDNESDAY

LESSON: MATTHEW 25.31-46

Through love be servants of one another. Galatians 5.13

One sin follows another. The rich man clothed in purple and faring sumptuously every day forgot his love towards his neighbour. He let poor Lazarus lie at his door and gave him no help. Even if he was disinclined to give Lazarus some help personally, he could still have ordered his servants to make a shed available to him where they could have done something for him.

This came about because he had no real understanding of God and had never experienced God's goodness. He who has experienced God's goodness also has some feeling for his neighbour's misfortune. But he who has never experienced God's goodness, also has no feeling for his neighbour's misfortune. Even as he finds no pleasure in God, so also his neighbour's plight never touches his heart.

Faith is so constituted that it looks to God for all that is good and relies on God alone. Out of such faith man learns to know God, how good and gracious He is. From this knowledge of God, man's heart is also softened and inclined to mercy, so that he readily does for everyone what he feels God has done for him.

The result of all this is love, by which a man begins to serve his neighbour with his whole heart, with body and life, with property and honour, with soul and spirit. He is ready to bestow everything on his neighbour, as God has done this for him. He does not look for healthy, high, strong, sick, noble and holy people, who have no need of him, but for the sick, the weak, the poor, the despised people who are sinners, to whom he can be useful. On these he can exercise his mercy and serve them as God has served him.

SL.XL.1197,7-8

PRAYER: Teach us, O Lord, that it is always better to give than to receive, better to serve than to be served, after your own example, that we may always help our needy neighbour, for your mercy and truth's sake. Amen.

THURSDAY

LESSON: PHILIPPIANS 3.7-11

Without faith it is impossible to please him /God/.
Hebrews 11.6

We should not form an estimate of Lazarus with his sores, poverty and troubles only from external factors. For there are many people who suffer want and trouble without ever deriving any benefit from it. King Herod had to endure terrible sufferings as we are reminded in the Acts of the Apostles (12.23). But his status before God did not improve thereby.

Poverty and suffering in themselves do not make men acceptable to God. But the poverty and suffering of one who is already acceptable to God is something precious in God's sight, as the psalmist declares, **"Precious in the sight of the Lord is the death of his saints". Psalm 116.15**.

We must look into the heart of Lazarus and search there for the treasure which made his sores so precious. This, without a doubt, was his faith and love, for without faith nothing can please God, as the writer of the Epistle to the Hebrews reminds us (11.6). The heart of Lazarus must have been so constituted that, even in the midst of his poverty and wretchedness he looked to God for all good, and found his only consolation in reliance on God.

Moreover, he experienced such rich satisfaction and pleasure in God's goodness and grace that he would have readily endured more suffering had that been the will of his gracious God. It was a real, living faith which, through the realization of God's goodness, softened his heart so that nothing was too onerous or difficult for him to endure or do. Faith makes the heart experienced when it experiences God's grace.

SL.XI.1199,12-14

PRAYER: Give us such faith in you and your sure purposes, heavenly Father, that we do not measure our lives simply by what we have done or failed to do, but by our obedience to your will, through Jesus Christ our Lord, who lives and reigns with you and the Holy Spirit for ever and ever. Amen.

FRIDAY

LESSON: LUKE 12.16-21

Abraham said, "Son, remember that you in your lifetime received your good things, and Lazarus in like manner evil things; but now he is comforted here, and you are in anguish." Luke 16.25

The inability of Lazarus to render bodily service to his neighbour has been more than recompensed by the rich spiritual service he has been enabled to render to others. For now, after his death, he serves the whole world with his sores, hunger and distress. His bodily hunger feeds our spiritual hunger; his bodily nakedness clothes our spiritual nakedness; his bodily sores heal our spiritual sores.

He teaches and comforts us by his example, reminding us that God can still be pleased with us even if things do not go well with us here on earth, provided that we have faith. He warns us that God's wrath can come upon us even if things go well for us in unbelief, even as God was pleased with him in his wretchedness and displeased with the rich man.

What king with all his wealth could render the whole world a service comparable with the service rendered us by Lazarus with his sores, hunger and poverty? How wonderful are God's works and judgements! In what a masterly manner He puts to shame the clever fool, with his reason and worldly wisdom, who prefers to see the beautiful purple of the rich man rather than the sores of poor Lazarus, who would rather look at a healthy man like the rich man than at an ugly naked body like that of Lazarus.

Christian faith brings about a complete change in our whole set of values.

SL.XI.1200,16-17

PRAYER: Enlighten us with your Holy Spirit, heavenly Father, that we may always get and keep our values straight as your children by faith in Jesus Christ, our Saviour and Redeemer. Amen.

SATURDAY

LESSON: HEBREWS 3.7-15

Abraham said, "They have Moses and the prophets; let them hear them . . . If they do not hear Moses and the prophets, neither will they be convinced if some one should rise from the dead".   Luke 16.29,31

In this Gospel you see how Abraham refuses to send someone from the dead to teach the living at the request of the rich man. He reminds the rich man that the living have Moses and the prophets to whom they should give heed.

In these words we are also reminded of God's prohibition against any kind of consultation of the dead on the part of the living (cf. Deuteronomy 18.10-12). It is certainly a devilish apparition when spirits make themselves known to men in response to various invocations, and request men to offer up masses for the dead, to undertake pilgrimages for them and to perform other works. There have also been claims that they have given assurances of success to those who have heeded their instructions.

In this way the devil has misled men into putting their trust in works and drawn them away from faith. He has created the illusion among men that works can perform great wonders. What St. Paul foretold is being fulfilled, that God sends upon those who perish and refuse to love the truth and be saved **"a strong delusion, to make them believe what is false". 2 Thessalonians 2.10,11**.

Therefore, be well advised and learn that God refuses to make known how the dead fare after this life. Here the only thing that can help us is faith through God's Word, faith which believes that after this life God receives believers into blessedness and condemns unbelievers. This is made abundantly clear in the Gospel of the rich man and poor Lazarus.

SL.XI.1207,31-32

PRAYER: Dear Lord Jesus, you are with us throughout our life; abide with us also at our death. Grant us not to die eternally but to rise to life everlasting with you and in you, who live and reign in the glory of the eternal Trinity, one God, for evermore. Amen.

SUNDAY

LESSON: LUKE 14.16-21

A man once gave a great banquet.   Luke 14.16

In this Gospel, as well as in the remainder of Holy Scripture, we must make an effort, to the best of our ability, to grasp the true, simple meaning of the text and to rest our heart and conscience on it. Anyone who wants to do battle with the devil must not waver to and fro or totter, but must be sure of his ground, armed with clear and certain Scripture. Otherwise, when the devil gets him on to his fork by means of an unsure understanding, he will toss him to and fro like the wind tosses a dry leaf.

In this Gospel we must also obtain a sure understanding so that we may stand our ground. It has nothing at all to do with the Lord's Supper, as has sometimes been claimed with the assistance of some really hair-splitting exegesis.

The sum and substance of this Gospel is that the Gospel has been preached and proclaimed in all the world but only few accept it. It is called a **"banquet"** or a supper because the Gospel will be the last, final word and doctrine which will bring this world to a close.

This supper, then, is nothing else but a rich, precious meal, which God has made ready by means of the Gospel, through Christ, in which He sets before us great blessings and rich treasures.

SL.XI.1210,1-3

PRAYER: Lord, you have set before us great blessings and rich treasures in the banquet prepared for us through your Son and offered to us in your Gospel. May we never lose sight of these blessings and treasures but ever regard them as our highest good, in and through our Saviour Jesus Christ. Amen.

MONDAY

LESSON: ISAIAH 55.1-7

A man once gave a great banquet, and invited many; and at the time for the banquet he sent his servant.

Luke 14.16,17

Jesus spoke to them in parables, saying, "The kingdom of heaven may be compared to a king who gave a marriage feast for his son, and sent his servants to call those who were invited to the marriage feast". Matthew 22.1-3

This invitation was sent out in the manner described in this Gospel. The man sent out his servant to invite guests to this great banquet. The Apostles were sent out by Christ into all the world with one and the same message: to invite men to this heavenly banquet with one voice, with one Gospel, with one message.

If St. Peter had ever preached at a place where St. Paul had previously preached the Gospel, it would have been one and the same proclamation, the one like the other. It would not have been difficult for the hearers to declare, "Peter preaches exactly the same message that we heard from Paul. They agree perfectly; they proclaim one and the same message."

To indicate this basic sameness in the proclamation of the message the evangelist says here, **"At the time for the banquet he sent his servant"**. He does not say "servants" or "many servants", but **"servant"**.

SL.XI.1211,4

PRAYER: We thank and praise you, heavenly Father, for the one, clear message of salvation, which you have given us in your Gospel of salvation. Strengthen us in such a way that we always cling to this with our whole hearts, for Christ's sake. Amen.

TUESDAY

LESSON: MATTHEW 22.1-14

Come; for all is now ready.   Luke 14.17

The message which the servant was to convey to the invited guests to urge them to come to the banquet was: "Come; for all is now ready". Christ died; He slaughtered sin and death in His death; He rose from the dead; the Holy Spirit was given; in short, everything that belonged to this banquet was prepared. Everything was prepared in such a way that it would cost us nothing. Through Christ, the Father assumed the whole cost so that we might enjoy His blessings without any merit or contribution on our part and become abundantly rich.

First of all He sent out His servant to the Jews to invite men to this banquet. The Jews had received special promises and undertakings from God about this banquet. The law of Moses and all the prophets were set up and appointed to prepare the people of Israel for God as the angel Gabriel also stated of John the Baptist to his father Zechariah:

"He will be filled with the Holy Spirit, even from his mother's womb. And he will turn many of the sons of Israel to the Lord their God, and he will go before him in the spirit and power of Elijah, to turn the hearts of the fathers to the children, and the disobedient to the wisdom of the just, to make ready for the Lord a people prepared." Luke 1.15-17.

When the Jews had trotted out all their excuses to John the Baptist and the apostles, to a very large extent rejecting Christ, the invitation to come to the banquet was extended to the Gentiles.

SL.XI.1211,5-6

PRAYER: Lord, you have made it quite plain in your all-embracing Gospel invitation that all are welcome in your kingdom. May we at all times receive this invitation whole-heartedly and treat it in all seriousness for ourselves and others, through Christ our Lord and for the glory of His name. Amen.

WEDNESDAY

LESSON: MATTHEW 9.9-13

But they all alike began to make excuses.   Luke 14.18

These words are a comment on Christ's words reported in Matthew: "He who loves father or mother more than me is not worthy of me; and he who loves son or daughter more than me is not worthy of me; and he who does not take his cross and follow me is not worthy of me". Matthew 10.37,38.

There are really only very few who are endowed with adequate resignation to accept this invitation. For anyone who would come to this banquet must stake everything on the Gospel — body and property, wife and child, friend and foe. He must give up everything that separates him from the Gospel, no matter how good, correct and holy it may be.

You should not suppose that the men who excuse themselves here were gross sinners or mixed up in unjust activities and action. By no means! They could all present a very good front. It is not at all wrong to buy and carry on business, to look after oneself well, to take a wife and marry. But we must not become involved in all these matters to such an extent that we cannot forsake them, clinging to them with all our heart. We must be prepared to forsake anything that is opposed to the Gospel. And self-denial will mean a cross.

The Gospel is a word of the cross. It will set up stumbling-blocks over which some will certainly falter. We must be prepared to forsake everything rather than cut ourselves off from God's Word or His love.

SL.XI.1212,7-9

PRAYER: Almighty God, whose beloved Son, for our sake, willingly offered himself to endure the cross, its agony and its shame, remove from us all coldness and cowardice of heart, and give us courage to take up our allotted task and follow Him, through the same Jesus Christ our Lord. Amen.

THURSDAY

LESSON: LUKE 14.25-33

He called to him the multitude with his disciples, and said to them, "If any man would come after me, let him deny himself and take up his cross and follow me. For whoever would save his life will lose it; and whoever loses his life for my sake and the gospel's will save it." Mark 8.34, 35

He who gives up something for the Gospel really loses nothing. Even if you lose your earthly life for Christ's sake, He will give you another, better life, eternal life, as Christ Himself says: **"He who finds his life will lose it, and he who loses his life for my sake will find it".** Matthew 10.39. If you have to leave child and wife, remember that God can take care of them and be a much better father to them than you have ever been. There is no doubt at all about this. Believe it with all your heart!

You have equally great assurance, together with rich promises and encouragement, that He will never fall down on His Word. He will keep His Word, as we shall also discover if we are ready to put our trust in it and to resign ourselves to it. He has given us His Word and promise; what more could we want or what could we desire that is greater?

Is something lacking? Only in our faith. Let no one come to this banquet unless he comes with a thorough-going faith which exalts God above all creatures and loves Him above all else.

SL.XI.1213,10

PRAYER: Almighty God, so reign in our heart and soul that Christ may always have dominion there. Grant that we may continue in true faith to confess Him with our tongues and glorify Him by our works with you, O Father, and the blessed Spirit, now and for ever. Amen.

FRIDAY

LESSON: JOHN 10.14-16

Then the householder in anger said to his servant, "Go out quickly to the streets and lanes of the city, and bring in the poor and maimed and blind and lame.   Luke 14.21

The householder's instruction to his servant to go out quickly **"to the streets and lanes of the city"** refers to the fact that the Jews proved themselves unworthy of the Gospel and turned away from it. As a result of this, the disciples of Christ turned to the Gentiles. Before His resurrection, Christ instructed His disciples not to turn to the Gentiles or to preach in the cities of the Samaritans. They were to busy themselves only with the sheep of the house of Israel and to pasture them. This they also did.

But later, after the resurrection of Jesus Christ, when the Jews opposed Christ's Word of salvation and refused to accept it, the apostles told the Jews, **"It was necessary that the word of God should be spoken first to you. Since you thrust it from you, and judge yourselves unworthy of eternal life, behold, we turn to the Gentiles. For so the Lord has commanded us."** Acts 13.46,47. The apostles then quoted a passage from the prophet Isaiah, **"I will give you as a light to the nations, that my salvation may reach to the end of the earth"**. Isaiah 49.6.

The same instruction is given by the householder to the servant here in this Gospel: **"Go out quickly to the streets and lanes of the city, and bring in the poor and maimed and blind and lame. Go out to the highways and hedges, and compel people to come in, that my house may be filled."** Luke 14.21,23.

SL.XI.1214,11

PRAYER: O God, in your great mercy and grace you have given us the good news of salvation in your Son Jesus Christ. Fill our hearts with thankfulness so that we may tell abroad the glad tidings which we have received, through the same Jesus Christ our Lord. Amen.

SATURDAY

LESSON: PSALM 84

Compel people to come in!   Luke 14.23

We must understand the compulsion referred to here as applying to those who have a despondent and feeble conscience. These people should also be invited to the banquet and compelled to come in. The reference, however, is not to any external compulsion but to an inner, spiritual compulsion.

This results when the Law is preached and sin is disclosed and brought to light, so that a man comes to realize what he really is. He is brought under compulsion, compelled to come in, when a vivid knowledge of sin is stirred up in his conscience. As a result of this, he also realizes that he is nothing in God's sight, that all his works are sinful and even condemnatory. His despondent conscience and tender, terrified heart so overwhelm him that he loses all confidence in himself and can see no help at hand anywhere to provide any comfort at all. In this wretched condition he is finally led to despair.

When a man has been brought under compulsion in this way you should not delay with the invitation to "**come in**" and help him out of this despondency. This is achieved when you comfort him with the Gospel, telling him how he has been freed from his sins with the words, "Believe in Christ, that He has freed you from your sins and you will be rid of your sins". This is what is meant in this Gospel by compelling men to come in so that the householder's home may be filled.

SL.XI.1214,12-13

PRAYER: Lord, you have reminded us in a very vivid manner that we are always confronted with a situation of grave urgency respecting our invitation to men to come in and partake of the banquet prepared for them in your kingdom of grace. Grant us wisdom and courage to perform our duties in this area with determination and love, in the name of Jesus Christ our Saviour. Amen.

SUNDAY

LESSON: LUKE 15.1-10

The tax collectors and sinners were all drawing near to him. And the Pharisees and the scribes murmured, saying, "This man receives sinners and eats with them".

Luke 15.1,2

It is not at all unusual for religious people to assume a very self-righteous attitude over against those whom they regard as "**sinners**", to turn up their noses at those who are not as holy as they themselves are, and to despise and shun them. This is always the way of human reason; it cannot be otherwise.

Self-righteous men are always close to hypocrisy and cannot help despising those who are not like themselves. Their own life counts for everything with them. They blow themselves up and cannot bring themselves to show any consideration at all for "**sinners**".

They know nothing at all about becoming servants of other men and never realize that their own piety should be of service to other men. They are also very proud and hard and do not understand how to manifest love to others. Confronted with a case of need, they are quite likely to argue as follows: "This bumpkin is not even worthy to undo my shoes; how can I be expected to show him my love?"

This is often where God comes in to play His part. He allows this proud spirit to take a heavy fall and to receive a sound rebuff. A marriage may break up and, at times, something even more terrible can happen, so that in the end this proud spirit is forced to lash out against himself, saying, "Keep quiet and get a grip on yourself, brother, you are no more than the material out of which this 'bumpkin's' trousers are made".

In this way he comes to realize that we are all the one cake and that one donkey does not have to become another donkey's pack animal. We are all born from the same flesh.

SL.XI.1236,5

PRAYER: Lord Jesus Christ, you have taught us that the greatest of all is the servant of all, and that the humble shall be exalted. Preserve within us a simple, humble heart and faith, ever ready to serve all men, for your name's sake. Amen.

MONDAY

LESSON: ROMANS 5.15-17

The tax collectors and sinners were all drawing near to him . . . the Pharisees and the scribes murmured.   Luke 15.1,2

In our Gospel two groups are set before us as an example and for our instruction. First of all, there are the Pharisees and hypocrites. These people were regarded as models of perfection in respect to all kinds of piety and godliness. They were immersed in holiness over their ears. Secondly, there are the open sinners and tax collectors. These people were immersed in sin over their ears. For this reason they were despised by the hypocritical "saints" and regarded as unworthy of all fellowship with them.

Christ comes in between these two groups and delivers a judgement. He points out to these "saints" that they must yield themselves in service to the "sinners", load up the "sinners" and carry them on their shoulders and take thought how to help them out of their sins with their righteousness and piety. The "saints" do not want to accept this role. But this is truly the proper procedure here and what must be done.

The correct Christian procedure is to fall down and become completely linked with the "sinner", no matter how deeply he is immersed in the mire of sin. This sin you must take upon yourself and wallow your way out of the mire with it, treating it just as if it were your own sin. Reproach and chastisement are necessary, and the whole matter must be treated in all earnestness. You must never despise a sinner, but love him with all your heart. If you are proud and despise a sinner there is no hope for you; you stand utterly condemned.

SL.XI.1236,6-7

PRAYER: Fill our hearts at all times with your grace and love, Lord Jesus, that with you we may love all sinners and lead them in faith to the victory over sin which you have achieved by your suffering and death on the cross and now offer to sinners in your Gospel, for your mercy and truth's sake. Amen.

TUESDAY

LESSON: MATTHEW 9.10-13

This man receives sinners and eats with them. Luke 15.2

To help and assist sinners in finding the true way out of their sins, and to conquer sin, are the really important and significant works in which we Christians should train ourselves. But not many are concerned about these works; most people by-pass them. The practice has died out and to a large extent become extinct. In preference, following the devil, one man goes to St. James; another builds a church; a third man establishes a mass. One man does this, another that. No one ever seems to think of making intercession for sinners. Hence, it is to be feared that the holiest of men are quite likely to end up in the very depths of hell and that heaven will be made up mostly of sinners.

It would be a real Christian work to interest yourself in some poor sinner; to go to the place where you pray to God in private and offer earnest prayer to Him, saying, "I hear that this poor sinner (naming him) has fallen and is held fast in sin. Help him up, dear God!" In this way you would be receiving a sinner with Jesus and serving him.

This is what Moses did when the Jews worshipped the molten calf. He became wrapped up in this sin and reproached them for it in all severity. Three thousand men were put to death when the avenging sword passed from gate to gate on this occasion (Exodus 32.27,28). But in the end Moses fell down before God and interceded with God to forgive them their sin, or blot him out of the book of life (Exodus 32.32). This was a man who knew that God loved him and had written his name in His book of life. But Moses said, "Lord, I would prefer it if you condemned me and forgave the people their sin". We have another example of this concern for sinners in the apostle Paul (Romans 9.3).

SL.XI.1237,8-9

PRAYER: Lord Jesus, your readiness to receive sinners and to help them with your grace and forgiveness has been made very plain to us in your Gospel. Grant us such a clear understanding of your Word and mission that we always manifest a similar concern for sinners and do our utmost to make known to them the help available in your Gospel. In your name we ask it. Amen.

WEDNESDAY

LESSON: 2 CORINTHIANS 7.5-13

I tell you, there will be more joy in heaven over one sinner who repents than over ninety-nine righteous persons who need no repentance.   Luke 15.7

In the example of Christ we are shown how we are to conduct ourselves towards sinners. Inwardly, in our heart, we must be prepared to serve them; outwardly, with the tongue, we should also instruct them in all earnestness.

This is what God expects of us, and this is also what Jesus, the captain of our salvation, has demonstrated for us. St. Paul also makes this quite plain to us when he says in his Epistle to the Philippians, **"Let each of you look not only to his own interests, but also to the interests of others. Have this mind among yourselves, which you have in Christ Jesus, who, though he was in the form of God, did not count equality with God a thing to be grasped, but emptied himself, taking the form of a servant, being born in the likeness of men. And being found in human form He humbled himself and became obedient unto death, even death on a cross." Philippians 2.4-8.**

Christ was absolutely perfect in all righteousness and He could have simply condemned all of us. But He does not do this. What does He do? He gives Himself to us as our servant. His righteousness served our sins; His perfection made up for our frailty; His life conquered our death.

We see this also quite clearly in this Gospel from Christ's friendly attitude towards sinners which made the Pharisees murmur.

SL.XI.1238,13-14

PRAYER: As your disciples, Lord Jesus, the interests of others are our interests. It is your clearly expressed will that we should always concern ourselves with the interests of others. May we apply this truth as your disciples, Lord Jesus, especially in our efforts to help sinners to repentance and the forgiveness of their sins, for your mercy and truth's sake. Amen.

THURSDAY

LESSON: MATTHEW 18.10-14

He told them this parable: "What man of you, having a hundred sheep, if he has lost one of them, does not leave the ninety-nine in the wilderness, and go after the one which is lost, until he finds it? And when he has found it, he lays it on his shoulders, rejoicing. And when he comes home, he calls together his friends and his neighbours, saying to them, 'Rejoice with me, for I have found my sheep which was lost'. . . . Or what woman, having ten silver coins, if she loses one coin, does not light a lamp and sweep the house and seek diligently until she finds it? And when she has found it, she calls together her friends and neighbours, saying, 'Rejoice with me, for I have found the coin which I had lost'."

Luke 15.3-6,8-9

Christ is the shepherd and He is also the woman. It is Christ who has lit the lamp, that is, the Gospel, and it is Christ who walks about in the wilderness, that is, the world, and who sweeps the house seeking the lost sheep and the lost coin. He does this seeking with His Word so that first of all sin is proclaimed to us and, thereafter, grace and mercy.

When we are told here that the shepherd takes up the lost sheep on His shoulders the reference is to the fact that our sin has been laid on Christ's shoulders. This certainly must strengthen our confidence in Christ, and this must also follow from the way in which tax collectors and other sinners flocked to Him and were received by Him. Had they regarded him as nothing but a stubborn judge they would never have come to Him. But these sinners recognized themselves as sinners in need of His grace. And when they heard tell of His attractive words, they came to Him.

Learn from this that we should seek out our neighbour to cover his shame with our honour, and to hide his sin with our piety.

SL.XI.1239,15-16

PRAYER: It is not your will, O Lord, that we should ever delight in the sins of others and gloat over them, but that we should rather help them to repentance and provide joy in heaven. Fix this truth in our hearts in such a way that we always act according to it, for the sake of Jesus our Saviour. Amen.

FRIDAY

LESSON: 2 CORINTHIANS 1.3-7

There is joy before the angels of God over one sinner who repents. Luke 15.10

When sinners come to Christ in response to the invitation of the Gospel, He does not reproach them with their sins. He remains silent and covers their sins. He could put us to shame and trample us underfoot as the Pharisees do; but He does not do that. At the last judgement He will certainly come forth, and all that has remained hidden will be revealed.

We must follow the example of Christ. A maiden must place her garland of chastity upon a whore, a pious wife must give her veil to an adultress, and we must be prepared to use any of our garments to cover sin. Every man will have his sheep and every woman her coin. All our gifts must be placed at each other's disposal.

In God's judgement there is no greater sin on this earth than that committed by pious men, women and maidens when they despise those who are held fast in their sins. At the same time, they are under the delusion that their natural endowment can help them out. They blow themselves up with their own perfections and self-importance and despise their neighbour.

Hence, this Gospel provides powerful consolation to poor sinners because it is so friendly to sinners, and at the same time it must be a source of some fear to the Pharisees.

SL.XI.1240,17-19

PRAYER: Have mercy on us at all times, O God, according to your steadfast love; according to your abundant mercy blot out all our sins in accordance with your promises, in and through Jesus Christ, our Lord and Saviour. Amen.

SATURDAY

LESSON: LUKE 19.1-10

The saying is sure and worthy of full acceptance, that Christ Jesus came into the world to save sinners.
1 Timothy 1.15

If you feel your sins biting you, and your heart is wavering and beginning to tremble, take your place on the side where the tax collectors are standing, for they are the people for whom the Gospel is intended.

Do this quite joyfully and say, "Dear God, according to your own words there is greater joy in heaven over one sinner who repents, than over ninety-nine just persons who need no repentance. All the angels and the righteous are interceding for this sinner and covering his sin. Now, dear God, here I am and I feel my sins. My case is already decided. All I now need is a shepherd to seek me out; I will entrust myself freely to your Gospel."

So you come to God and you are already the sheep that God has taken on His shoulders; you have already found your shepherd. You are the coin already lying in the hand; you are the one over whom all the angels of heaven are rejoicing.

Whether you feel all this right away or not must not disturb you in any way. Sin falls away gradually, and the bite in your conscience will impel you to keep on seeking God. You must fight with your faith against your feeling and say, "Dear God; I know what you have said; to this Word I will cling. I am the sheep and the coin; you are the shepherd and the woman."

SL.XI.1241,21-22

PRAYER: I thank and praise you, heavenly Father, for your grace and mercy in seeking me out and finding me with your Gospel of salvation. Preserve and keep me in your mercy and grace, in and through Jesus Christ the Saviour. Amen.

SUNDAY

LESSON: LUKE 6.36-42

Be merciful, even as your Father is merciful.   Luke 6.36

Jesus is not speaking here of the kind of mercy that human reason commends and suggests to us. This is a mercy which is selfish and self-seeking, which gives to those who are important and learned, to those who have earned it and merited it, to those whom it loves or who are beautiful, to those from whom it can expect some benefit or advantage. This is a particular, beggarly, tattered and tousled mercy. For if I give to him who has earned it, or if I consider beauty or friendship, I am only performing a duty or paying a debt and not carrying out an act of mercy at all.

This is what the Lord meant when He said in the section immediately preceding this Gospel, **"If you love those who love you, what credit is that to you? For even sinners love those who love them. And if you do good to those who do good to you, what credit is that to you? For even sinners do the same. And if you lend to those from whom you hope to receive, what credit is that to you? Even sinners lend to sinners, to receive as much again." Luke 6.32-34**.

The mercy of Christians does not seek its own advantage or repayment of any kind. It must always be extended in all directions. We must open our eyes and keep them fixed on all men alike, on friend and foe, and be merciful, even as our heavenly Father is merciful.

SL.XI.1274,11

PRAYER: Your steadfast love, O Lord, never ceases, and your mercy towards us knows no ending; it is new every morning and accompanies us in the night seasons. Grant us grace to follow and practise a similar mercy towards our fellowmen, for your name's sake. Amen.

MONDAY

LESSON: PSALM 89.1-4

The Lord, the Lord, a God merciful and gracious, slow to anger, and abounding in steadfast love and faithfulness.
Exodus 34.6

Where mercy is not practised, there is no Christian faith. If your heart is established in faith, so that you know and realize how merciful and good God has proved Himself to be as far as you are concerned, without any merit on your part, and absolutely for nothing on His part, when you were still His enemy and a child of eternal damnation — if you really believe all this, you have no other alternative at all but to manifest a similar spirit towards your neighbour. And you do all this out of love for God, and for the benefit of your neighbour.

Take care, then, that you make no distinction between friend and foe, between worthy and unworthy. All who have experienced God's mercy deserved anything but mercy. This will be the case also when we show mercy to others. This is what our Lord Himself wanted to emphasize for us when He said, **"Love your enemies, and do good, and lend, expecting nothing in return; and your reward will be great, and you will be sons of the Most High; for he is kind to the ungrateful and the selfish".** Luke 6.35.

Mercy will be a constant fruit of true Christian faith.

SL.XI.1275,12

PRAYER: O Lord Jesus Christ, your mercy and compassion were always freely extended to all who had gone astray. Inflame our hearts with the fire of your love that we also may extend our mercy and compassion to all our fellowmen, whether friend or foe. In your name we ask it. Amen.

TUESDAY

LESSON: HEBREWS 11.17-19

Abide in me, and I in you. As the branch cannot bear fruit by itself, unless it abides in the vine, neither can you, unless you abide in me. I am the vine, you are the branches. He who abides in me, and I in him, he it is that bears much fruit, for apart from me you can do nothing.   John 15.4,5

Someone may wonder how we can reconcile what Jesus teaches in this Gospel with our frequent contention that works count for nothing with God, and play no part at all in obtaining a favourable judgement from Him. How does it come to pass that the very opposite seems to be set forth by Christ in this Gospel? Christ says, "Be merciful, even as your Father is merciful. Judge not, and you will not be judged; condemn not, and you will not be condemned; forgive, and you will be forgiven; give, and it will be given to you." Luke 6.36-38.

The gist of all these statements seems to be that we must gain God's favour for ourselves by means of our works, and that by our works we must win God over so that He is merciful to us and forgives us. We, on the other hand, have always been most emphatic in insisting that it is faith alone that achieves all this.

Note well, then, that St. Paul, with the whole testimony of Scripture oft-repeated on his side, insists on the necessity of faith, that we must have dealings with God through pure faith alone. Hence you must understand passages like the ones which we have here in our Gospel as teaching that works are the proof and verification of faith. If I have faith, then I must be merciful, refrain from judging and condemning, forgive and give to my neighbour.

SL.XI.1275,13-14

PRAYER: Grant us your grace, O God, that we may always demonstrate the genuineness of our faith in abundant works of mercy towards our neighbour for Christ's sake. Amen.

WEDNESDAY

LESSON: 2 CORINTHIANS 6.1,2

What have you that you did not receive? If then you received it, why do you boast as if it were not a gift?

1 Corinthians 4.7

We must always receive before we can give. Before we practise mercy, we must receive mercy from God. We never lay the first stone. The sheep does not seek out the shepherd, but the shepherd the sheep.

See to it, then, that you always keep works in their proper place. You do not obtain anything from God by your works. You obtain all that you receive from God without any merit or worthiness on your part at all, as God says to us in Isaiah, **"I was ready to be sought by those who did not ask for me; I was ready to be found by those who did not seek me". Isaiah 65.1.** At the end of the same chapter God says: **"Before they call I will answer, while they are yet speaking I will hear". Isaiah 65.24.** Before we seek Him, He finds us; before we ask after Him, He already hears us.

This is also what Paul says in the famous section of Romans, **"All have sinned and fall short of the glory of God, they are justified by his grace as a gift, through the redemption which is in Christ Jesus, whom God put forward as an expiation by his blood, to be received by faith. This was to show God's righteousness, because in his divine forbearance he had passed over former sins; it was to prove at the present time that he himself is righteous and that he justifies him who has faith in Jesus." Romans 3.23-26.**

Paul explains it all very neatly when he says later on in Romans, **"If it is by grace, it is no longer on the basis of works; otherwise grace would no longer be grace". Romans 11.6.**

SL.XI.1276,15

PRAYER: O God our Father, let us find mercy in your sight so that we have grace to serve you acceptably with due reverence and godly fear, and further grace not to receive your undeserved love in vain, or to neglect it, or fall away from it, but to stir us up to grow in it and persevere therein, through Jesus Christ our Lord. Amen.

THURSDAY

LESSON: JAMES 2.14-17

Brethren, be the more zealous to confirm your call and election, for if you do this you will never fall; so there will be richly provided for you an entrance into the eternal kingdom of our Lord and Saviour Jesus Christ.   2 Peter 1.10,11

Good works should always be a sure sign to me, resembling a seal on a letter, to make me certain that my faith is right. If I feel in my heart that a certain work has flowed from the love in my heart, I can be certain that my faith is as it should be. If I forgive, my forgiveness should assure me that my own faith is a living reality. It guarantees and proves my own faith that God has forgiven me and forgives me daily. But if I do not forgive, I should quickly have to conclude that there is something lacking in my faith.

This was also Abraham's experience. Works made his own faith known to him. God certainly knew that he had faith, but Abraham also had to know this and prove his faith.

Works are therefore the fruits and proof which freely follow faith. Of what use would it be to me if I had a strong faith, but did not know it? It would be like having a chest full of florins and not knowing it. This would be of no use to me. But if someone made this known to me, his service to me would seem like a gift.

So also with faith. If I have faith and do not know it, it is of no use to me. Therefore it must break forth and become known to me by the works which follow it. Peter urges us to do good works, not that we should thereby be called, but to confirm our call and offer proof of it.

SL.XI.1277,16-17

PRAYER: Lord God, heavenly Father, endow us with a true, living faith which always proves itself in works of love to our neighbour, for the Saviour's sake. Amen.

FRIDAY

LESSON: MATTHEW 6.1-4

Do good, and lend, expecting nothing in return.

Luke 6.35

In these words Jesus outlines a basic Christian principle which involves our earthly property and its use in relieving the needs of our neighbour and helping him. Our earthly property should always be at the disposal of our neighbour. We should lend to our neighbour and give to him where and when he wills it.

These are real commandments and not merely counsels, as has sometimes been suggested. Jesus does not mean here, "He who wants to attain perfection must follow this course". In an effort to observe this counsel of perfection, men withdrew from the world into monasteries seeking this perfection. For this reason alone all monasteries are a devil's delusion. For no people are greedier and less inclined to break off their wrong practices than those in monasteries.

If one wants to be a Christian, one should be prepared, as Jesus says, to lend **"expecting nothing in return"**. If we are confronted with a case of need, where there is no possibility of repayment, we should make a free gift and remit all indebtedness, as Nehemiah did (Nehemiah 5.9-12).

God gave you your property, and He can certainly give you more if you continue to trust Him. If you are wrongfully deprived of something, do not demand it again for yourself. Let your neighbour step forth on your behalf and help you, so that you do not have to suffer excessively. Your neighbour should help you and protect you against wrong and violence. If you want to be Christians you must lend and give, and even suffer the deprivation of your goods, or your faith will be lacking.

SL.XI.1279,20-21

PRAYER: You have given us everything, O God. Train us in your ways so that we, too, may learn to give everything for the welfare of our neighbour, for Jesus' sake. Amen.

SATURDAY

LESSON: MATTHEW 7.1-5

Judge not and you will not be judged; condemn not, and you will not be condemned.   Luke 6.37

Jesus is speaking here of uncharitable judging and condemnation, forming a good or bad opinion about something that cannot really be seen from the outside but is a judgement that only God can make. It can happen that you see your neighbour sinning on the one day and God accepts him on the next day. You can also put on a very pious front and blot out all remembrance of your own sins.

Christ has forbidden judging, for there can be no love or unity where such judging and condemning is current among men. To judge or condemn another man is nothing else but having a log in one's eye such as all hypocrites have in their eyes. Those who have the idea that their piety exceeds that of other men always find something wrong with their brethren. No matter what their brethren do, they find fault with it, but they cannot see their own sins.

If you see nothing but sin in others, without ever noticing the log in your own eye, you are falling under the judgement of God. You, who are so ready to judge and condemn another man, are a greater sinner before God than the worst scoundrel and the worst harlot, of whom God alone knows who is saved or condemned.

All sin that other men commit is as nothing when compared with the sin that you commit with your uncharitable judgement of others.

SL.XI.1281,26

PRAYER: To you and to no one else, O God, belongs all judgement and condemnation. Keep us always aware of this basic fact whenever we are tempted to judge and condemn our neighbour in defiance of the love that we should always manifest to him, in and through our Saviour Jesus Christ. Amen.

SUNDAY

LESSON: LUKE 5.1-11

When they had done this, they enclosed a great shoal of fish; and as their nets were breaking, they beckoned to their partners in the other boat to come and help them. And they came and filled both the boats, so that they began to sink.

Luke 5.6,7

First of all, let us note here that those who believe in Christ will also have enough for their bodily needs. Christ attends to this matter here in supplying Peter and his partners with such a large number of fish, more than they would ever have dared to hope for.

We see here how Christ is genuinely concerned for the bodily welfare of His disciples. If only there were not so much accursed unbelief! Take the example of St. Peter in this Gospel. Look into his heart and you will find that he did not reckon with the possibility of catching so many fish. But God intervenes here, and brings the fish into the net in greater numbers than any of them had desired.

This example shows us that believers in Christ receive enough for their bodily needs. Unbelievers never have enough of anything. They never experience any real rest, and are continually engrossed in the piling up of earthly possessions. This is how they become enmeshed in all kinds of harmful vices.

What Paul writes to Timothy is only too true: **"Those who desire to be rich fall into temptation, into a snare, into many senseless and hurtful desires that plunge men into ruin and destruction. For the love of money is the root of all evils; it is through this craving that some have wandered away from the faith and pierced their hearts with many pangs." 1 Timothy 6.9,10.**

SL.XI.1304,2-3

PRAYER: You have given us the strongest of assurances, heavenly Father, that you will always watch over the needs of all your children, even the needs of their bodies. Grant us the grace of contentment so that we always receive your blessings with thanksgiving and with real benefit to ourselves and our neighbour, in and through Jesus Christ our Saviour. Amen.

MONDAY

LESSON: LUKE 12.13-21

Jesus said to his disciples, "Truly, I say to you, it will be hard for a rich man to enter the kingdom of heaven. Again I tell you, it is easier for a camel to go through the eye of a needle than for a rich man to enter the kingdom of God."

Matthew 19.23,24

Paul gives a vivid description of what happens when men give way to unbelief (1 Timothy 6.6-10). The man who is solely bent on piling up earthly possessions and becoming rich, falls into temptations and snares of the devil. This cannot be seen; it is something spiritual. If we could really see the damage that the devil does in spiritual things in the same degree that we can see the damage that he does in bodily matters, we would really have something to preach about. For we have external evidence of how an unbelieving man keeps on scraping earthly property together, doing violence to every man so that he may have no opposition and stand alone in his scraping operations so that finally he may rely on what he has scraped together and say: "Now I have enough".

What a mean and unfriendly thing this unbelief is! It does no one any good; it is friendly to no one; it will sell to no one; it considers nothing but its own advantage. It is certainly an accursed thing, this unbelief, refusing to trust God for the sake of our benefit, and actually believing that if we do not adopt all possible methods and procedures for insuring our bodily welfare, even at the expense of our neighbour's welfare, we will die of hunger.

SL.XI.1306,4-5

PRAYER: Lord, you have shown us in very clear precept and example that we should never be greedy and covetous, but contented and generous. Fill our hearts with such trust in your wonderful care and providence, that we overcome all temptations to selfishness, and use our blessings to help all in need, for your name's sake. Amen.

TUESDAY

LESSON: 2 THESSALONIANS 3.6-13

When he had ceased speaking, he said to Simon, "Put out into the deep and let down your nets for a catch". Luke 5.4

Jesus says here in effect: "Let down your nets and do the work that belongs to a fisherman and let Me do the worrying. I do not want you to worry but to work." We always want to change this procedure. We want to do the worrying and let Him do the work. This is one reason why so much usury is practised today. Men want to make money to avoid the necessity of working.

If you want to live like a real Christian, leave the worrying to your God. Let Him bring the fish into the net and you take up a position in which you have to work. All of us would prefer positions in which we do not have to work. For this attitude the devil is responsible. There was only one reason why such large numbers formerly became monks and priests: we all wanted to live like aristocrats and avoid the necessity of work. Parents even sent their children to school so that they might subsequently enjoy good days in the service of God. In the end, no one really knew any longer what good days were.

God has indicated that it is His pleasure that man should eat his bread in the sweat of his brow, and He has therefore ordered man to work. He said to Adam, **"In the sweat of your face you shall eat bread". Genesis 3.19**. The more closely you stick to God's law in this respect, the better it is for you. Do your work in faith and let God freely exercise His government.

SL.XI.1308,10-11

PRAYER: It is your will, heavenly Father, that your children here on earth should be honest and reliable workers in whatever calling or position you may place them. May we ever remember that it is your will that we should work in faith and trust to your governance of all times, in and through Christ our Lord. Amen.

WEDNESDAY

LESSON: ROMANS 8.31-39

Hope does not disappoint us, because God's love has been poured into our hearts through the Holy Spirit which has been given to us.   Romans 5.5

God's children must learn to combine their works with hope. God can delay results, and sometimes deems it fitting to do so. If God keeps you in suspense for a time and lets you work in the sweat of your brow without immediate result, do not straightway conclude that your work has been in vain. You must be wise and learn to recognize your God and know how to put your trust in Him. In the end, He will make His presence felt for you and give you more than you need.

If God keeps you in suspense for a time, say to yourself: "St. Peter was also kept in suspense for a time and later endowed with rich gifts". So entrust the matter to His good and gracious will and do not lose hope, and your works will become golden and acceptable to Him.

Hope waits patiently and perseveres when God delays His help and does not intervene as soon as we would prefer it. He has to make additional contribution here and hang some costly stones on your works to make them important. The most precious stone is faith, but the works of unbelievers are of straw. They are not built on faith.

SL.XI.1309,14

PRAYER: Your promises and assurances to us, heavenly Father, are always sure and certain. May we always work in the certain hope that, when it is best for us, you will help us and bestow rich blessings on us, in and through Christ our Saviour. Amen.

THURSDAY

LESSON: ROMANS 5.18-21

When Simon Peter saw it, he fell down at Jesus' knees, saying, "Depart from me, for I am a sinful man, O Lord". For he was astonished, and all that were with him, at the catch of fish which they had taken.   Luke 5.8,9

We may take Peter here as an example of those who are to believe in the eternal blessings and actually see them. A sinful conscience is by nature so constituted that it does what Peter does here, it flees from its Saviour and thinks, "I am not worthy of being saved and sitting among the saints and angels. The experience of all this good is too much for me." The straitened conscience cannot comprehend the greatest of blessings but thinks as follows, "If I were like St. Peter or St. Paul, I might be able to believe it all."

This is all very foolish, for if you wanted to take your stand on your own holiness you would be building on sand. Do not do this, but follow St. Peter. In regarding himself quite unworthy of such grace he is really proving his worthiness.

It is just because you are a sinner, and realize this fact, that you must trust yourself entirely to God's grace. You must open up your conscience to its widest extent and let your heart swell so that grace may enter in.

SL.XI.1310,16

PRAYER: We thank and praise you, heavenly Father, for your friendly approach to us sinners and for the wonderful riches of your goodness toward us. May this ever be an incentive and an invitation to us to draw even closer to you, and readily accept your grace whenever it is offered to us. In Jesus' name we ask it. Amen.

FRIDAY

LESSON: PSALM 143

If thou, O Lord, shouldst mark iniquities, Lord, who could stand? But there is forgiveness with thee, that thou mayest be feared.   Psalm 130.3,4

When you feel your sins and become like Peter, with a desire to run away from God, you must turn around and get closer and closer to Him. For if God were disposed to flee from you and were not willing to take away your sins, He would never have come to you or pursued you. Therefore, the more you feel that you are a sinner, and the more you want to run away from God, the more importunately you should seek Him.

Mark this well! For as St. Peter re-acted here, so all consciences re-act in fear because of their sins, trying to escape from God and seeking some false god. Do not end your struggle like this. You cannot possibly end it like this. Present a bold front and cling to God. Otherwise, when you run off in search of works to seek help with another god, and then later want to come back to the true God, you may well have the same experience that the foolish virgins had after going off to buy oil for their lamps, returning only to find the doors locked (Matthew 25.10).

But what did Jesus do after Peter had humbled himself to such an extent that in great fear and terror he requested the Lord to depart from him? Did He allow Peter to remain in his despondency? By no means! He proceeded to comfort Peter with the words, **"Do not be afraid; henceforth you will be catching men".** Luke 5.10.

SL.XI.1311,18-20

PRAYER: It is your assurance, heavenly Father, that the more we feel our sins, the nearer we always are to the forgiveness of sins. Keep us ever steadfast in our faith and hope that you will help and save us, in and through our Saviour Jesus Christ. Amen.

SATURDAY

LESSON: 2 CORINTHIANS 5.11-15

Do not be afraid; henceforth you will be catching men.
Luke 5.10

This is an evangelical word by which weak hearts may obtain consolation. We have seen in this Gospel how God looks after our bodily needs. He provided Peter with so many fish when he would have probably had enough with two or so. God also fills Peter so richly spiritually that he should have enough also in this respect to share it with others. He makes Peter a fisherman both bodily and spiritually. In a bodily manner Peter catches so many fish that he can sell them; spiritually, however, he is to become a fisher of men, for he has the Gospel with which he is to bring in others and extend the kingdom of Christ.

When men come to faith, God gives them so much that they are in a position to help all men, outwardly with their property and goods, and from their spiritual resources they are equipped to teach others and make them rich inwardly. When men come to faith they must proclaim it to others, and tell others of their experiences.

The psalmist knew all about this when he wrote, **"Create in me a clean heart, O God, and put a new and right spirit within me. Cast me not away from thy presence, and take not thy holy Spirit from me. Restore to me the joy of thy salvation, and uphold me with a willing spirit. Then I will teach transgressors thy ways, and sinners will return to thee." Psalm 51.10-13.**

When I believe, I come to know God. Then I also see what others are lacking, and proceed to proclaim the Gospel to them. I am in a position as a believer to feed the hungry both bodily and spiritually.

SL.XI.1312,21-23

PRAYER: Thanks and praise be yours, heavenly Father, for the riches of both bodily and spiritual blessings which you continue to shower upon us. Grant us the insights to use all these blessings to relieve the needs of our neighbours, and for the glory of your kingdom, in Jesus' name. Amen.

SUNDAY

LESSON: MATTHEW 5.20-26

I tell you, unless your righteousness exceeds that of the scribes and Pharisees, you will never enter the kingdom of heaven.   Matthew 5.20

The scribes and Pharisees led a life of such a kind that both they themselves as well as other people were of the opinion that they would gain the kingdom of heaven as a result. But they were very wide of the mark. Christ censures them and tells His disciples that unless their righteousness exceeds that of the scribes and Pharisees they will never even enter the kingdom of heaven.

This naturally prompts the question, "What then shall we do to become righteous?" Here all works that any man can perform are given up and abrogated and the most pious exponents of work-righteousness are struck down. No work can ever be performed whereby any man can save himself and rescue himself from sin. To make this statement today invites the charge of heresy.

There were certainly also those who would have been inclined to say to Christ here: "You are a heretic; do you really want to reject good works?" Christ is not disturbed by the possibility of such a charge. He openly concludes that the works of the scribes and Pharisees are worthless and nothing in God's sight. These men, too, may have felt like answering Christ here with a counter-argument, "If works do not make a man righteous before God, why do we have the Law through which we have good reason to trust that we will save ourselves, provided that we obey it in our lives?" This gives Christ a reason for introducing a discussion on the commandments in His Sermon on the Mount.

SL.XI.1336,3-4

PRAYER: In your revelation of the Gospel, heavenly Father, you have shown us with the utmost clarity that all reliance on our own efforts to gain righteousness in your sight are vain and hopeless. May we always trust your promises and assurances in firm faith and reliance, and thereby experience the full joy of salvation, in and through our Saviour, Jesus Christ. Amen.

MONDAY

LESSON: PSALM 1

You have heard that it was said to the men of old, "You shall not kill; and whoever kills shall be liable to judgement". But I say to you that every one who is angry with his brother shall be liable to judgement; whoever insults his brother shall be liable to the council, and whoever says, "You fool!" shall be liable to the hell of fire.

Matthew 5.21,22

This word is so lofty and deep at one and the same time that it defies all and any efforts to render it perfect obedience. This is not only attested here by the Lord; it is also proved in every man's experience and feelings. Christ here touches on four areas: thoughts, gestures or signs, words and deeds. No one can wriggle his way out here; we must acknowledge a verdict of "Guilty!"

It makes little difference what pious man or woman you take here as an example. They are normally quite friendly with people who do not get too close to them. But if they suffer some kind of abuse, if someone gets a little too close to them, they can become very angry on the slightest provocation. They can become incensed almost at the drop of a hat. Reason can never see its way clear to be well-disposed to those who do us an injury. Secular literature is full of instructive examples of all this, and there is also our own experience to teach us.

This, of course, is not satisfactory as far as God is concerned, but flesh and blood cannot do anything for us here. We must carefully note what God's Word actually says to us in the commandment, **"You shall not kill"**. Who is meant by **"you"**? The hand? No! The tongue? No! He means **"you"**, with all that you are and all that is in you. Your hand, your heart, your thoughts shall not kill.   SL.XI.1337,5-6

PRAYER: Dear Father in heaven, even our best efforts to render your Law the obedience it deserves fall far short of the mark of perfection. Help us in our efforts to improve our obedience to your holy will, and forgive us our many shortcomings in this connection, in the name of our Saviour. Amen.

TUESDAY

LESSON: ROMANS 10.5-13

Whoever kills shall be liable to judgement.   Matthew 5.21

Christ here interprets the law of Moses and pronounces a judgement which applies all over the world. What man on this earth is not guilty of breaking this commandment? What will we do now in the face of the necessity of keeping this commandment while not being able to do so? We cannot sweep away the mire. We are faced with despair and must judge ourselves accordingly. Hence God's laws are only a mirror in which we see our filth and wickedness; they shut all of us up under sin, so that we cannot work our way out of this situation by our own strength and free will. Something else has to come to our assistance.

Christ continues and says, "**Whoever shall say to his brother, 'Raca'** *['you fool']*, **shall be liable to the hell of fire**". "Raca" is an abusive name manifesting anger or hatred. Anger or hatred, of course, is no excuse for breaking one of God's commandments. Even though I am obliged to regard someone with whom I am at enmity in a friendly manner, signs of hatred and anger like abusive names will make it clear that my heart is not really behind my friendly exterior.

Dig into your own experience. Take a close look at others as well as yourself, and you will find that no one can help himself out of the dilemma into which his wicked disposition continually drags him, and which is deeply implanted by human nature. You may adopt a friendly attitude to your brother, but you cannot give him your heart, even if you were to tear yourself apart in the effort. In this matter we are beyond human help. Only God and His Holy Spirit can bring about the necessary change here which can spell success for us.

SL.XI.1338, 7-8

PRAYER: Change our hearts by your Holy Spirit, heavenly Father, that we may receive the necessary strength to run the way of your commandments in the service we render to our neighbour in faith and love, through Jesus our Saviour. Amen.

WEDNESDAY

LESSON: 1 PETER 1.22-25

Any one who hates his brother is a murderer, and you know that no murderer has eternal life abiding in him.
1 John 3.15

It is quite clear from Christ's interpretation in this Gospel that we are all guilty of breaking the commandment, "**You shall not kill**".

He who is not born again from God cannot possibly ever throw off the charge of murder. Even though a man refrains from the act of murder, he cannot get rid of his murderous thoughts and his acquiescence in a murder. How often do we not say when someone is murdered, "He got his deserts! It served him right!" All such reactions are clearly contrary to this commandment. God does not merely consider external works, He looks into the heart. And so this commandment, "**You shall not kill**", is a very wide-reaching commandment with a very wide application.

Without spiritual rebirth it is beyond us. Here, too, it is necessary to become a new creature. Christ has fulfilled the whole Law for us by His perfect obedience to His heavenly Father in life and in death. He has "**redeemed us from the curse of the law, having become a curse for us — for it is written, 'Cursed be every one who hangs on a tree'**". **Galatians 3.13.**

By faith in Christ all our sins against God's law are fully and freely forgiven. For our sakes God made Him to be sin who knew no sin, that we might be made the righteousness which avails before God in Him. By faith in Christ we become new creatures, we are born again, we love to run the way of God's commandment. But even as new creatures we are still far from perfection. We must always remain linked with Christ or else we must surely fail. SL.XI.1339,10-11

PRAYER: Renew us by your Holy Spirit, O God, that we may begin to love your holy Law and observe it in our relations with our neighbour as new creatures in and through Christ our Saviour. Amen.

THURSDAY

LESSON: MATTHEW 18.21-35

If you are offering your gift at the altar, and there remember that your brother has something against you, leave your gift there before the altar and go; first be reconciled to your brother, and then come and offer your gift.
Matthew 5.23,24

There are two parties here. One has committed a wrong against another man; he must ask forgiveness. The other man has been wronged; he must offer forgiveness in a friendly and ready manner, even if he has not been requested to do this.

This is very hard for human nature. It is true, of course, that it does come along once in a while with a plea, saying, "Dear friend, forgive me!" But if it were not compelled to do so in fear of hell and God's wrath, it would never do so. In any case, the old resentment still continues in the heart. On the other hand, the man who suffers the injury also finds it very difficult to forgive it in his heart. And just as the former man comes with a hypocritical plea, so he also offers a hypocritical forgiveness.

All this means nothing at all before God. **"If you are offering your gift at the altar"**, He says, **"and there remember that your brother has something against you, leave your gift there before the altar and go; first be reconciled to your brother, and then come and offer your gift"**.

Reconciliation must come from the heart; forgiveness must come from the heart. Therefore mark this text very well.

SL.XI.1340,13

PRAYER: Awaken in us a loving spirit, O Lord, which is always ready to forgive and bring about reconciliation where hostility and strife have caused discord and grief. We ask this in Jesus' name. Amen.

FRIDAY

LESSON: LUKE 12.57-59

Make friends quickly with your accuser, while you are going with him to court, lest your accuser hand you over to the judge, and the judge to the guard, and you be put in prison; truly, I say to you, you will never get out till you have paid the last penny.   Matthew 5.25,26

We do injury to our neighbour in many ways. When I do not protect his good name to the best of my ability, and when I am unfriendly to him and refuse to help him, I am already his enemy. If I want to be acceptable to God, I must first become reconciled to my neighbour. If I do not do this I cannot be acceptable to Him. God rejects any service I may render Him, if I have previously failed in service to my neighbour.

Our lives hitherto have left much to be desired. In our insane rush to secure personal benefits for ourselves from the saints, we have almost completely neglected our neighbour. The Lord reminds us here that instead of doing such wonderful things for departed saints we should be doing things for our living neighbours. We should pay the closest attention to the services we render our neighbour. God attaches no importance to a church we build for Him if it means that we have neglected the needs of our neighbour.

We have been taught the very opposite of this. We have been taught to put everything into pretentious foundations and institutions at the expense of our needy neighbour.

It is God's will that we serve our neighbour, render him his due, put all matters right with him and become reconciled to him, otherwise He does not want to see us or hear us. Moreover, if my adversary makes an approach to me, I should willingly forgive him.

SL.XI.1341,15-18

PRAYER: You have shown us, O Lord, that there is never any gain in putting off reconciliation and even great danger to our faith and piety in postponing it. Give us an open heart and spirit that is ever ready to forgive and forget, after your own example and for your name's sake. Amen.

SATURDAY

LESSON: ROMANS 8.1-9

Think not that I have come to abolish the law and the prophets; I have come not to abolish them but to fulfil them.
Matthew 5.17

What are we to learn from Christ's interpretation of the Law in His Sermon on the Mount? First, you should learn that if you were to be judged by your obedience to the Law, you would have to be condemned as a child of sin and the devil. From this lost condition you cannot possibly rescue yourself by your own resources. You have no alternative but to seek refuge in God and beseech Him to change you. Otherwise all is lost and you are ruined.

Therefore, take hold of God's Word and promises that He is willing to change you, and this will prove itself a source of great help to you. Say to God, "See here, my God, you have set up Christ, your beloved Son, as an example for me. You want me to live as He did. I cannot do this. Change me, dear God, and grant me your peace."

God comes to our assistance and says, "Because you acknowledge your need of help and seek grace from Me, I will change you and make a new man of you. And though you are not perfect like Christ, as you should be, My Son's life and perfection shall come to your assistance." There must always be something to humble us and inspire us with healthy fear.

This is real comfort — depending not on our own ability but on the fact that we have a gracious God who forgives us, and on our faith in Christ, not on our own "worthiness". This also purifies us from day to day and, wherever there is something still lacking, we trust in Christ to provide us with adequate consolation. This is also the chief thrust of this particular Gospel (Matthew 5.20-26).

SL.XI.1350,11-12

PRAYER: Thanks be to you, Lord Jesus Christ, for the hope of salvation which you have provided in the perfect fulfilment of your heavenly Father's Law for us which you offer us in your Gospel of salvation, for your mercy and truth's sake. Amen.

THE WEEK OF TRINITY VII

SUNDAY

LESSON: MARK 8.1-9

The law was given through Moses; grace and truth came through Jesus Christ.   John 1.17

Scripture holds up a twofold picture before us: a picture of fear, that is, a picture of the boundless and strict wrath of God before which no one can stand the test, a picture which would mean utter despair for every one of us, if we did not have faith. Over against this, the picture of grace is held up before us, so that faith should regard it very closely and draw from it a friendly, comforting confidence, with the hope that we can never over-estimate God's goodness towards us. There is always still much more with Him.

You have often heard that there are two kinds of blessings, spiritual and bodily. This Gospel (Mark 8.1-9) deals with temporal and bodily blessings. It teaches us children's faith; it is a Gospel for the weak.

In this Gospel we are taught to look to God as the source of all good, and to learn to trust Him. From our experience of God's blessings in the temporal sphere we should also learn to trust Him in regard to spiritual blessings. This Gospel reminds us of the fact that Christ does look after our bodily needs. From this we may well infer that He also wants to nourish our soul with spiritual blessings.

If I am not prepared to entrust the sustenance of my body to Him, I will be much less disposed to entrust the eternal welfare of my soul to Him. If I cannot trust a man to give me one florin, how can I trust him to give me ten? If I cannot look to someone for a piece of bread, much less can I entertain any hope that he will give me house and home and a whole estate.

SL.XI.1367,2-3

PRAYER: Heavenly Father, source of everything that is good for our bodies and souls, continue to pour your good blessings upon us in accordance with the promises and assurances you have given us in and through Christ, our Saviour. Amen.

266

MONDAY

LESSON: EPHESIANS 3.14-21

Now faith is the assurance of things hoped for, the conviction of things not seen. Hebrews 11.1

Here the writer of the Epistle to the Hebrews reminds us that faith is the basis on which we rely for blessings which we do not yet see, or, in other words, I must wait for a blessing that I can neither see nor hear but can only hope for.

This was also the situation in the Gospel (for this week, Mark 8.1-9). Here we have a large group of men, almost four thousand of them, who with their wives and children had been with Jesus and His disciples for three days with nothing to eat. This was real fasting, I would have you understand. They are now hungry, far from home and without the necessary provisions to sustain themselves. The writer of Hebrews says that faith is an assurance whereby I hope for blessings that I cannot see. This is the kind of faith that we find here in this multitude: they see no food at all, but they still hope that God will sustain them.

What does Jesus do here? What attitude does He take in this business? It would almost seem that He has no clues at all, for He goes to the apostles and asks them what to do about the problem of feeding these people. Their reply is characteristic enough, **"How can one feed these men with bread here in the desert?"** Here we see how human reason and faith not infrequently walk along together. We see that the smarter human reason is, the less it is in line with the works of God.

Jesus put His question to the disciples so that each of them should learn and recognize from the way his own reason reacted, that there is really no way in which reason and faith can be brought together. Here we learn that as soon as faith begins, reason must be shut out from that time, or granted "leave of absence".　　　　　　　　　　　　SL.XI.1368,6-7

PRAYER: Loving Father, on whose bountiful providence we wholly depend, give us at your pleasure whatever necessities this life requires. Above all, continue to feed our souls with spiritual food, the bread of life from heaven, through Jesus Christ our Lord. Amen.

TUESDAY

LESSON: PSALM 37.16-26

With God nothing will be impossible.   Luke 1.37

Faith is the firm foundation upon which I wait for that which I do not see. Hence I must always have enough. Before faith would ever experience dire need, the angels would come from heaven and dig bread out of the earth so that a believer with such faith should be fed. Heaven and earth would have to pass away before God allowed such a person to suffer want in clothing or any other necessity. The comforting, powerful words of God's assurances and promises call for such certainty and conviction on our part.

But if one took counsel with human reason, one would soon get the reply, "It is not possible. You will have to wait a long time before roast ducks fly into your mouth." Reason sees nothing and grasps nothing. There is nothing there.

This was also the reaction of the apostles with their question, "**How can one feed these men with bread here in the desert?**" They thought, of course, that it would be quite impossible. Had they seen a big heap of money, butchers' stalls and bakers' shops ready at hand, they would have found it easy to offer advice and to afford some comfort here. This would have provided them with a good rational solution to their problems. But when they saw nothing, they could offer no useful advice. They regarded the feeding of these people as an impossibility in the absence of the wherewithal to do this.

SL.XI.1370,9-10

PRAYER: Your mercy and goodness towards us, heavenly Father, are unending and beyond all our powers of telling. We praise and thank you for all this goodness which we experience in body and soul, in the name of Jesus our Saviour. Amen.

WEDNESDAY

LESSON: PSALM 145.14-21

He has filled the hungry with good things.   Luke 1.53

In the discussion on this Gospel of the feeding of the four thousand we have said quite a lot about entrusting our bodily welfare to God, and God's assurances to us that we will never lack the temporal blessings we need.

We also want to say something about the spiritual blessings which we need, more particularly in the face of death. When we have death before our eyes, we will find that we would rather continue to live; we will see hell before us and would much rather have heaven; we will be conscious of God's judgement and would much rather have His grace. In short, we will see nothing of what we would like to have before our eyes.

Against death, hell and God's judgement no creature can come to our help but, if I have faith, I say to myself, "Faith is a basis on which I obtain what I do not see; if I believe, nothing can harm me. Even though I see nothing before me but death, hell and God's judgement, I must pay attention to none of these, but wholly believe that God, by virtue of this assurance, and not through my own merits, will give me grace, salvation and life."

This is what it means to cling to God in true faith. This is pictured in the living example of the four thousand people who clung to God with this faith alone. They were sure that God would feed them and refused to be side-tracked by any sophistries of human reason.

SL.XI.1370,11-12

PRAYER: Comfort us with your gracious promises and assurances, heavenly Father, in the days of our pilgrimage here on earth, but especially also when death comes upon us. Let us depart this life without any of the uncertain props of human reason, trusting only and solely in your grace, through Jesus Christ our Lord. Amen.

THURSDAY

LESSON: PSALM 33.8-22

I have compassion on the crowd, because they have been with me now three days, and have nothing to eat; and if I send them away hungry to their homes, they will faint on the way; and some of them have come a long way. Mark 8.2,3

What a friend we have in Jesus! He is even concerned about the welfare of those despicable stomachs of ours. Our hopes must be aroused and we must certainly find comfort in Christ's words regarding the multitude on this occasion. They have been waiting upon Him for three days with nothing to eat, and Christ is determined to meet their needs. Here you see that all those who cling steadfastly to God's Word are fed by God Himself. Here we have an example of the true nature and power of faith; it flows solely from God's Word.

Hence, my dear friends, let us really make a beginning of believing. Unbelief is the over-all reason for all the sin and vice which has gained the upper hand in all social ranks in our day. How does it come about that there are so many silly women and rogues everywhere, so many traitors, thieves, robbers, usurers, murderers, and those who have ecclesiastical livings for sale? All this results from unbelief. All these people form their judgements on human reason alone. Reason follows nothing but what it can see, and what it cannot see it cannot comprehend. And so reason cannot comprehend how ultimately, by refusing to place its trust in God through faith, it must end in self-despair in the presence of so many rascals and scoundrels. This is what results where men allow reason to assume all controls and shut out faith in God.

SL.XI.1371,13-14

PRAYER: Lord of all power and might, the author and giver of all good things, graft in our hearts true love of your name. Increase in us true religion, nourish us with true goodness and, of your great mercy, ever keep us in the same, through Jesus Christ our Lord. Amen.

FRIDAY

LESSON: ROMANS 12.1-8

Christ . . . suffered for you, leaving you an example, that you should follow in his steps.   1 Peter 2.21

In the Gospels we are taught both faith and love. Christ is portrayed to us from two viewpoints: from the viewpoint of faith, that we should repose our whole faith and trust in Him and not indulge in anxious care and worry; and from the viewpoint of love. Just as He does to us in His concern for us, feeding us, giving us drink and clothing us out of free love alone — and not just to be useful to us, or as a reward for our merits — so also we should do good freely to our neighbours so that, just as He is Christ for us, we should also be Christ for them.

Here we see that many of the works performed in times past by the religious are vain and even damned. For they were not performed in the interests of the neighbour, but for the sole reason of piling up personal merits before God.

True Christian works must never be done with any ulterior motive; they must always be quite free, so that they redound to our neighbour's welfare, and are a completely free gift to him. They are, so to say, thrown into a common pool from which anyone can draw.

This is what Christ Himself did. He threw all His benefits into a common pool. He gave His doctrine, Word and life to the congregation as His free gift to them. Blessed are those who accept this gift of Christ with thanksgiving.

SL.XI.1372,15-16

PRAYER: Shine in our darkened hearts and lives with your Holy Spirit, Lord Jesus, that we may learn to love others as you have loved us, and that, as you are Christ for us, we may also be Christ for them. Grant us this for your mercy, truth and love's sake. Amen.

SATURDAY

LESSON: COLOSSIANS 1.15-20

He [Christ] is before all things, and in him all things hold together.   Colossians 1.17

This Gospel (Mark 8.1-9) sets Christ before us as a rich, powerful lord and steward. To be sure, He is a rich miller and baker in one, better than any other that the world has ever seen, and He has learnt His trade very well. He really draws on a number of trades at once and without any human help at all. He ploughs and harvests, threshes, grinds and bakes, almost all in the twinkling of an eye.

It is a miracle and incomprehensible to human reason how He could feed so many thousand men, without counting women and children, so that they were satisfied, and much more was taken up in broken pieces than they had at the outset. And He did it all on the instant with a word. He merely touches the bread and hands it out for distribution and enough has been ground, baked and prepared for four thousand or more people.

The five thousand whom He fed on another occasion wanted to take Him by force and make Him their King (John 6.15). They thought that a man who simply had to put his hand into one basket or one pocket to provide all their needs could prove himself an excellent leader for them. He could actually do this and become such a king. Remember also the coin which Peter found in the mouth of the fish (Matthew 17.27).

He can certainly perform His wonders when, where and how He wills. He could bring enough bread and water out of a stone to feed the world. He actually does perform such miracles daily for the whole world. All that the world has, is provided by His miracles which are no less, as St. Augustine also has shown, than His feeding of the four thousand.

SL.XI.1379,15-16

PRAYER: Lord Jesus Christ, our God and Lord, in whom all things in this world hold together, provide us with all that we need for our faith and lives now and always, in your name and for your mercy's sake. Amen.

SUNDAY

LESSON: MATTHEW 7.15-23

Whatever you wish that men would do to you, do so to them; for this is the law and the prophets.   Matthew 7.12

After explaining the commandments of God as reported in Matthew, chapters five and six, and in the earlier part of chapter seven, the Lord concludes His discussion with the words, "**Whatever you wish that men would do to you, do so to them; for this is the law and the prophets**". This is a Christian doctrine and a neat summary of the whole of Christianity.

Following on this, we have the present Gospel (Matthew 7.15-23), in which the Lord performs the office of a godly shepherd and teacher, and warns us to beware of false teachers. It is as though He meant to say, "There you have your doctrine; from now on, beware of other doctrines. For it is certain that wicked teachers and false prophets will arise wherever this Word is preached."

This we must consider very carefully, that there are two brands of doctrine: correct and good, and false, misleading doctrine. There are two brands of doctrine, one always to be found alongside the other. This is how matters have stood from the beginning, and this is how it will be until the end of the world. We achieve nothing at all by withdrawing in silence and seeking security without trouble and annoyances. The wicked doctrine of men, the devil's doctrine and all our foes will oppose us unceasingly. We must never imagine that all our battles are over. We are not yet "out of the woods". Hence the Lord gives us a very serious warning and says, "**Beware of false prophets, who come to you in sheep's clothing but inwardly are ravenous wolves**".

SL.XI.1394,1-2

PRAYER: Lord Jesus, you have given us very clear, precise teaching and instruction on what we are to believe as your disciples. Implant your Word in our hearts in such a way that we understand and keep it, for your truth's sake. Amen.

MONDAY

LESSON: ROMANS 11.17-20

Beware of false prophets, who come to you in sheep's clothing but inwardly are ravenous wolves.   Matthew 7.15

We should note very carefully that the Lord Jesus orders Christians and gives them authority to be judges over all doctrine, to pronounce judgement on whether it is correct or not. This authority was filched from us by false Christians for something like a thousand years, so that we had no authority to pronounce judgement on any doctrine but simply had to accept, without expressing any judgement, whatever the pope and the councils determined.

This Gospel completely overthrows the papacy and all councils. We are not obliged to accept what the pope enjoins or what men set up. Therefore I say once more, take careful note of this Gospel. Neither the pope nor the councils have received the command to set up and determine what faith is. Christ says here, **"Beware of false prophets"**. Either the Gospel must be lying, or the pope with the councils.

Christ tells us that as Christians we have the right to judge all doctrine and what has been set up for us to hold or not to hold. Christ is not speaking only to the pope but to all Christians. Just as Christ's former words are spoken to all, **"Whatever you wish that men would do to you, do so to them"** *[v.12]*, so also these words exclude no one, **"Beware of false prophets"**. From these words it is quite clear that I have the right and duty to judge doctrine.

Hence I am obliged to say here, "Pope, you and your councils have made decisions. I now have to judge whether I can accept these decisions or not, for you will not be at my side to answer for me when I have to die. So I have to see to it where I stand and I must be sure of my ground."

SL.XI.1394,3-5

PRAYER: Heavenly Father, your Word is the truth and you have given us full and ready access to this Word of truth. Grant us a sure and certain understanding of your Word, that we may always stand fast in our faith and openly confess the truth of your Word, through Jesus Christ our Lord. Amen.

TUESDAY

LESSON: 2 PETER 1.19-21

**Whoever speaks, [speak] as one who utters oracles of God.
1 Peter 4.11**

You must be just as sure and certain about the Word of
God as you are sure and certain that you live, and even more
so. For on this Word alone your conscience must take its
stand.

No matter how many men come along, or even angels and
the whole world, with some sort of conclusion, if you cannot
make such a judgement or reach such a conclusion, you are
lost. You cannot simply accept the judgement of the pope or
of anyone else. You must be so constituted that you can say,
"This is what God says; God does not say this. This is
correct; that is not correct." Otherwise you cannot stand
your ground.

If you are on your deathbed and take up your stand on the
pope and the councils, saying, "The pope says this; the
councils have decided that; the holy fathers like Augustine
and Ambrose have concluded this", the devil will
immediately shoot holes in your claims with the question,
"What if these statements were incorrect? What if they
erred?" If such temptation comes upon you, you have
already succumbed. Here you must be quite sure and say,
"This is God's Word. On this I will surrender body and life
and a hundred thousand necks if I had them."

St. Paul says to the Corinthians, **"I was with you in
weakness and in much fear and trembling; and my speech
and my message were not in plausible words of wisdom, but
in demonstration of the Spirit and power, that your faith
might not rest in the wisdom of men but in the power of
God". 1 Corinthians 2.3-5.**   SL.XI.1395,6-7

*PRAYER: Lord, you have given us a sure and certain
Word to establish us in the faith, and to remove far from us
all uncertainty and doubt. Enable us at all times to live up to
our convictions, and to confess your holy name without fear
or favour, in Jesus' name. Amen.*

WEDNESDAY

LESSON: PSALM 119.89-96

We also thank God constantly for this, that when you received the word of God which you heard from us, you accepted it not as the word of men but as what it really is, the word of God, which is at work in you believers.

1 Thessalonians 2.13

God makes His Word known to us through men, and He proclaimed it and had it written down especially through the apostles. St. Peter and St. Paul did not speak their own words, but God's Word, as St. Paul also assures the Thessalonians when he says to them, **"We also thank God constantly for this, that when you received the word of God which you heard from us, you accepted it not as the word of men but as what it really is, the word of God, which is at work in you believers"**.

The Word may well be preached to me, but no one can implant it in my heart except God alone. God must speak His Word to my heart, otherwise nothing comes of it. If God keeps silent, the Word is not really spoken to my heart. Hence no one will ever force me to give up the Word which God Himself has taught me. This I must know as certainly as I know that two and three make five. This remains true even if all councils say otherwise. If they say otherwise, I know that they are lying. Likewise, one yard is more than half a yard, this is certain. Even if the whole world says otherwise, I know that this does not change such facts. Who forces me to this conclusion? No one but the truth alone, which is so complete and so certain that no one can deny it.

This is also the case with the truth which God has implanted in our hearts. I am not so concerned about the opinion of Augustine, Jerome, St. Peter, St. Paul or even of the archangel Gabriel from heaven — I want to have God's Word and what God Himself says.

SL.XI.1396,8-10

PRAYER: Lord God, heavenly Father, we praise and thank you for the sure and certain truth which you have set forth in your Word. Make us steadfast and immovable in this truth, in and through our Saviour Jesus Christ. Amen.

THURSDAY

LESSON: PSALM 119.105-112

Even if we, or an angel from heaven, should preach to you a gospel contrary to that which we preached to you, let him be accursed. As we have said before, so now I say again, If any one is preaching to you a gospel contrary to that which you received, let him be accursed.   Galatians 1.8,9

In regard to God's Word, you must reach the point when you say, "That is how matters stand; no one will ever move me from my stand on God's Word". When you hear the Word say, **"You shall not kill"**, or **"Whatever you wish that men would do to you, do so to them"**, then you must know that this is Christ's doctrine over against the decisions of all the councils, even though all men say otherwise.

This is also the case with the doctrine that we cannot help ourselves in the matter of our salvation but must look to Christ as our Saviour who, by His suffering and death, has obtained the forgiveness of sins for us. This doctrine you must know and confess in your heart as the truth.

If this is not your conviction, you do not have the Christian faith. You may have the Word hanging on your ears or on the tip of your tongue like froth on the water, as Hosea says that Samaria has **"her king cut off as foam upon the water"** Hosea 10.7 A.V.. You must believe God's Word, not just as though it is made up of words preached by Peter, but as a Word which God has commanded you to believe.

I say all this so that we should return once again to the Gospel and note from what fountain the foundation of our faith flows, and to remind you that you have the authority to pronounce judgement on all that is set before you. I do not build my faith on any man and should not do so. I must answer for myself when I am confronted by death.

SL.XI.1397,11

PRAYER: The truth of your Word, O God, is a sure and certain guide for us in all matters of faith and life. Bestow your Holy Spirit upon us in such a measure that we understand, believe and confess your Word, for Christ the Saviour's sake. Amen.

FRIDAY

LESSON: 1 JOHN 4.1-6

He who is of God hears the words of God; the reason why you do not hear them is that you are not of God.   John 8.47

Do not let yourself be persuaded to believe in all simplicity what the pope says or what the councils have decided. If you recognize God in the truth of His Word, you have the rule, the measure and the yardstick whereby you may form a judgement on all the doctrine of the fathers, namely, when you know that Christ is our salvation, that He rules us, and that we are sinners.

So, if someone suggests that you must become a monk, or that you must do this or that to make sure of your salvation because faith alone is not enough for salvation, you can say in all certainty, "You are lying; your doctrine is false because he who believes in Christ is saved".

From where have we learnt this? From the faith in our hearts which believes this, and this alone. No one can take adequate precautions against error unless he is led by the Spirit of God Himself. St. Pauls says to the Corinthians: **"The spiritual man judges all things, but is himself to be judged by no one".** 1 Corinthians 2.15. False doctrine can be properly judged only by the believer who is led by the Holy Spirit.

SL.XI.1397,12

PRAYER: Your Spirit, O God, is the Spirit of truth and understanding. Lead us by your Spirit into the truth and keep us therein. We ask it in Jesus' name. Amen.

SATURDAY

LESSON: LUKE 6.46-49

No other foundation can any one lay than that which is laid, which is Jesus Christ.   1 Corinthians 3.11

We must remain free judges with authority to judge, accept or reject even what popes or councils decide. If we accept anything, we should accept it because it agrees with our conscience as instructed by Holy Scripture, not just because pope or council orders it. St. Paul says in Romans that if a man has prophecy it should be in agreement with the faith (Romans 12.6). All prophecy slanted towards works and not leading genuinely to Christ or to your own consolation is not in agreement with faith, no matter how pleasant it may be, like the revelations of the hobgoblins, masses, pilgrimages, fasts and the search after the merits of the saints.

In these matters many of the fathers have erred, including Gregory (the Great), Augustine and many others. Not the least of their errors was to take away our authority to judge doctrine for ourselves. The false idea that we owe obedience to the pope and councils without question is a heart-breaking affliction which began at a definite point in history. So you must also once again begin to say, "God has said this; God has not said this". As soon as you are compelled to say, "Man has said this", or "The councils have decided this", you are building on sand.

There is no other judge on earth in spiritual matters and on Christian doctrine than a human being who has the true faith in his heart, whether it be a man or a woman, young or old, servant or maid, learned or unlearned. God is no respecter of persons. All who live according to His commandments are alike dear to Him, and so they all have authority to judge doctrine.

SL.XI.1398,14-15

PRAYER: Heavenly Father, you have bestowed great and wonderful privileges upon us as your children by faith in Christ Jesus. May it please you to preserve and keep us in these privileges, strong in faith and hope, for Christ our Saviour's sake. Amen.

SUNDAY

LESSON: LUKE 16.1-9

He who trusts in his riches will wither, but the righteous will flourish like a green leaf. Proverbs 11.28

In this Gospel, "mammon" means surplus sustenance, including money, with which one can help others without injury to oneself. It is called "**unrighteous mammon**" by our Lord because of its daily use for unrighteous purposes and because it incites men to all kinds of unrighteousness.

"**Mammon**" is also God's creation, like wine and corn, and God's creatures are good. But men can misuse God's good creatures and can fall into much sin in acquiring them. St. Paul tells the Ephesians that they should make the most of the time "**because the days are evil**". **Ephesians 5.16**. The "**time**" or "**the days**" are not evil in themselves, but much evil occurs during these days or this time.

Similarly, he speaks in Romans of "**the day of wrath**", **Romans 2.5**, although the "**day**" in itself is quite good. But because God's "**wrath**" will be manifested on this day it derives its name from this fact. So also, because "**mammon**" is used for all kinds of unrighteous ends, Christ here calls it "**unrighteous mammon**". It is surplus sustenance which we should use to relieve the needs of our neighbour and to help him. If we do not use it for this purpose it becomes "**unrighteous mammon**" for us; we possess it unjustly and it is stolen in God's sight.

Before God we are in duty bound to give, to lend, and even to let men take what we have. According to the common proverb, the biggest money-bags are the greatest thieves. They have the biggest surplus and give away the least.

SL.XI.1447,2-4

PRAYER: Heavenly Father, may the good gifts of your creation never become a snare to us nor incite us to all sorts of acts of unrighteousness, either in sins of omission or sins of commission. Grant us grace to use these gifts for our own welfare and the sustenance of our neighbour, for Jesus' sake. Amen.

THE WEEK OF TRINITY IX

MONDAY

LESSON: 1 TIMOTHY 6.17-19

The master commended the dishonest steward for his prudence; for the sons of this world are wiser in their own generation than the sons of light.   Luke 16.8

We shall understand the story by which Jesus makes his point in this week's Gospel (Luke 16.1-9) in its simple meaning, without introducing a large number of subtleties into it, as Jerome has done. It is not always necessary to search out such a pointed meaning; the milk of the story is enough for us.

We do not necessarily have to explain here in what way this steward had wasted his master's goods, and how it comes to pass that even after this he still succeeds in using up his master's property for himself treacherously, fraudulently and falsely.

Christ concludes that the steward acted prudently or astutely. He does not praise him for being good. He actually finds fault with him for having wasted his master's goods, and also for ensuring the continuance of his comfortable existence by treacherously playing fast and loose with his master's goods. What the master in the story commends is that this man did not forget his self-interest in a critical situation; he commends the steward's craftiness. It is like saying of a harlot who has the whole world at her feet, "She is a clever harlot".

From all this Christ draws the conclusion: just as this steward displays outstanding craftiness in matters concerning his earthly welfare, we also should be deeply concerned about our eternal welfare and eternal life.

SL.XI.1448,5

PRAYER: Lord God, heavenly Father, the treasures and riches of heaven and its glories far outweigh the most desirable riches and treasures that our earthly life affords. Grant us a zeal and concern for our spiritual welfare that is at least the equal of the craftiness and shrewdness whereby men sell their souls for earthly happiness. We ask it in Jesus' name. Amen.

TUESDAY

LESSON: MATTHEW 10.16-23

The sons of this world are wiser in their own generation than the sons of light. Luke 16.8

To understand the story in this week's Gospel (Luke 16.1-9) correctly, consider St. Paul's statement, **"Adam . . . was a type of the one who was to come". Romans 5.14.** Adam was a type of Christ. How can the apostle compare Adam with Christ when Adam brought sin and death upon us, and Christ has brought us righteousness and life?

St. Paul compares Adam with Christ in respect to origin and race, not in regard to fruit and work. Adam is the origin and head of all sinners, whereas Christ is the origin and head of all saints. We have inherited nothing else from Adam but sin, condemnation and our eternal curse; from Christ, however, we have obtained righteousness and salvation. You cannot make these two extremes agree, for sin is punishable and righteousness is praiseworthy. But in respect to origin there is a comparison: even as sin and death have penetrated to all men through Adam, so, through Christ, righteousness and life have become available for all men.

So in the Gospel Christ compares the unrighteous man with the righteous man. As the unrighteous man acts shrewdly with his unrighteousness and villainy, so we should act wisely in matters of justice and piety. This is the point of the comparison, as Jesus Himself explains when He says, **"The sons of this world are wiser in their own generation than the sons of light".** The **"sons of light"** should learn prudence from **"the sons of darkness"**, or the world. Even as they are clever in all their doings, so also should **"the sons of light"** be clever in their doings. That is also why Christ adds the words, **"in their own generation".**   SL.XI.1448,6-7

PRAYER: Lord God, heavenly Father, it is your will that we should be just as wise and prudent in regard to what is good, as unbelieving men are in regard to what is evil. Establish us in everything that is good, that we always prove ourselves your wise and prudent followers, through Jesus Christ, in whom you have given us all treasures of wisdom and knowledge. Amen.

WEDNESDAY

LESSON: MATTHEW 12.33-37

The good man out of the good treasure of his heart produces good, and the evil man out of his evil treasure produces evil; for out of the abundance of the heart his mouth speaks. Luke 6.45

When Christ declares that we should make friends for ourselves by means of the unrighteous mammon, it is quite clear that He means that we should do good works on the basis of which these friends will receive us into the eternal habitations (Luke 16.9).

This may sound rather strange to those who have been accustomed to the proclamation of salvation by faith alone. But there is nothing in this Gospel which conflicts with this proclamation. With a Christian, faith and love are everything. We are accounted righteous before God by faith alone; we prove or demonstrate this faith by works of love. I cannot perform any acts of piety unless God's grace has previously taken possession of my heart. If I am to make friends for myself by means of the mammon of unrighteousness, I must first be accounted righteous before God.

Two facts hold good here: a bad tree cannot produce good fruit, and, contrariwise, a good tree cannot produce bad fruit. The conclusion, then, is not so difficult. If I am to do good by my use of mammon, I must be truly righteous in my heart beforehand, for God looks at the heart; He regards my works according to the disposition of my heart. I point out these distinctions lest you attempt to force works into the heart.

Before I can do good works I must be accounted righteous in God's sight by faith in Christ. You do not build here from the outside inwards, nor do you start building from the roof. You commence with the foundation, and in things Christian this is faith.

SL.XI.1450,9-10

PRAYER: Heavenly Father, it is faith and the imputation of Christ's righteousness that forms the beginning of everything in us and our works, that is really good in your sight and in the true interests of our neighbour. Preserve us in the faith which always rests and trusts in you alone, for Christ our Saviour's sake. Amen.

THURSDAY

LESSON: PSALM 15

Faith working through love.   Galatians 5.6

Scripture also speaks of our walk of life externally, of how we are to walk with our fellowmen as human beings made up of flesh and blood. That I am accounted truly righteous before God is something that you do not know and I myself cannot simply take it for granted. I must make my faith sure and certain for myself and other people as well. I must do good to my neighbour so that my faith proves itself.

External works are signs of inward faith. These works do not actually make me godly and pious, but they demonstrate that I am godly and pious, and attest that I have the right faith. This is how I must understand the injunction of the Gospel, **"Make friends for yourselves by means of unrighteous mammon"**, that is, do good to make your faith sure and certain. So we must distinguish between the Spirit and the fruit of the Spirit.

Luke describes the fruit of faith as giving to the poor and making friends for ourselves in this way. He means to say to us: "I do not want to speak to you now about faith as such, but about how you should prove your faith. Do good to your neighbour and if you can really give to him out of the goodness of your heart, you can be quite sure about your faith."

Scripture at times speaks about the fruits of faith, at other times about faith as such. It speaks to us about the fruits of faith when we are told in Matthew that on judgement day the Lord will say to those who have been rejected on His left hand, **"I was hungry and you gave me no food, I was thirsty and you gave me no drink"**. **Matthew 25.42**. He will point out to those on His left hand that they did not really believe in Him and will demonstrate their unbelief from their lack of fruits of faith.   SL.XI.1451,11-12

PRAYER: Lord God, faith that does not prove itself in works of love is a dead faith and of no value at all, as you plainly demonstrate in many clear passages of your holy Word. Grant us your grace and strength at all times to prove that our faith is a faith that works by love, in and through our Saviour Jesus Christ. Amen.

FRIDAY

LESSON: HEBREWS 12.18-24

Enter not into judgement with thy servant; for no man living is righteous before thee. Psalm 143.2

It seems, on the surface, that Christ in this week's Gospel (Luke 16.1-9) actually suggests that we should do good works by means of unrighteous mammon, so that we may obtain eternal life thereby, and that those whom we have helped with our mammon may receive us into eternal habitations.

Our opponents are not slow to remind us that we have always taught we should not do good works to inherit eternal life, and that what we read here seems to be the direct opposite of this doctrine. What are we going to say to this? There are many passages here and there in Scripture which speak of our merits. With these, our opponents think they can set God's mercy at naught, and force us to adopt the position that we must satisfy God's justice with our good works. Be on your guard against such views and take up your stand on God's pure grace and mercy alone, saying, "I am a poor sinner, O God; forgive me my sins. I will gladly keep silent about my merits if you will only keep silent about your judgement."

Why was Christ given us as our Mediator? If we want God to enter into judgement with us on the basis of good works, we push Christ aside as our Mediator. And without Christ's work of mediation we cannot stand before God. Hence, let Him remain your mediator. Seek the cover of His wings as the psalmist advises: "**He will cover you with his pinions, and under his wings you will find refuge**". **Psalm 91.4.**

Let this be your prayer: "O God, I do not presume to claim any merit before you from my works, but devote them to the service of my neighbour, placing all my faith and trust in your pure mercy alone".

SL.XI.1452,14

PRAYER: We give you eternal thanks and praise, heavenly Father, for the riches of your grace and mercy continually bestowed upon us poor, lost and condemned sinners, in and through our Saviour and Mediator, your Son Jesus Christ. Amen.

SATURDAY

LESSON: MATTHEW 25.31-46

And the King will answer them, "Truly, I say to you, as you did it to one of the least of these my brethren, you did it to me". Matthew 25.40

How will the people whom we help by means of the unrighteous mammon receive us into the eternal habitations? Will they take us by the hand and lead us in? By no means!

When we come before God's judgement, some poor man to whom I have done good will stand up in heaven and say, "He washed my feet; he gave me drink, food, clothing, and so on". This man will really prove himself a friend to me and a witness to attest my faith. Such a poor beggar will be more useful to me than St. Peter or St. Paul, for they will not be able to help me then. But when a poor beggar will come and say, "O God, this is what he did for me as a member of your flock", this is going to help me, for God will say, "What you did for him, you did for Me".

These same poor brethren will not be our helpers but our witnesses, so that God may receive us. In saying this, I do not want you to withhold due honour from St. Peter and the other saints, for the saints, too, are members of God and of Christ. But you do better in giving your neighbour a penny, than you do in building a gilded church for St. Peter, for to succour the poor is something you are commanded to do, but you are not commanded to build a church for St. Peter.

Nowadays men are prepared to do anything and everything for the saints who are dead and beyond all assistance from us, but the poor people, whom we should really treat as a holy shrine, are left sitting or lying on the street.

SL.XI.1454,20

PRAYER: Heavenly Father, let us never fall into the error of seeking showy works to impress our fellowmen rather than the works of love which help our needy neighbour, works truly pleasing to you, in and through our Saviour Jesus Christ. Amen.

SUNDAY

LESSON: LUKE 19.41-48

When he drew near and saw the city he wept over it.

Luke 19.41

The events described in this Gospel occurred on the day we usually call Palm Sunday when Jesus, amidst public acclaim, entered Jerusalem as the king of grace. On that occasion He proceeded at once to the temple and there He preached for three days on end. This He had never done before. The sum and content of this Gospel is Christ's deep concern over those who despise God's Word and His lament over their ultimate distress.

You have often heard what the Word of God is, what it brings with it, and what kind of students it encounters. This Gospel tells us nothing of these aspects. It simply sets before us the punishment and distress which will come upon the Jews because they did not know the time of their visitation. We must take a close look at all this because it also concerns us. If those are punished who do not know the time of their visitation, what will be the fate of those who knowingly persecute, blaspheme and dishonour the Gospel and the Word of God? Here, however, Jesus speaks only of those who do not know the time of their visitation.

There are two ways of preaching against those who despise the Word of God. Christ illustrates one method when He pronounces His woes upon Chorazin, Bethsaida and Capernaum, declaring that it will be more tolerable for Tyre, Sidon and Sodom on the day of judgement than for these places (Matthew 11.20-24).

The other method of dealing with those who reject God's Word is illustrated here in this Gospel when Jesus weeps over Jerusalem. He feels the deepest of compassion for these poor, blind people. He does not reprove or threaten them as hardened and deluded sinners. His heart melts in love for them, He has compassion for these enemies. SL.XI.1468,1-4

PRAYER: Lord Jesus, as you shed tears of mercy and compassion over Jerusalem, so also let us experience your love and compassion whenever we stand before you as sinners in need of salvation, for your mercy and truth's sake. Amen.

MONDAY

LESSON: ROMANS 13.11-14

Would that even today you knew the things that make for peace!   Luke 19.42

There are many ways in which God can punish men for despising and neglecting the Gospel and His Word. He can send them false prophets and sectarians who preach with such assurance that one would imagine they had swallowed the Holy Spirit. Even men in whom we had every confidence can become their victims and fall into error, so that they no longer know what they should do or leave undone.

There is no greater affliction or calamity than for God to send us sects and false teachers, because they are so bold, keen and daring that it is really pitiable. On the other hand, the Word of God is such a great treasure that no one can adequately grasp it. God values His treasure very highly, and when He visits us in His grace it would please Him greatly if we accepted His visitation with love and thanksgiving.

He does not bring us under compulsion here, as well He might, but He wants us to follow Him gladly, with joy and love. However, He does not wait for us to come to Him; He gets in first and comes to us. He comes into the world; He becomes man; He serves us, dies for us, rises again and sends us His Holy Spirit. He also gives us His Word and opens up heaven so widely that all stands open. In addition He gives us rich promises and assurances of His temporal and eternal care here on earth and in heaven, and pours out His grace upon us in full measure.

We are now living in a rich time of grace, but we despise it and throw it to the winds. This He cannot disregard.

SL.XI.1472,12-13

PRAYER: In your Word and Gospel, O God, you have bestowed rich and precious gifts upon us, and by your mercy and grace we have enjoyed a rich season of grace. May we never lose the appreciation of the precious nature of your rich blessings to us, but ever continue in their full enjoyment, in and through Jesus Christ our Saviour. Amen.

TUESDAY

LESSON: PSALM 95.6-11

The days shall come upon you, when your enemies will cast up a bank about you and surround you, and hem you in on every side, and dash you to the ground, you and your children within you, and they will not leave one stone upon another in you; because you did not know the time of your visitation.   Luke 19.43,44

These words of Jesus were fulfilled about forty years after this when Jerusalem was destroyed by the Romans in the manner described by Jesus. Let us learn a lesson from this, because it certainly concerns us and all other men.

This is no joking matter, and we have no reason at all to suppose that our experience will be so different. The Jews refused to believe it until they experienced it personally. We are now being visited by God. He has opened to us His treasure, His holy Gospel, by which we learn to know His will and to see how we have been held fast in the devil's power.

No one is prepared to accept it in all seriousness. We even despise it and make fun of it. No city, no prince or ruler, is really thankful to God for this gift. And what is even more serious, there are those who persecute and revile the Gospel.

God is patient and bides His time for a while. If we simply misread open facts and push matters too far, however, He can take His Word away from us, and the same wrath which fell upon the Jews can also fall on us. For we have the same Word, and the same God and Christ that the Jews had. We, too, will suffer the same punishment that the Jews suffered, for the same sin that they committed, despising and rejecting God's Word and, more particularly, His Gospel of salvation in Christ. **"Today, when you hear his voice, do not harden your hearts." Hebrews 3.7.**   SL.XI.1471,10-14

PRAYER: Lord God, your warning voice is always quite plain. We have no one but ourselves to blame if we fail to recognize the day of your visitation. Keep us always fully aware of the serious nature of your offer of salvation, in and through Christ our Saviour. Amen.

WEDNESDAY

LESSON: PSALM 19.1-4

Finally, brethren, pray for us, that the word of the Lord may speed on and triumph, as it did among you.
2 Thessalonians 3.1

In our day, praise God, the Gospel is being proclaimed with a fullness and clarity that has not been known since the days of the apostles. We should appreciate this time of visitation and pray earnestly to God to continue it among us, especially also by continuing the blessings of peace.

The princes and rulers are always only too ready to decide matters with the sword. They are too bold in grabbing hold of God by His beard and God will strike them on the mouth accordingly. It is high time to pray earnestly to God to keep on making His Gospel known in ever-widening circles among those who have not yet heard it. Should punishment suddenly fall upon us, it would be too late and many souls would be left behind whom the Word had not yet reached.

This is why I deeply regret the fact that we despise the Gospel in such a horrible manner. This is not said simply for our own sakes, but also for the sake of those who are still going to hear the Gospel. Matters have settled down a little, and, God grant, I hope that this continues and that both the princes and the peasants do not become any crazier. If hostilities break out again I have grave fears that they will not end.

SL.XI.1473,14-15

PRAYER: Preserve unto us times of peace, O Lord, in which your Word may have free course and still reach many who do not yet know it and believe it, for your name's sake. Amen.

THURSDAY

LESSON: 1 PETER 4.12-19

Every one who has left houses or brothers or sisters or father or mother or children or lands, for my name's sake, will receive a hundredfold, and inherit eternal life.
Matthew 19.29

In many ways we resemble the Jews. They were more concerned about their bellies than about God, more intent on filling their bellies than on learning God's plan of salvation for them. Ultimately, therefore, they lost out in both directions, and deservedly so. Inasmuch as they refused to accept eternal life and joy, God also deprived them of their bodily welfare, and so they lost both body and soul.

They offer an excuse which rings much like those we also hear today from our contemporaries, "We would have been quite glad to accept the Gospel had it not endangered our body and property, and perhaps even cost us wife and children". "If we let him go on thus", some of them said in reference to Christ, "every one will believe in him, and the Romans will come and destroy both our holy place and our nation". John 11.48.

What they here feared would happen did happen, for as Solomon said, "What the wicked dreads, will come upon him". Proverbs 10.24. These fears prevented the Jews from believing in God. They did not regard the great and rich promises which God had made to them.

We also pass over such matters and do not see the mighty, comforting promises which our Lord has made us. Even if we do lose our earthly property, heaven and earth are the Lord's, and He will certainly repay us freely and richly.

SL.XI.1474,16

PRAYER: Heavenly Father, your blessings and benefits to us are many and great, and are all the free gifts of your love and mercy. Open our hearts in such a way that we never offer any hindrance to the operation of your free and wonderful grace, and so that we may be prepared at all times to suffer everything and risk everything for Christ's sake. Amen.

FRIDAY

LESSON: 2 THESSALONIANS 2.12-16

And he entered the temple and began to drive out those who sold, saying to them, "It is written, 'My house shall be a house of prayer'; but you have made it a den of robbers".
Luke 19.45,46

The temple and the whole priesthood was established to promote God's Word and for the praise of His grace and mercy. This was to be attested with the external service of sacrifices and in public thanksgivings. But the temple services were not simply regarded by the Jews as opportunities for praising and thanking God for His grace and mercy; they turned their temple worship into a monkish doctrine of works. With their sacrifices in the temple they believed that they could earn God's grace for themselves, and that by the making of many sacrifices they could influence God to give them heaven and all earthly blessings as well.

All that they should have expected from God on the basis of God's pure goodness and grace, they based on their own works and merits. In addition, in the devil's name they went so far in all this that in their greed they set up tables for money-changers and seats for those who sold pigeons and other animals to offer as sacrifices right in the temple, so that those who came from distant lands and cities might find enough to purchase or exchange their money there. This they did to increase the trade in sacrificial animals and to enrich themselves in the process.

In the name of worship and under the excuse of worship they absolutely distorted all worship and destroyed it. They changed God's grace and mercy into human merit, and His gift into human work which He had to accept from them and for which He had to thank them.

SL.XI.1482,36

PRAYER: In your Word, O Lord, you are giving to us; we are not giving to you. Keep us ever mindful of the fact that you are the source of all blessing, and that we are always receivers solely dependent on your grace, in and through Christ our Saviour. Amen.

SATURDAY

LESSON: LUKE 21.21-24

They will not leave one stone upon another in you.
Luke 19.44

Jesus becomes angry at the desecration of His temple by these greedy money-grubbers. They not only despise and neglect the true worship of God, but turn it completely upside down and trample it under foot. Out of the temple which God set up to teach men God's Word and bring them into heaven, they made nothing else but a den of robbers and murderers.

It was, indeed, a den of murderers, for nothing but the utter corruption and murder of souls took place there. God's Word, through which alone souls are saved, was never heard there. In its place, men were directed to the devil's lies.

This is really the chief sin, the reason for which they merited utter destruction together with their temple. Because they are bent on the destruction of God's kingdom, God no longer wants to build up their kingdom. He says to them in effect, "Because you proceed to build up the devil's kingdom in place of My kingdom, I will adopt a similar procedure with you and absolutely destroy everything that I have built up among you".

Of this He gave them a prelude when He went on the rampage in their temple just before the end of His public ministry. Later on, when He had left this earthly scene, the Romans would carry out His words to the letter. Then they would be completely carried off from Jerusalem with all their possessions, just as He had removed them from the temple. They would no longer have any worship, temple or priesthood, land or people.

SL.XI.1483,39

PRAYER: O God, let us not forget the example which you made of your chosen people, the Jews, when they hardened themselves in unbelief. Keep us always truly humble and free from false presumptions, as we trust solely and only in your grace, through Jesus Christ our Saviour. Amen.

SUNDAY

LESSON: LUKE 18.9-14

Two men went up into the temple to pray, one a Pharisee and the other a tax collector.   Luke 18.10

You have already heard that before any man can do what is good and pleasing in God's sight he must already be a pious man, that is, he must be accounted as justified and righteous before God by faith in Christ. At all times it remains universally true that a good tree cannot bear bad fruit, and, contrariwise, that a bad tree cannot produce good fruit. If a man is to do what is good, he must be good beforehand. So also here. The tax collector beats his breast, and this act may be regarded as a mark of the faith he already had in his heart.

This took place and was recorded so that we should really open our eyes and not judge people merely by outward appearances. We must try to discover what was in the heart of these two men and not simply form a judgement according to works. If the heart is godly, all is godly. If this tax collector is judged by works, you soon come to a false conclusion. It appears that in him there is nothing but sin. Likewise, when I judge the hypocritical Pharisee here according to works, I also finish up with a wrong conclusion. He stands in the holy place, makes a fine prayer, praises and thanks God with impressive works, fasts, gives tithes and harms no one. Everything about this man glitters. His standards find universal approval.

It is not easy to reject the testimony of such an honourable, virtuous life. Who would venture to assert that fasting is not good, that praising God and rendering to every man his due is something evil? When I look at a priest, monk, or nun I regard them as godly. Who can gainsay me? But if I am to determine that this man is evil and that man godly, I must look into their hearts. This I cannot do.   SL.XI.1486,2-4

PRAYER: We know that it is quite useless, heavenly Father, to play the role of a hypocrite, because you can always look into our hearts and judge us accordingly. Purify our hearts from all base motives, that the services we render you may truly please you and benefit our neighbour, for Christ's sake. Amen.

MONDAY

LESSON: 1 PETER 5.6-11

The tax collector, standing far off, would not even lift up his eyes to heaven, but beat his breast, saying, "God, be merciful to me a sinner!"   Luke 18.13

It seems that the tax collector must have heard something of God's Word beforehand, that he believed this Word and became a godly man as a result of this, as Paul says, **"Faith comes from what is heard, and what is heard comes by the preaching of Christ". Romans 10.17.** When God's Word takes hold of a man's heart, it purifies him and makes him truly pious and godly. The evangelist does not expressly say here that the tax collector had heard the Gospel, but he gives certain indications that he had heard it somewhere or other, for he makes the tax collector exclaim, **"God, be merciful to me a sinner!"**

Such an exclamation is beyond all the powers of human reason. Therefore he must have become acquainted previously with the fact that God is gracious, merciful and friendly to all who recognize their sins, who call upon Him and desire His grace. He had heard that God in His heart of hearts is gracious to all who humble themselves, and who look to Him for comfort and consolation.

The beginning of all true piety must never be sought in ourselves but in the Word of God. God must first let His Word sound forth in our hearts. Through this Word we learn to know God and come to faith in Him. After this, we are equipped for good works. Accordingly, we must also infer here that the tax collector in some way or other heard the Word of God. If this were not so, it would certainly have been quite impossible for him to confess himself to be a sinner as the Gospel reports it. He would not have been humbled and beaten his breast unless there were true faith in his heart beforehand.

SL.XI.1487,5-6

PRAYER: Thanks and praise be to you, heavenly Father, for the precious gift of your Word. Grant that we may always accept your Word with our whole heart so that it always proves itself a powerful influence in our lives, fully sanctifying us, for Christ the Saviour's sake. Amen.

TUESDAY

LESSON: 2 CORINTHIANS 4.13-15

I tell you, this man went down to his house justified rather than the other.   Luke 18.14

The tax collector's faith certainly proves itself by its fruits. How do we explain Christ's statement here that he **"went down to his house justified rather than the other"**? We have suggested that this tax collector was justified before the happenings recorded in this Gospel and before he beat upon his breast as here reported. What does Christ mean here, then, with the statement that **"he went down to his house justified"**?

This refers to something I have frequently stressed previously: if faith is as it should be, it will break out and produce fruit. If the tree is green and good, there is no coming to a standstill; it must sprout and produce fruit and leaves. Nature sees to this. I do not have to command the tree and say, "Listen to me, tree, produce apples!" If the tree is there and it is a good tree, fruit comes of its own accord. If true faith exists anywhere, works must follow.

If I confess myself to be a sinner, it follows that I must also say, "Dear God, I am a rogue; make me godly!" So also the tax collector here. He does not hold back, but speaks out quite freely. He is not afraid of disgracing himself before other people. He must come out with his faith, saying, **"God, be merciful to me a sinner!"** It is as though he meant to say, "Now I see that all is shattered for me; I am a rogue and acknowledge my sin. There is nothing else for me now but to believe in God and cling to His mercy, to implore His grace; otherwise I am ruined."

In this way faith casts itself upon God. It breaks forth and establishes itself through works. When that happens in a man, I can recognize him as a believer and so can others.

SL.XI.1488,8-9

PRAYER: When you bring men to true faith, heavenly Father, you also empower them to prove their faith in their lives. Make our faith such a power in our lives that all men will know that we are your children and glorify your holy name, in and through Jesus Christ our Saviour. Amen.

WEDNESDAY

LESSON: 1 CORINTHIANS 2.1-5

By God's power *[we]* are guarded through faith for a salvation ready to be revealed in the last time.   1 Peter 1.5

The reason why St. Luke and St. James put considerable emphasis on works is to prevent men from labouring under the false delusion that faith is merely some vague sort of feeling that floats about on the heart like froth on the beer. This is absolutely wrong!

Faith is a vital, living reality, making a man quite new, changing his whole disposition, giving his life a completely different direction. Faith brings a man right down to the grass roots of existence, and a complete renewal of the whole man takes place. Hence, if I formerly knew a man to be a sinner, I can see from his changed behaviour, his altered being, and his different life that he is now a believer. Faith is always a most important factor.

The Holy Spirit has also seen fit to emphasize works because they are witnesses of faith. If there are those who produce no evidence in the form of works, we can quickly conclude, "They heard the message of faith but it never penetrated to any depth in their case".

If you want to persist in pride and immorality, in greed and wrath, while continuing to chatter a lot about faith, St. Paul will come to you and say, **"The kingdom of God does not consist in talk but in power"**. 1 Corinthians 4.20. The kingdom of God must be lived and put into action; it cannot be adequately attended to with little more than idle chatter.

SL.XI.1489,11

PRAYER: Heavenly Father, faith is the power which you use to bring men to salvation and to keep them as your children and disciples. May we never lose this faith but may it ever increase in us, continuing to manifest itself in rich fruits of faith for the welfare of your kingdom and in the interests of our neighbour. In Jesus' name. Amen.

THURSDAY

LESSON: PSALM 9.7-12

The tax collector, standing far off, would not even lift up his eyes to heaven, but beat his breast. Luke 18.13

We are urged to produce works as evidence of faith, not that we should pile up merits by them. Doing works freely and gratuitously for the benefit of our neighbour must become our normal procedure. In urging such works upon us, God is saying to us in effect, "If you have faith, heaven is yours. But even so, in order not to deceive yourselves, do some works."

The Lord pointed this out in an excellent manner when He said to His disciples, **"This I command you, to love one another". John 15.17**. And just before this, during evening supper, He said, **"A new commandment I give to you, that you love one another; even as I have loved you, that you also love one another. By this all men will know that you are my disciples, if you have love for one another." John 13.34,35**.

Before this He stated, **"I have given you an example, that you also should do as I have done to you". John 13.15**. Christ means to say here, "You are My friends, but no one can detect this from your faith. But if you show forth fruits of faith, and your love bursts forth, people will be able to recognize you as My friends. The fruits will not save you or make you My friends; you must prove yourselves to be My friends, and that you are saved by your fruits of faith."

Therefore, note this well! Faith alone makes you godly. Although it is a living force and a great treasure, because it lies hidden in you, works must emerge and attest your faith to the praise of God's grace and the condemnation of the works of men. You must lower your eyes and humble yourself before everyone so as to win over your neighbour by your service to him. For this reason also God prolongs your life, otherwise you would have deserved to lose your head long since. This you see well illustrated in this pious tax collector.   SL.XI.1490,13

PRAYER: Strengthen our faith, heavenly Father, by your means of grace, that we may always produce abundant proof of our faith in good works to our neighbour, for Christ's sake. Amen.

FRIDAY

LESSON: LUKE 14.7-11

Every one who exalts himself will be humbled, but he who humbles himself will be exalted.   Luke 18.14

We must take a look here at the foolish hypocrite, the Pharisee. He is adorned with the most beautiful works. First, he gives thanks to God, fasts twice in the week, and gives a tithe on his whole income to God, not to St. Nicholas or St. Barbara. He has not broken up his marriage or committed an act of violence against anyone. He is not the kind of man to insist on his rights; he has always preserved an unblemished record of piety. If that is not a fine, honourable life, I would like to know what is! No one could really fault this man; as far as the world is concerned he deserved nothing but praise. In fact, he praises himself.

God intervenes here to demonstrate that the works of this Pharisee are blasphemies. Lord God forbid! What judgement is this! Nuns and priests might well be dismayed here and tremble in the marrow of their bones. None of them are half as pious as this Pharisee. Would to God that there were still many such hypocrites and Pharisees today!

What is there lacking in this pious man? The simple fact is that he does not really know his own heart. Here you see that we are our own greatest enemies, inasmuch as we close our eyes and heart. This man tells us how he feels. If I were to ask such a hypocrite, "My dear man, do you really mean what you say?" he would affirm with an oath that he has his facts quite straight. Note, however, how deep God's sword cuts, **"piercing to the division of soul and spirit"**. Hebrews 4.12. Here everything must crash in ruins and fall to the ground. Without humility, no one can stand before God.

SL.XI.1492,17-19

PRAYER: Open our eyes and hearts, O Lord, that we really recognize ourselves for what we are, miserable and wretched sinners, utterly lost and condemned if left to our own resources. Fill up our emptiness with your grace and mercy, and continue to shower your blessings upon us, in and through our Saviour Jesus Christ. Amen.

SATURDAY

LESSON: LUKE 7.36-50

Now may our Lord Jesus Christ himself, and God our Father, who loved us and gave us eternal comfort and good hope through grace, comfort your hearts and establish them in every good work and word.   2 Thessalonians 2.16

The tax collector (Luke 18.9-14) stands there and humbles himself. He mentions no fasting, no good work; he mentions nothing at all. And yet the Lord says that this man's sins are not as great as the hypocrite's. A man must really be bold if, in the face of all this, he would feel inclined to exalt himself above the least of sinners. If I draw myself up even a finger's breadth above my neighbour, or above the worst of sinners, I am thrown down. The tax collector during his whole life did not commit so many and so great sins as this Pharisee here committed when he said, **"God, I thank thee that I am not like other men"**, and lied so that heaven might well have thundered in reply. You hear no word here like the tax collector's plea: **"God, be merciful to me a sinner!"** God's mercy, tender-heartedness and love are clean forgotten.

God is nothing but sheer and pure mercy, and he who does not see this does not believe in God at all, as the psalmist also declares, **"The fool says in his heart, 'There is no God' "**. **Psalm 14.1.** This is where the unbeliever finishes up with his lack of self-knowledge.

I will add just one more remark here. Even if this man had committed the very worst of sins like deflowering virgins it would not have been as bad as saying, **"God, I thank thee that I am not like other men, extortioners, unjust, adulterers"**. To be sure, Pharisee, do I hear you? Do you have no need of God, do you despise His goodness, mercy, love and all that He is? These are real sins. It is not a question here of open sins breaking out. It is a matter of unbelief in the heart, which we cannot see. This is always the real sin.   SL.XI.1493,20

PRAYER: Heavenly Father, the consequences of unbelief, cutting ourselves off from all grace and mercy, are truly fearsome and must lead to despair. Keep us firm in faith and duly humble by keeping us close to our Saviour, in whose name we also ask this. Amen.

SUNDAY

LESSON: MARK 7.31-37

How are men to call upon him in whom they have not believed? And how are they to believe in him of whom they have not heard? And how are they to hear without a preacher? Romans 10.14

The external history of this Gospel or the example it sets before us is good in itself. For here we see how many adopted the pressing need of this poor man as their own need and brought him to Jesus that He should help him. In this action there is set forth an example of both faith and love. It is an example of faith. They had heard that the Lord is good and merciful and helped all who came to Him. The Word, portraying God's goodness to us, must be heard beforehand and reach our hearts so that we cling to it in faith. Christ's words must have taught these people these basic facts about God; otherwise, in the absence of that Word, faith and works are also absent.

Although the actual details are not recorded here, we must infer from what actually took place that before these people brought this man to Jesus they must have heard the good news, the Gospel concerning the Lord Jesus Christ, by which they were brought to faith. For the Gospel in its real essence is good news, a good report, not written on paper but promulgated and made known in the world in the living voice. Accordingly, they had no doubt heard that Christ is good, friendly and beneficial, helping everyone. This was the beginning of their faith.

So you must take a firm grip of the Gospel. You will always find that the good news must first go out and bring us to God. God must lay the first stone or otherwise all is lost. Secondly, they adhered to this good news, they came to Jesus and expected to obtain from Him what they had heard about Him.

SL.XI.1516,2-4

PRAYER: The Gospel which you have made known to us, O God, is a message of good news. May this message ever draw us closer and nearer to our Saviour and keep us with Him. In His name we ask it, and for His sake. Amen.

MONDAY

LESSON: PSALM 57.1-3

Bear one another's burdens and so fulfil the law of Christ.
Galatians 6.2

The Gospel for this week (Mark 7.31-37) describes works of love. These men seize the initiative and go to the poor, deaf man with speech troubles to lend him a hand. Without their merits or any initiative from them, Christ sends forth His Word and attends to the spreading of His goodness and mercy. Accordingly, after drawing from the fountain, there is an outflowing from them which is quite spontaneous. They now share gratuitously with their neighbour, without any condemnation of merits.

Love must always do its work in this way, quite freely and with no other consideration but the neighbour's welfare. Among other things, St. Paul says of love that it **"does not insist on its own way"**. **1 Corinthians 13.5**. To the Philippians he writes, **"Let each of you look not only to his own interests, but also to the interests of others"**. **Philippians 2.4**.

This is the attitude which we find here also among these pious people. They do not need the work in question. They do not consider simply their own interests; they think only of the poor deaf man and of how they can help him. They seek no reward. They render their services to this man quite gratuitously.

This is also the kind of sincerity which should mark your good deeds to your neighbour or otherwise you are not Christians. Mark well, then, how love is described here. It takes upon itself another man's troubles. If we follow this example, good for us. If we refuse to follow it, God can punish us with the blindness which afflicted our forbears for almost four hundred years.

SL.XI.1517,5-6

PRAYER: It is your will, heavenly Father, that we should always practise our faith, especially in the love which we show to each other. Grant us your grace that we love each other without any self-interest, looking not to our own things but to the things of our neighbour, in and through Christ our Saviour. Amen.

THE WEEK OF TRINITY XII

TUESDAY

LESSON: GALATIANS 3.23-29

In Christ Jesus you are all sons of God, through faith.
Galatians 3.26

You know now that man is accounted righteous before God and becomes acceptable to God on no other ground but on the basis of faith alone. Hence it is nothing but a false fabrication to teach what has hitherto been taught on this matter in the church, namely, that we must have dealings with God on the basis of our works.

Over and above all this, it was even more foolish for the church to direct men to other sources of help besides faith and works. It was asserted that nuns, priests and monks could help others with their nocturnal howling in their cloisters and distribute their treasures among others.

We should note that no one should ever make up his mind to be saved through another's faith and work. Your salvation is beyond the work and faith of Mary or any other saint. It cannot even result from the work and faith of Christ Himself.

To be saved you must believe for yourself. You can be saved only by your own faith. God will not give His consent to permit Mary, or any other saint, not even Christ, to take your place in this respect. You can be accounted righteous in His sight and justified before Him only by your own faith. If Christ's own faith and work are of no account here, you will achieve even much less with the work and faith of all monks and priests.

SL.XI.1518,7

PRAYER: We praise and thank you, heavenly Father, for the gift of faith which you have bestowed upon us in your free and unmerited grace. Let this faith now become a real fountain of good works in us which we perform in the interests of our neighbour, for Christ our Saviour's sake. Amen.

WEDNESDAY

LESSON: MATTHEW 9.18-22

He said to the woman, "Your faith has saved you; go in peace".   Luke 7.50

This Gospel (Mark 7.31-37) suggests discussion on the part played by another's faith in our salvation. These men brought the deaf man to Jesus as a fruit of their faith in Jesus. The deaf man made no contribution at all; he played an entirely passive role.

We should note at the outset that it is quite impossible to be saved by another man's faith in the sense that the other man does the believing for you and in your place. But it may well happen, that through another man's faith, you yourself come to personal faith. In a similar way, the works of another man can help me or influence me to perform works of my own. Those people are lying who claim that we can be saved through the works and faith of others, whether we have personal faith for ourselves or not. It is not so! Unless you derive a personal faith for yourself from God's goodness and mercy, you cannot be saved.

This is how the case stands. If you do not have your own personal faith, neither the faith nor work of another man will help you, not even Christ who is a Saviour for the whole world. His goodness and His help avails you nothing unless you yourself have faith in Him, and are thereby enlightened. Therefore, be on your guard against anyone who directs you for help to another's faith. Tell such a would-be helper, "If you want to serve me with your works, make an approach to God and say to Him, 'Dear heavenly Father, through your grace I have come to faith, therefore I beseech you, my God, give this poor man faith also'. This could help me, but it is impossible for you to give me your own faith. And even if you could do so, it would help me not at all."

SL.XI.1518,7-9

PRAYER: Heavenly Father, of all the many gifts which you have bestowed upon us in your grace and mercy, none is more important to us than the gift of faith. Make our faith strong and a powerful source of good works, through your holy Gospel and for Christ's sake. Amen.

THE WEEK OF TRINITY XII

THURSDAY.

LESSON: LUKE 12.35-40

Then all those maidens rose and trimmed their lamps. And the foolish said to the wise, "Give us some of your oil for our lamps are going out". But the wise replied, "Perhaps there will not be enough for us and for you; go rather to the dealers and buy for yourselves". Matthew 25.7-9

It is important for you to know how far another man's faith can help you. The merits of others can prompt you to acquire merits of your own, but that is their limit. Even if all the angels and God's mercy itself took your part, it would not help you, unless you adhered to that mercy with a faith of your own. One thing another man's faith can do for you is to help you acquire a personal faith for yourself.

Similarly, even if Christ, after dying for us and giving His body and life, blood and flesh for us, were to intercede for us, it would still not help us, unless we believed in Him. But He can help us by interceding for us with His heavenly Father and saying, "Dear Father, all this I have done for men; give them faith that they may avail themselves of it". This also helps us after we regard His works and merits as our very own possession. The same thing applies in respect to all the other saints. Their intercession and merits are of no avail at all to us unless we have personal faith.

You see this also from the events set forth in this Gospel (Mark 7.31-37). The poor man lies there helpless; he cannot speak or hear anything. Those who brought him to the Lord can speak and hear. He does not acquire the ability to speak through their hearing and speaking. Even if they had all come forward and said, "We want to speak and hear for you", he would have remained speechless and deaf for ever and never have acquired the ability to speak.

If you make use of your faith to help me to personal faith for myself, that is helping me. Otherwise no work or ties of brotherhood are of any avail. SL.XI.1520,11-12

PRAYER: Lord God, heavenly Father, make our faith a living power in our lives, not only to believe all that you have promised us, but also to do all you command us, for Jesus' sake. Amen.

305

FRIDAY

LESSON: 1 PETER 2.9,10

I do not say to you that I shall pray the Father for you; for the Father himself loves you, because you have loved me and have believed that I came from the Father.   John 16.26,27

I should never rely on your works and you should not rely on mine, but with my faith I will pray to God for you to give you a personal faith of your own. John says that Christ has **"made us a kingdom, priests to his God and Father". Revelation 1.6.** Like Christ Himself, we may now step forth on behalf of others and pray that God may bestow a personal faith on them. Hence, if I see that you do not have such a faith, or a weak faith, I go off and pray to God to help you to such a faith. I do not give you my own faith and works, but I pray God to give you your own faith and works. I pray to God that Christ may give you all His works and salvation through faith, as He has given us His blessings through faith.

This is also the point in the passage quoted above from John's Gospel. Christ means to say here, "I have prayed and had dealings with God on your behalf so that He may give you what is Mine. Therefore acknowledge My name. Through My prayer for you He has accepted you and given you faith, so that from now on you may pray for yourselves. I do not have to do it for you, but you should do it for yourselves in My name."

Here God crowned us, consecrated us, and anointed us with the Holy Spirit so that we are all priests and each one should pray for the other. We are a royal priesthood of believers.

SL.XI.1521,13-14

PRAYER: Among our greatest distinctions, Lord Jesus, is this, that you have given us individually the status of being kings and priests before God, our heavenly Father. Grant us at all times a clear understanding of our privileges as priests, especially in intercessions for the needs of our brethren. We pray in your name, Lord Jesus. Amen.

SATURDAY

LESSON: 1 JOHN 5.9-15

Whatever you ask in prayer, you will receive, if you have faith.   Matthew 21.22

As Christians who are priests before God we should say, "Christ was certainly a priest in the fact that He prayed for me and acquired personal faith and the gift of the Spirit for me. Hence, I also am a priest who should continue to pray to God that He should give faith to this man or that man." We should have the firm persuasion that we shall receive what we pray for boldly in faith, in accordance with Christ's promise, **"Ask, and you will receive". John 16.24.**

To pray boldly is not always in our power. The Spirit does not always give the ability to pray boldly. Paul prayed to God for Israel that they might be saved (Romans 10.1). Why was his prayer not successful? It was a matter of faith. The Holy Spirit withheld it. Had Paul been able to pray for this with boldness it would most certainly have happened. Had Paul said, "I pray for the whole of Israel", and had he believed boldly and said, "Lord, I am certain that you will do it", it would certainly have happened. It was certainly his heart's desire and one which he often expressed, but the Holy Spirit never enabled him to believe it with confidence.

It is not within our power to pray with bold confidence; the Holy Spirit must give us this confidence. When we pray for anyone with the confident addition, "It will certainly happen", it will certainly happen. But normally we Christians must pray with the addition, "Your will be done!" If I must leave it to His will, then I cannot prescribe person, time or manner to Him, but leave it to His good pleasure. This gives me adequate certainty. This is also what Christ did. He prayed in the garden, **"My father, if it be possible, let this cup pass from me; nevertheless, not as I will, but as thou wilt". Matthew 26.39.**   SL.XI.1522,15-16

PRAYER: Heavenly Father, give us a full measure of your Holy Spirit, enabling us to pray at all times in faith and confidence, through Jesus Christ our Saviour. Amen.

SUNDAY

LESSON: LUKE 10.23-37

Turning to the disciples he said privately, "Blessed are the eyes which see what you see! For I tell you that many prophets and kings desired to see what you see, and did not see it, and to hear what you hear, and did not hear it".

Luke 10.23,24

This seeing and hearing must be understood quite simply as external seeing and hearing, namely, that they saw Christ in His own person and in the office He fulfilled, heard His preaching, and witnessed the miracles which He performed among the Jews. They were all in a position to confess with Peter, **"You are the Christ, the Son of the living God".** **Matthew 16.16.**

Many prophets and kings also saw Christ, but only in spirit. The Lord Himself said to the Jews, **"Your father Abraham rejoiced that he was to see my day; he saw it and was glad". John 8.56.** On that occasion the Jews thought that Jesus was speaking about a physical seeing; but Jesus was referring to the spiritual seeing whereby all pious Christian hearts saw Jesus before He was born and still see Him today. If Abraham saw Him in this way, there is no doubt that many prophets, in whom the Holy Spirit resided, also saw Him thus. This spiritual seeing brought salvation to the holy fathers and prophets, but they also experienced a heart-felt desire and longing to see the Lord Jesus Christ in the flesh. This is indicated here and there in the prophets.

The Lord here says to His disciples, who both heard and saw Him in the flesh, **"Blessed are the eyes which see what you see!"** He means to say, "This is a blessed time, an acceptable year, a time of grace. What is now present before you is so precious, that the eyes which see it are quite rightly called blessed. Never before has the Gospel been proclaimed to every man with such publicity and clarity."

SL.XI.1536,2-4

PRAYER: Jesus, Lord and Saviour, you pronounced your disciples blessed for being able to see and hear your works of grace and your Gospel of salvation. Help us to a similar experience of blessedness in connection with your Gospel of salvation, for your name's sake. Amen.

MONDAY

LESSON: ROMANS 13.8-10

A lawyer stood up to put him to the test, saying, "Teacher, what shall I do to inherit eternal life?" He said to him, "What is written in the law? How do you read?" And he answered, "You shall love the Lord your God with all your heart, and with all your soul, and with all your strength, and with all your mind; and your neighbour as yourself". And he said to him, "You have answered right; do this, and you will live". Luke 10.25-28

I think that the Lord set out to teach this pious man a very elementary lesson. And yet, such treatment of such a fine man can hardly be right. Surely, He should have shown more consideration for this man! He puts him to shame before the whole world. How can this help the man? He shows this man who had imagined that he had done everything, that he has really done nothing. He asks: **"What shall I do?"** When Jesus was finished with him, he certainly had enough and more than enough to do.

A great deal of very necessary comment could easily be supplied on the two commandments which this man quotes for Jesus. They are the most significant and most important parts of Moses. As Jesus says, **"On these two commandments depend all the law and the prophets".** Matthew 22.40.

If we examine all the laws in Moses, we shall see that they all have reference to love. I cannot explain or interpret the commandment, **"You shall have no other gods before me"**, **Exodus 20.3**, as having any other meaning than "You shall love God alone". This is how Moses himself explains it in Deuteronomy when he says, **"Hear, O Israel: The Lord our God is one Lord; and you shall love the Lord your God with all your heart, and with all your soul and with all your might".** Deuteronomy 6.4,5.

SL.XI.1538,6-8

PRAYER: Lord God, heavenly Father, guide us at all times by your Holy Spirit to a full and correct understanding of your holy Word, so that it achieves in us the purposes for which you have given it to us and receives its full meaning for us, in and through Jesus Christ. Amen.

TUESDAY

LESSON: MATTHEW 23.27,28

The aim of our charge is love that issues from a pure heart and a good conscience and sincere faith. 1 Timothy 1.5

God's Law says to us, "**You shall have no other gods before me**". **Exodus 20.3**. "**You**" it says. It means you and all that you are. In particular, however, it means your heart, your soul, all your might. Nothing is said about the tongue, the hand or the knees. It is really referring to your whole body, and to everything that you have and are.

If I am to have no other gods before the one true God, it means that I must truly have the one true God in my heart, that is, I must love Him with my whole heart, always cling to Him, rely on Him and trust Him. I must find joy and pleasure in Him and keep Him continually in my thoughts.

Even in ordinary matters which please us we are accustomed to say: "It really does my heart good to taste this". When a person reads or laughs and is not in earnest and does not mean it from his heart we say: "You are laughing, but it is not coming from your heart". The heart is something quite different from the mouth. In Scripture "heart" means the strong, intense love which we should always have for God. Those who serve God merely with the mouth, the hand or the knees are hypocrites and God does not regard them. God does not want to have only one part of you; He wants to have the whole of you.

The Jews withheld themselves outwardly from idolatry but served God only with their mouth. Their heart was far from Him, filled with mistrust and unbelief. Outwardly they presented quite a beautiful appearance, as though they worshipped God in full earnestness; inwardly, however, they were full of idolatry.

SL.XI.1538,9-10

PRAYER: Purify our hearts, heavenly Father, that you may reign in them alone and that they may become a fixed habitation of the Holy Spirit within us to lead and direct us in all our ways, in and through Jesus Christ. Amen.

WEDNESDAY

LESSON: 1 CORINTHIANS 5.6-8

Far be it from me to glory except in the cross of our Lord Jesus Christ. Galatians 6.14

The really wicked people in God's sight are those who are proud of their external performances, who want to justify themselves and be accounted righteous before God because of their works. The lawyer in the Gospel belonged to this class of men. What a proud ass he is! And like a proud ass, he comes to the fore. He imagines that Christ can find no fault in him. He probably even thinks that the Lord will commend and praise his life right here before all the people. It never entered his head that he might have something to learn from the Lord; he was seeking only his personal honour and glory. This coxcomb was expecting a song of praise from the Man to whom the people looked up and about whom everyone wondered.

The Lord does not really do this man a service in shaming him like He does. Christ can really be quite unfriendly and anything but kind, especially when He tells people the plain, unvarnished truth. One can understand why some people became so cross with Him. This pious, holy lawyer is still standing on his head. He has but one aim in view: to cash in on the very high reputation he has won by his holy living. He is quite sure that he has fulfilled all the commandments. He hopes to hear from Christ the commendation, "My good man, you have done everything; all is well with you". But Christ says: **"Do this!"** In plain language Christ means to tell him, "You are a complete fake; you have never at any time kept this law, not even a letter of it". He shows this man his wickedness. The poor simpleton thinks that he should be in one of the upper seats. It would be fine and clean. He would rather take his place among the angels than among these people. At times Christ can certainly be a very strange Christ.   SL.XI.1539,11-12

PRAYER: You have made it perfectly clear, O God, that self-righteousness never has any room to spare for your grace and mercy. Empty our hearts of all false pride and self-righteousness, that your grace and mercy may enter and abide there, in and through our Saviour Jesus Christ. Amen.

THURSDAY

LESSON: ROMANS 1.18-25

You shall worship the Lord your God and him only shall you serve.   Matthew 4.10

God allows us to love His creatures; that is why He created them and made them good. The sun is a fine creation of God; gold and silver and everything that is fair and beautiful quite naturally engender love in us. God readily permits us to love these creatures. But to cling to them and equate our love for them with our love for Him, this He neither will nor can tolerate. Indeed, it is His will that I should deny and forsake all if He wants me to do so, and that I should be satisfied even if I never saw the sun, money or any of my property again.

Love of creatures must always stand a very long distance beneath love of Himself. Even as He is the supreme good, so He wants us to love Him in the highest manner before everything else. If He does not want me to love anything beside Himself, much less does He want anything to be loved above Himself, although both of these alternatives amount to the same thing.

Now, I believe, you can see what it means to love God with your whole heart, and your whole soul, and your whole mind. To love God with your whole heart is to love Him above all creatures. Although many creatures are quite lovable and please me well and I love them, I should still be fully prepared to disregard them and let them go for God's sake, if God, my Lord, so wills it.

SL.XI.1541,13-14

PRAYER: We thank and praise you, heavenly Father, for all the good gifts of your creation. Grant us the moderation and understanding to use these creatures according to your will and for our neighbour's benefit, in Christ's name and for His sake. Amen.

FRIDAY

LESSON: COLOSSIANS 1.9-12

Thy will be done, on earth as it is in heaven.
Matthew 6.10

We have seen in our consideration of this Gospel (Luke 10.23-37) what God means when He says, "**You shall love the Lord your God**". He means you, the whole you, not only your hands, your mouth or your knees. When we love God with such a fullness of our being, we fulfil this law.

But there is not a single person on this earth who fulfils it in this manner. Indeed, we all do the very opposite. This law makes sinners of all of us, so that not even the smallest letter of this commandment is fulfilled, not even by the greatest saint in the world. No one adheres to God with his whole heart in such a way that he could forsake everything for God's sake. We have, praise God, advanced so far that we cannot endure giving up even one little word, yes, not even a farthing for God's sake!

How is it possible to love God if His will is not pleasing to us? If I love God, I also love His will. When God sends us sickness, poverty, disgrace and shame, that is His will. But what do we do? We rampage, snort and groan, and accept matters with much impatience. This is the least of our problems. What would we do if we had to give up body and life for God and Christ's sake? Then I suppose we would show quite another front! In the meantime I act like this Pharisee and lawyer. I lead a fine life outwardly, honour God and serve Him, fast, pray and always put on a very pious and holy front. But God does not look for this. He wants His will to be accepted joyfully and in love. In this respect we continue to drag our feet.

SL.XI.1542,18

PRAYER: O God, make us ready and willing at all times to obey your holy will, not grudgingly and impatiently, but whole-heartedly, freely and openly, for Christ our Saviour's sake. Amen.

SATURDAY

LESSON: PHILIPPIANS 2.1-4

And who is my neighbour? . . . Go and do likewise.
Luke 10.29,37

The lawyer does not ask, "Who is my God?" It seems that he feels that he owes God nothing. As far as God is concerned, he is quite sure that there is nothing amiss. Nor is he conscious of any shortcomings as far as his neighbour is concerned. But he still comes up with the question, "**And who is my neighbour?**"

The Lord answered him by telling him a parable which shows that we are all neighbours one of another, both the man who does a good deed to another man, and the man who needs that act of kindness. In this parable, however, Christ more particulary presents the man who does an act of kindness to another as a neighbour. But Scripture uses the term "neighbour" in both senses; it calls the man who does the act of kindness a neighbour, and at times it speaks of the recipient of such an act as a neighbour.

From this parable Jesus draws the conclusion, "Go and do likewise". This lawyer had not only sinned against God but also against his neighbour. He failed not only in his love to God but also in his love to his neighbour. He did not do good to his neighbour. We can imagine how the poor man began to sweat at the suggestion that there was nothing but evil in him from the top of his head to the soles of his feet. How could he have been so remiss, this highly learned and pious man?

This is how he came to overlook important duties: he led a pharisaical, dissembling, hypocritical life. In this sort of life he never stooped to consider the interests or welfare of his neighbour. He never even thought of helping others with his life; he thought only of his personal honour and glory before his fellowmen, and so he always kept gaping at heaven. He led the very opposite of a God-pleasing life.

SL.XI.1543,22-24

PRAYER: Grant us your grace, heavenly Father, that we always keep our priorities in correct perspective, loving you with a pure heart and loving our neighbour as ourselves, in Christ's name and to His glory. Amen.

SUNDAY

LESSON: LUKE 17.11-19

The Son of man came not to be served but to serve, and to give his life as a ransom for many.   Matthew 20.28

One point of difference between St. Luke and the other evangelists is that Luke did not concentrate only on the work and doctrine of Christ, like the others; he also described the order of His journeys and the routes by which He travelled. Up to chapter thirteen, Luke's Gospel points out how Jesus began to preach and to do signs in Capernaum to which He went from Nazareth and where He lived.

From the end of chapter nine till the end of his Gospel, Luke tells us how He preached and performed miracles on His journey from Capernaum to Jerusalem. This was the last journey during His life here on earth and took place during the last year of that life. This is also what Luke is referring to here when he says that **"on the way to Jerusalem he was passing along between Samaria and Galilee"**.

This was not the usual route from Capernaum to Jerusalem. He passed along **"between Samaria and Galilee"** lengthening His journey. The nearest route lay along the borders of these territories. The evangelist is at some pains to remind us here that Jesus did not travel by the usual route to Jerusalem but that He took a time-consuming, more distant and circuitous route on this journey to Jerusalem.

He did not do this for any personal reasons but to seize extra opportunities to proclaim the Gospel and to extend His help to people who needed it. He makes His way through the midst of this territory so that His progress might be quite public, and that he might be at everyone's service. In this way, the people could approach Him from all sides and receive His help. He was sent to make Himself available to all, so that everyone might freely enjoy His goodness and grace.

SL.XI.1572,1-2

PRAYER: Thanks and praise be yours, heavenly Father, for sending us your Son to be such a ready and willing helper. May this fact draw us ever closer to Him in all our needs, in the full assurance of His most tender grace and looking to Him for full salvation. In His name we ask it. Amen.

315

MONDAY

LESSON: MATTHEW 17.14-21

If I have all faith, so as to remove mountains, but have not love, I am nothing.   1 Corinthians 13.2

This Gospel (Luke 17.11-19) places before us a simple story or event that is quite easy to understand and requires little explanation. But although it is quite simple it sets before us a most important example. In the case of the lepers it teaches us faith; in respect to Christ it teaches us love. And faith and love constitute the whole essence of a Christian, as I have so frequently stated.

Faith receives; love gives. Faith brings a man to God; love brings him to his neighbour. Through faith, man lets himself be benefited by God; through love, he does good to his neighbour. He who has faith has all things from God and is blessed and rich; henceforth he needs nothing more. All that he does, he arranges for the good and benefit of his neighbour, and he does all this through love, even as God has done all things for him through faith. He draws good from above through faith, and he dispenses it here below through love.

The saints who have acquired their holy status by works violently oppose all this; their merits and good works concern themselves rather than their neighbour. They live for themselves alone. They do their good without faith. These two sides of the Christian life, faith and love, are well illustrated in this story of the cleansing of the ten lepers.

SL.XI.1575,4

PRAYER: Lord God, heavenly Father, strengthen our faith that it becomes the real fountain and source of all that is good and blessed in our lives as Christians, and produces a rich harvest in fruits of love to our neighbour, for Jesus' sake. Amen.

TUESDAY

LESSON: ROMANS 9.30-33

As he entered a village, he was met by ten lepers, who stood at a distance and lifted up their voices and said, "Jesus, Master, have mercy on us". Luke 17.12,13

It is not enough for you to believe that there is a God, and that you make long prayers, as is now the abominable custom. In the case of the lepers, you see how it is a mark of faith to teach men fruitful prayer without any professional instruction. Here you see how they had formed a good opinion about Christ and had acquired a degree of confidence in Him. They also entertained the firm expectation that He would regard them graciously.

This same expectation made them bold and thirsty, so that they placed their need before Him and with all seriousness and in a loud voice requested His help. Had they not previously gained this high opinion and expectation in regard to Him, they would probably have stayed at home and not come out to meet Him, crying out to Him in a loud voice. In that case, too, doubt would probably have gained the upper hand as they asked themselves: "What are we up to? Who knows if He will react kindly to our requests? Perhaps He will not even look at us!"

True faith has no doubt at all about the good and gracious will of God. And so the prayer of true faith is strong, just as faith itself is strong and firm. St. Luke underlines three things in the conduct of these lepers: first, they came out to meet Jesus; secondly, they stood; and thirdly, they lifted up their voices. In these three points Luke praises their strong faith and sets them before us as examples.

SL.XI.1575,6

PRAYER: Lord God, heavenly Father, all that you have revealed to us about Jesus and His Gospel of salvation is the strongest of incentives to faith and confidence. Grant us your grace to accept in firm faith all that your Gospel offers us, in and through Jesus Christ our Saviour. Amen.

WEDNESDAY

LESSON: PSALM 103.1-5

Jesus, Master, have mercy on us.   Luke 17.13

Faith never asserts merits or tries to purchase God's grace with works. It pleads only its utter lack of merits, or its demerits, and clings only to the pure, unmerited goodness and grace of God. This is also demonstrated very well by the lepers who have confident expectations in regard to Christ's grace, without the performance of any works.

What good thing could they have done beforehand to impress Him? They had never seen Him before; much less did they have opportunities of serving Him. Then, too, they were lepers whom He would have been compelled to avoid according to the Law (Leviticus 13). It would have been necessary for Him to tell them the rights and wrongs of their situation. Basically, He would have been compelled to tell them the truth that He could have nothing to do with them, and they nothing with Him. That is also why they stand "at a distance", as those who are well aware of their unworthiness.

Faith also stands at a distance from God; yet it runs to meet Him and cries out to Him. Faith fully recognizes the truth that it is unworthy of God's goodness and has nothing on which to rely except His highly celebrated goodness. The soul which stands at a distance and is empty also seeks God's goodness. This goodness cannot be linked in any way with our merits or works; it will come only of its own accord as Christ comes in this village to the lepers so that their praise might remain free and pure.

There is complete agreement here. God's love dispenses His goodness freely and gratuitously. It receives nothing or seeks nothing in payment. Faith receives this goodness as a pure and simple gift, without making any payment of any kind for it.   SL.XI.1578,12-14

PRAYER: There is never anything in us, O God, which merits your grace and goodness, but rather the very opposite of this. Thanks and praise be yours, heavenly Father, for the riches of your grace and mercy freely bestowed upon us, in and through our Saviour Jesus Christ. Amen.

THURSDAY

LESSON: JAMES 1.2-8

When he saw them he said to them, "Go and show yourselves to the priests".   Luke 17.14

In this Gospel we are given a very warm and friendly invitation to draw near to Christ, to put our faith and trust in Him. There is no doubt that He wants to do for everyone what He did for these lepers. All that is necessary is for us to cast ourselves freely upon Him in the expectation of receiving from Him all His grace and goodness.

In this regard, true faith and a Christian heart should act and does act as these lepers act and teach us to act. That it pleases Christ that we should joyfully and freely determine to build upon His goodness even before we have experienced it or felt it, is sufficiently attested here in the way in which He so willingly lends an ear to them without any delay at all. Nor does He tell them that He is about to help them. He simply deals with them as if what they desired had already happened. He does not say to them, "Yes, I will have mercy on you; you will be clean". He simply says, **"Go and show yourselves to the priests".**

It is as though He says to them, "You do not have to make any entreaty. Your faith has already obtained and acquired what you want before you ask for it. You were already clean, as far as I was concerned, when you began to expect all this from Me. Nothing more is needed, then, but that you should go to show the priests that you have been cleansed. As I regard you, and as you believe, so you are and so you will be." He would not have sent them to the priests had He not regarded them as clean.

Behold, how powerful faith is! It acquires everything it desires from God, and God regards it as accomplished even before it is asked for. Isaiah speaks of faith when he says, **"Before they call I will answer, while they are yet speaking I will hear".** Isaiah 65.24.   SL.XI.1579,16-17

PRAYER: Faith is the means whereby you bestow all your blessings upon us, heavenly Father. When our faith is right, all is right with us as your children. Preserve us and strengthen us in faith, in and through Christ, the author and finisher of our faith. Amen.

FRIDAY

LESSON: 1 PETER 2.13-17

Let each of you look not only to his own interests, but also to the interests of others.   Philippians 2.4

The lepers teach us faith; Christ teaches us love. Love deals with the neighbour in the manner in which it discovers that Christ has dealt with us. Jesus said to His disciples, **"I have given you an example, that you should do as I have done to you". John 13.15.** Soon after this He said, **"A new commandment I give to you, that you love one another; even as I have loved you, that you also love one another". John 13.34.**

What else is Jesus saying to us here but this, "Through Me you now have in faith everything that I am and have; I am your very own. You are now rich and fully satisfied through Me. For all that I do and love is not for My sake but for you that you should have nothing but the one thought, namely, how I can be useful and helpful to you and fulfil all that you desire and need. Therefore never lose sight of Me as your example. Do to one another as I have done for you. Consider also henceforth how you can live for the benefit of your neighbour and do whatever you see to be useful and of benefit to him. Your faith has enough in My love and goodness; therefore you should now give your love to others."

SL.XI.1580,18

PRAYER: It is your will, heavenly Father, that we should always give you our full and complete faith and trust. Grant us also the privilege to prove our faith in you with the love that we show our neighbour, in and through Christ our Saviour. Amen.

SATURDAY

LESSON: 1 THESSALONIANS 2.11-13

As the body apart from the spirit is dead, so faith apart from works is dead.   James 2.26

We prove the genuineness of our love as Christians by works of love. Jesus said, **"By this all men will know that you are my disciples, if you have love for one another".** **John 13.35.** James declares, **"Faith apart from works is dead". James 2.26.** His meaning clearly is: If your life is so arranged that it is not of service to others, that you are living for yourself alone without any consideration for your neighbour, your faith is certainly nothing. In such a case, you are not doing as Christ has done for you. You do not really believe that Christ has done you any good at all, for if you did, you would be compelled by an inner necessity to do good to your neighbour. This is also what Paul means in the celebrated passage in Corinthians: **"If I have all faith, so as to remove mountains, but have not love, I am nothing".** **1 Corinthians 13.2.**

We do not say all this to suggest that faith is not enough to obtain righteousness for you before God, but because in a Christian life these two, faith and love, must always be attached to each other and never separated. There are presumptuous people who think that they can separate them. They want to believe without loving. They despise their neighbour and still want to have Christ. This is a false and wrong view. So we say: faith is everything and saves, so that a man requires nothing more for his salvation.

But faith is never inactive or lazy. It is always very busy; but it works for the good of the neighbour and not for self. It needs nothing for itself, for it already has all things in Christ. If this is not how faith reacts, there is something wrong with it. Its reaction must be love.   SL.XI.1583,23

PRAYER: Preserve us, O God, against the error of errors that we are saved by works of righteousness which we ourselves have performed. Keep us ever firm and steadfast in the conviction that we are saved only by God's grace, through faith in our Saviour Jesus Christ. Amen.

SUNDAY

LESSON: MATTHEW 6.24-34

Be doers of the word, and not hearers only, deceiving yourselves.   James 1.22

In this Gospel we see how God separates the Christians from the heathen. The Lord does not offer this doctrine to heathen because they do not accept it: this doctrine is given to Christians. But He does not regard those as His Christians who hear the Word only to learn and recite it by heart like many of the religious do with the psalter.

The devil also hears the Word of God and the Gospel in this way; in fact, he knows it better than we do. He could also preach it just as well as we do if he wanted to do so. But the Gospel is a doctrine of such a kind that it always aims at becoming a living force in men's lives. It must result in action, strengthen men and comfort them, make them courageous and bold.

Therefore, those who hear the Gospel only to obtain an external knowledge of it, so that they may be able to discourse learnedly about the wisdom of God, should not be numbered among true Christians. The only real Christians are those who actually put into practice what the Gospel teaches. You will not find so many of these. We see many who are hearers of the Word, but not so many who are doers.

May God grant us His grace that we may always become doers of His Word so that His Gospel does not remain only in our ears and on our tongues, but that it may really reach our hearts and then burst forth in active works of love to our neighbour.

SL.XI.1614,1-2,35

PRAYER: Lord God, heavenly Father, we praise and thank you for the precious gift of your Word and Gospel in which you reveal all that it is necessary for us to know and believe for our faith and life as Christians. Bestow your Holy Spirit upon us in rich measure that we never become merely hearers of your Word, but actual doers of the same, for Christ our Saviour's sake. Amen.

THE WEEK OF TRINITY XV

MONDAY

LESSON: MATTHEW 15.1-9

No one can serve two masters; for either he will hate the one and love the other, or he will be devoted to the one and despise the other. You cannot serve God and mammon.

Matthew 6.24

The man who wants to serve two masters will always find himself in a relationship to one of them which is not service in any sense at all. Matters must always take a course like the one described by the Lord in this week's Gospel (Matthew 6.24-34). You can force a servant to do something to which he is opposed and which annoys him. But no one can compel him to do it gladly or from his heart. Perhaps he will do it as long as his master is present, but as soon as his master leaves, he also hurries away and does not really make a good job of things.

It is the Lord's will that our service should flow from love and be done willingly. If this is not the case, it is not real service. No one is pleased with what we do unwillingly. This is quite natural and we have experience of this daily. Now, if it commonly applies among all ranks and situations among men that no one can serve two masters, it will apply much more to our service of God.

Our service of God can never be a divided service. We must serve Him alone, and our service must come from the heart. That is why our Lord states quite categorically, "**You cannot serve God and mammon**". God cannot suffer us to have another master beside Him. He is a jealous God, as He Himself declares, and cannot tolerate us serving Him and His enemy. "You must be Mine alone", He says, "or not at all".

SL.XI.1614,3-4

PRAYER: O Lord, our God, you leave us in no doubt at all with your "either . . . or" instructions about the kind of service which alone can please you. Take our hearts into your keeping and purify them with your Holy Spirit, so that we always serve you with our whole hearts, for your name's sake. Amen.

TUESDAY

LESSON: PSALM 37.1-11

Either he will hate the one and love the other, or he will be devoted to the one and despise the other.   Matthew 6.24

You will find very few people who do not sin against this Gospel (Matthew 6.24-34). The Lord pronounces a very strict judgement here, and it is alarming to hear Him make this judgement which might very well apply to us. No one likes admitting it. No one is very pleased to hear someone telling us that we hate and despise God and are, in fact, His enemies. Almost all of us, on being asked if we loved God and were attached to Him would reply, "Yes, I love Him". But this Gospel seems to suggest that we all hate God and despise Him in our love of mammon and our attachment to it.

God certainly puts up with such a mixed state of affairs in regard to our service of Himself. He bides His time with much patience. But when He deems it fitting, He can also intervene in a very drastic manner sooner than we expect it. He who loves his money and property, and clings to it with strong attachment, must hate God; it cannot be otherwise. Jesus places two alternatives alongside of each other here which are mutually hostile and concludes: If you love one of these two and become attached to it, you must hate the other one and despise it.

Therefore, no matter how pleasantly one lives here on this earth, clinging to one's property, in such a case there must be hatred of God; it cannot possibly be otherwise. Contrariwise, he who is not attached to money and property in this way, loves God. This is certain.

SL.XI.1615,5

PRAYER: Lord, give us, in all the days of our earthly pilgrimage, a proper understanding and appreciation of the most important priorities in our life of service in your kingdom. Let us never become slaves of mammon, but ever remain your true servants, in and through Jesus Christ our Saviour. Amen.

WEDNESDAY

LESSON: COLOSSIANS 3.5-11

Be sure of this, that no immoral or impure man, or one who is covetous (that is, an idolater), has any inheritance in the kingdom of Christ and of God.   Ephesians 5.5

Where are these people who love God and have no hankering at all after money and property? Take a close look at the whole world, including the Christians, to see whether they despise money and property. To hear the Gospel, and to live according to it, requires some effort and serious attention. We have the Gospel, God be praised; no one can deny that. But what is our response to it? Our one concern is to hear it and learn it, and nothing more comes of it. We allow ourselves to be persuaded that it is enough for us to know it; we never bother ourselves with actually doing it. What does cause grave concern is if anyone leaves a florin or two, or it may be only a cent or two, on the windowsill or somewhere else in a room unguarded. This could cause concern and even fear that the money might be stolen. But it does not concern the same people very much to be without the Gospel for a whole year or so. And such fellows want to be classed as evangelicals!

Here we see what and who such people really are. If we were true Christians, we would despise earthly property and become really concerned about the Gospel. We would also live by it and prove this by our deeds. We see too little of such Christians. We must hear the judgement of the Gospel (Matthew 6.24-34) that we despise God and hate His Word for the sake of earthly riches and blessings. What a fine reputation that is! We should be ashamed in the very depths of our heart. We are really in a bad way.

SL.XI.1615,6-7

PRAYER: Heavenly Father, forgive us our many sins of omission when it comes to really putting your Word and Gospel into practice. Enlighten us by your Holy Spirit that the Gospel becomes our greatest treasure, bestowing upon us the power to live as your true children, through Christ our Lord. Amen.

THURSDAY

LESSON: PSALM 49.16-20

The kingdom of heaven is like a treasure hidden in a field, which a man found and covered up; then in his joy he goes and sells all that he has and buys that field.   Matthew 13.44

The world cannot hide its unbelief in its gross public sins. I can plainly see that it has more love for a florin than it has for Christ and all His apostles. Even if the latter were all present and preached in person, it would not change the world's attitude so much.

I, too, can hear the Gospel proclaimed daily, but it does not necessarily benefit me daily. But it can also happen, after I have heard the Gospel for a whole year, that the Holy Spirit visits me with a favourable hour. If I obtain such an hour, I do not merely obtain five hundred florins; the riches of the whole world is mine. What would I not have if I had the Gospel? I would receive God who is the maker of silver and gold and everything that is on this earth. For I have received a Spirit of such a kind that through Him I know that I will be preserved for ever. This is far more than having a church full of florins.

See whether our heart is not a rogue full of wickedness and unbelief! If I were a real Christian, I would say, "At the hour when the Gospel comes, a hundred thousand florins, to be sure infinitely more, come to me". When I have this treasure I have everything in heaven and on earth. But to this treasure one must devote one's whole service; one cannot serve God and mammon. Either you must love God and hate money, or you must hate God and love money. This is how matters stand and not otherwise.

SL.XI.1616,8

PRAYER: O God, guard and defend us especially against the idolatry of loving earthly things, wealth, happiness, success and honour, more than we love you and the blessings of your Gospel. Give us the Holy Spirit of truth and understanding that we may always treasure the blessings which you have conferred on us in your Gospel, in and through our Saviour Jesus Christ. Amen.

FRIDAY

LESSON: LUKE 12.13-21

A man's life does not consist in the abundance of his possessions.   Luke 12.15

How does it come about that the Gospel and St. Paul single out greed and call it idolatry? They do not do this in the case of other gross sins like impurity, harlotry, evil lusts and thoughts, unchastity, and many other vices opposed to God. It is a very great disgrace that gold should be our god whom we serve, in whom we trust and on whom we rely. This god of gold cannot preserve us or save us; he cannot stand or walk, hear or see; he has no power or might, neither consolation nor help.

What help to the emperor are his great treasures and riches when the hour comes that he must die? Money is a disgraceful, hateful and powerless god, who cannot help you even with one of your little sores and cannot even protect himself. There he lies in his box and must be waited on. Indeed, one must pay attention to him as something powerless, impotent and weak. The master who possesses him must take precautions day and night that a thief does not steal him. This powerless god cannot help himself or any-one else. What a god this is, a dead god who cannot give the slightest help, a god deserving of our loathing, and yet a costly god! He lets himself be waited on in the most magnificent manner, to be guarded with great chests and castles. His master must always be dancing attendance on him, taking care that he is not destroyed by fire or any other calamity. If this treasure or god consists of rich clothing or fabrics, he must also become an object of special care and guarded against the tiniest of worms and moths who might so easily spoil him and eat him up. What a shocking and accursed thing is unbelief!

SL.XI.1617,10-12

PRAYER: You have warned us against the sin of covetousness, heavenly Father, because it is a sin that can so easily take complete possession and control of our hearts and lives. Keep this idolatry out of our lives by instilling in us the ideals of true Christian service, in and through our Saviour Jesus Christ. Amen.

SATURDAY

LESSON: JAMES 5.1-6

**Do not lay up for yourselves treasures on earth, where
moth and rust consume and where thieves break in and steal,
but lay up for yourselves treasures in heaven, where neither
moth nor rust consumes and where thieves do not break in
and steal.   Matthew 6.19,20**

There are sins that bring at least some kind of joy; we get
something out of them, like gluttony and drunkenness, for
example. The same can also be said for fornication; it does at
times provide relaxation for the people who practise it. Even
anger provides a certain amount of satisfaction. The same
could be claimed for other vices as well.

But covetousness or greed always claims complete and full
service from its devotees. It plagues and torments its victims
ceaselessly and never provides anything in the shape of
pleasure or joy. There the money lies in a heap and claims
your full attention and service. It defies you to buy yourself
even a pint of wine out of it. Rust comes along and eats away
at it but it must not be touched; that would make this god
angry. And after protecting this god for so long, the servants
of this god have no more than any poor beggar.

Who brings this about? God, the Lord, arranged matters
in this way. They may well be plagued with a sickness which
prevents them from eating. They may have something wrong
with their digestive processes, so that they have no taste for
food. They have weak stomachs; their lungs and liver have
packed up. They suffer from this or that sickness. Here
something is lacking; something else there. They never have
a really pleasant hour in which to enjoy eating and drinking.

This is how those who serve mammon fare. The true God
puts Himself at the service of His own and serves men;
mammon never does this. He wants to enjoy perpetual quiet
and receive service from men.
SL.XI.1618,13-14

*PRAYER: Heavenly Father, in your grace and mercy you
supply us with all that we need for our bodies and lives. We
thank and praise you for the riches of all your goodness
towards us, above all for all the blessings bestowed upon us
in and through our Saviour Jesus Christ. Amen.*

SUNDAY

LESSON: LUKE 7.11-17

It depends not upon man's will or exertion, but upon God's mercy. Romans 9.16

In this Gospel the evangelist once again sets before us a divine miracle. In it he wants to encourage us to direct our hearts to God if we find ourselves in a situation like the one in which the widow found herself. This account was not written for the sake of this widow, but for the sake of those who would hear the Gospel until the end of the world. We must also be counted among the latter.

In the first place, it should be quite obvious to all of us, that the kindness and grace conferred on this woman by Christ was altogether gratuitous; she did not earn it or merit it. She goes through the city with her friends, where there is nothing but wailing and weeping. It never even entered the thought of this good woman that she would bring back her son into the city alive. This is not her desire and she does not ask for it. Even less did she merit it. Any idea of Christ's intervention had never occurred to her; she did not know Christ, nor did she know that He helped people. All preceding merit and preparation are ruled out here.

This has all been recorded so that we may draw a general conclusion from this which applies in the case of all benefits received from God. Just as this widow obtained a blessing freely and out of pure grace alone, solely and only because Christ was moved to pity, so we, too, receive such blessings without any merit on our part and even without seeking them. It is always God who takes the initiative. He always lays the first stone.

What is the reason for this? He takes pity on us, hence it remains God's grace. If our merits counted here, it would not be grace. Accordingly, as a result of this, we can say, "You are a gracious God; you do good to those who do not deserve it".

SL.XI.1646,1-3

PRAYER: Heavenly Father, your mercy and grace towards us are never-ending and always abounding. Continue to bestow your free mercy and grace upon us, in and through our Saviour. Amen.

MONDAY

LESSON: PSALM 100

Your Father who is in heaven ... makes his sun rise on the evil and on the good, and sends rain on the just and on the unjust.   Matthew 5.45

If I only duly considered what God has done for me in giving me my eyes, truly, a very great treasure, it would not be very surprising if I died of shame for my thanklessness in never having thanked God for this great blessing. We do not recognize the blessing and the noble treasure because it is common. But when a child has been born blind we realize what a painful affliction the absence of sight can be and what a precious thing even a single eye is.

A fresh, healthy countenance is certainly one of God's good gifts to us. It serves us throughout our whole life. Without it we would prefer to be dead. But how few there are who ever think of thanking God for something like this! Take a closer look at your body and you will find indications of God's grace and goodness everywhere. The psalmist does not overstate the case when he says, **"The earth is full of the steadfast love of the Lord". Psalm 33.5.** He had clear eyes and depth of vision so that he could see that the whole earth was full of God's goodness and blessings.

What moves God to bestow His goodness upon us? Have we deserved such treatment? Not at all! It is simply God's good pleasure to cast forth His gifts and blessings upon the world in this manner. They embrace the thankless and the thankful without distinction. It annoys us when we have to part with one or two florins, or perhaps even less, and even if it is given to the poor. But how many blessings does not God shed abroad on this world daily, even when no one ever thanks Him for one of them? For that matter, who still acknowledges God's goodness at all?

SL.XI.1648,5

PRAYER: Your bounteous goodness and mercy towards us, heavenly Father, is altogether wonderful. Grant us at all times the ability to evaluate your goodness correctly, in and through Christ our Saviour. Amen.

TUESDAY

LESSON: PSALM 86.8-15

**If many died through one man's trespass, much more have
the grace of God and the free gift in the grace of that one man
Jesus Christ abounded for many.   Romans 5.15**

At times God suffers a man to experience fear and
distress, pain and sorrow. He suddenly finds himself in a
world which seems to have no God. A man loses his sight; he
becomes lame; he develops dropsy. God even lets him die like
the widow's son in this Gospel. All men are God's creatures
and He can do with them as He pleases.

Why does God create or suffer such situations? He is
resorting here to extreme measures to keep us ever mindful
of His goodness. John reports that on one occasion Jesus and
His disciples came upon a man who was **"blind from his
birth. And his disciples asked him, 'Rabbi, who sinned, this
man or his parents, that he was born blind?' Jesus answered,
'It was not that this man sinned, or his parents, but that the
works of God might be made manifest in him'."** John 9.1-3.

He means to say, "God wants to be praised in this blind
man. God sees that the treasures of the whole world do not
move us. Hence He must take some drastic action. Out of
pure grace, He sets a blind man before our eyes so that we
come to realize what a precious gift we possess in the gift of
sight. And since we do not recognize His goodness and grace
in something advantageous, we are compelled to note it and
recognize it from something disadvantageous."

This man was born blind so that men might come to their
senses and declare, "Merciful God, what a precious gift and
what a blessing it is to have a healthy body and a fresh
countenance!" But no one takes it to heart in this way.

SL.XI.1649,7

*PRAYER: Grant us grace at all times, heavenly Father, to
interpret your blessings for what they are, acts of your grace
and mercy, so that we may both acknowledge your mercy
and grace and return you due thanks for it, in and through
Christ our Saviour. Amen.*

WEDNESDAY

LESSON: 2 CORINTHIANS 9.10-15

O how abundant is thy goodness, which thou hast laid up for those who fear thee, and wrought for those who take refuge in thee, in the sight of the sons of men! Psalm 31.19

In what happened to the widow at Nain, God lets us see what kind of God He is, how He regards us, and how we should regard Him.

This woman was the subject of two misfortunes. In the first place, she was a widow. This is misfortune enough for one woman. She is forlorn and alone, with no one to look to for any comfort. This is why God is often spoken of in Scripture as the God of widows and orphans.

Secondly, she has an only son who dies. This son should have been a consolation for her. But God intervenes and takes away her husband and her son. She would undoubtedly have preferred to lose her house and home, and even her own life, than this son and her husband.

God certainly makes some changes here. While her husband was alive, this woman failed to recognize what a gift a husband can be; when he died, she really recognized this for the first time. So also with her son. While he was hale and healthy, she did not recognize him as God's good gift to her; but after he died, she really recognized for the first time what a treasure she had lost.

This is how matters stand with us. There are many people who begrudge the investment of ten florins in their child's education. If the child dies, they suddenly change their mind and say, "Would to God that he was still alive! I would be prepared to spend hundreds of florins, anything, on him."

SL.XI.1649,8

PRAYER: Lord God, heavenly Father, provide us with open minds and hearts so that we always clearly and readily acknowledge the riches of your goodness toward us, and give you due thanks with grateful hearts, through Jesus Christ our Saviour. Amen.

THURSDAY

LESSON: PSALM 119.121-128

I will not leave you desolate; I will come to you.

John 14.18

The common lesson taught in all the Gospels is that we should learn from them what kind of God we have. In this week's Gospel (Luke 7.11-17), the point that is made quite clear is that God forsakes no one. And so He lets this widow see once again what kind of God she has. When she is forlorn and without a husband or son, Christ demonstrates to her that He is still at her side and says to her in effect, "Learn to believe and trust in God. Recognize Him to whom death and life are both alike. Be brave-hearted and courageous. Do not weep; there is no need for that."

Then Jesus steps up, awakens the dead man and gives him to his mother.

These and similar miracles are recorded in God's Word that we may learn in our hearts what attitude to adopt over against God, and what we should expect from Him. This woman had certainly made up her mind that she had lost her son, and that it was impossible for her to receive him back again. Even if someone had assured her that within an hour her son would be alive again, she would have regarded it as impossible and declared, "It is more likely that the heavens will collapse than that my son should live again". Before she has time to look about her, God intervenes and does what she had never even dared to regard as a possibility and restores her son to life.

Why does God follow such a course? He allows a person to fall into such danger and fear that there is no longer any hope at all of counsel or help. But it is not His intention to lead us to despair. He wants us to put our faith and trust in Him alone who can bring forth a possibility from an impossibility, something out of nothing.

SL.XI.1651,10-11

PRAYER: As far as we are concerned, O God, you are never far off but ever ready to help us, ever at our side and along all our paths and ways. Continue to support us with your boundless grace, in and through Christ our Saviour. Amen.

FRIDAY

LESSON: 2 TIMOTHY 1.8-10

When the perishable puts on the imperishable, and the mortal puts on immortality, then shall come to pass the saying that is written: "Death is swallowed up in victory. O death, where is thy victory? O death, where is thy sting?" The sting of death is sin, and the power of sin is the law. But thanks be to God, who gives us the victory through our Lord Jesus Christ.   1 Corinthians 15.54-57

In our eyes all miracles and works of God are impossible, and it is also impossible for nature to grasp them. The reason for this is that God wants us to recognize Him as an almighty Creator who brings forth a possibility from an impossibility and makes something out of nothing.

It is impossible for me to become alive again after I have died. Even if I prayed to all the angels and saints for help in this respect, nothing would come of it. What could I hope for from my own free will here? Yet even in death I am bound to say, "I will live". This does not take place because of anything in myself or due to myself. I know that I have a God who does not make something out of a piece of wood that might be lying before my eyes, but a God who can make a possibility out of an impossibility and something out of nothing. Otherwise He would not be in reality the true God.

Hence, if death came to me and I could live no longer, I would still be able to say, "I am still going to live and I want to live. The death which is hovering over me is like a tiny spark of fire and the life that I hope to live looms as large as the ocean."

Reason cannot grasp how this comes to pass. But he who has faith, knows this for certain. To the man with faith, death is as a tiny spark of fire in the middle of a great ocean of life, and the little spark is extinguished in a moment. God is almighty; and he who has faith, is in God.

SL.XI.1652,12-13

PRAYER: Dear Lord Jesus, you are the conqueror of sin and death. In your victory we are also conquerors of these bitter enemies. Be with us all the time of our earthly pilgrimage, especially in the hour of our death, for your truth and name's sake. Amen.

SATURDAY

LESSON: ROMANS 8.28-30

For a brief moment I forsook you, but with great compassion I will gather you. In overflowing wrath for a moment I hid my face from you, but with everlasting love I will have compassion on you, says the Lord, your Redeemer.
Isaiah 54.7,8

The poor widow in this week's Gospel (Luke 7.11-17) is so closely beset by very great sorrow and fear that she thinks that God, heaven, earth and everything is opposed to her. Because she looks at all this from the viewpoint of the flesh, and as it appears outwardly before her eyes, she must come to the conclusion that it is impossible for her to be released from such anxiety and fear.

But when her son was awakened from death, it seemed just as if heaven and earth, wood and stone were laughing with her and that everything was rejoicing with her. She forgot all her pain and sorrow. It disappeared just like a little spark of fire is extinguished when it falls into the middle of the sea.

Isaiah speaks of a **"brief moment"**. Sometimes I do not see it that way and the **"brief moment"** seems an eternity. But in reality it is only **"a brief moment"** and it is followed by much joy as the psalmist also reminds us, saying, **"Thou hast made him little less than God, and dost crown him with glory and honour". Psalm 8.5.** But that can still be hidden for us and, like the widow here in the Gospel, we do not see it. This deceased son is in the midst of life for God has him in His bosom and it was God's intention to awaken him from death. There is a little spark of death there which proved itself his undoing for **"a brief moment"**. Of course, none of the people present saw it that way. But when he was restored to life again, that which was previously hidden before all the world became manifest.

SL.XI.1653,14

PRAYER: Your ultimate purposes, O God, are sometimes hidden from us but we are assured that you are always concerned for our good. So direct and govern us by your Holy Spirit that whatever befalls us we are nevertheless convinced that all things must work for our good, in and through Jesus Christ our Saviour. Amen.

SUNDAY

LESSON: LUKE 14.1-11

I am the true vine, and my Father is the vinedresser. Every branch of mine that bears no fruit, he takes away, and every branch that does bear fruit he prunes that it may bear more fruit. You are already made clean by the word which I have spoken to you. Abide in me, and I in you. As the branch cannot bear fruit by itself, unless it abides in the vine, neither can you, unless you abide in me. I am the vine, you are the branches. He who abides in me, and I in him, he it is that bears much fruit, for apart from me you can do nothing. If a man does not abide in me, he is cast forth as a branch and withers; and the branches are gathered, thrown into the fire and burned. If you abide in me, and my words abide in you, ask whatever you will, and it shall be done for you.

John 15.1-7

Two main points must be considered in this Gospel. One is a point which all the Gospels have in common, and the second one is something special.

The first point, the point which all the Gospels have in common, is that they portray Christ for us, showing us who and what He is, and what we should expect from Him. In this respect the Gospels all teach us faith and love. They continually remind us of the importance of faith.

The man who had dropsy illustrates this point. He had heard something of the Gospel beforehand. Some report had probably reached him of how the Lord Jesus Christ was such a friendly, good and kind man, helping everyone and sending no one away without help and consolation. Had he not heard such a report about Christ he would hardly have followed Him right into the Pharisee's house. He must have received information on Christ and heard something very encouraging about Christ and believed it.

SL.XI.1674,1-2

PRAYER: Your promises and assurances, O Lord, are always most encouraging. Stir up within our hearts the faith and trust always to accept your promises and assurances in all confidence, for your mercy and truth's sake. Amen.

MONDAY

LESSON: PSALM 34.1-10

Offer to God a sacrifice of thanksgiving, and pay your vows to the Most High; and call upon me in the day of trouble; I will deliver you, and you shall glorify me.

Psalm 50.14,15

Before we can come to faith, the Gospel must be proclaimed to us. To come to faith, we must know that God is so friendly and merciful to us that He sent us His Son from heaven to help us. This our conscience must hear and believe. Even if all creatures were friendly to us it would not help us at all in the event of God being ungracious and unfriendly to us. On the other hand, if God is satisfied with us, no creature can harm us as Paul reminds us when he says in the Epistle to the Romans, **"If God is for us, who is against us?"** **Romans 8.31.** Therefore let death, the devil, hell and all creatures rave and rage; they can harm us none.

It is the function of the Gospel graciously to portray the man to us who is none other than God Himself. From this source, our heart draws faith and a friendly confidence towards God, namely, that He will help us through life and death. We also see this in the case of the man whom Jesus cured of dropsy. He had heard of the friendliness of Jesus, and he had come to believe that Jesus would also demonstrate His friendliness and goodness as far as he was concerned. The Pharisees had Jesus before them but they never really believed in Him; they rejected Him in unbelief. The Gospel goes out to all men in general, but not all accept it. It is often rejected.

SL.XI.1676,3-4

PRAYER: Remove from our hearts all distrust and unbelief, heavenly Father, and fill our hearts with firm confidence in your grace, mercy and love as promised to us and bestowed upon us in and through our Saviour. Amen.

TUESDAY

LESSON: MATTHEW 15.1-9

Jesus spoke to the lawyers and Pharisees, saying, "Is it lawful to heal on the sabbath, or not?" Luke 14.3

The lawyers and Pharisees, of course, did not believe that it was lawful to heal or to do anything else on the sabbath day. In this Gospel (Luke 14.1-11) Jesus shows them that all laws, divine or human, bind us only as far as love permits. For Christians, love must always make the final decision in the interpretation of all laws. Where there is no love, all is over. The Law can only be harmful, no matter what the situation may be.

It is even a principle of canon law that if any law runs counter to love, it should be set aside as soon as possible. This, in a word, is stated both of divine and human commandments. The reason for this is that all laws have been enacted for the sole purpose of setting up the principle of love, as Paul also reminds us in Romans when he says, **"Owe no one anything, except to love one another; for he who loves his neighbour has fulfilled the law".** Likewise: **"Love does no wrong to a neighbour; therefore love is the fulfilling of the law". Romans 13.8,10.**

We owe no one anything but to love one another. If I love my neighbour, I help him, protect him, accord him his due honours, and do to him what I would have others do to me.

Therefore, since all laws should help to establish the principle of love, they must cease immediately that they run counter to love. In this Gospel, Christ's deed of love to the man with the dropsy was far above any of the regulations pertaining to sabbath observance.

SL.XI.1677,8-9

PRAYER: O God, let us never become so immersed in useless quibbles about rules and regulations that we forget our real duties of love to our neighbour. Keep our vision pure and unblurred, in Jesus' name. Amen.

WEDNESDAY

LESSON: 1 CORINTHIANS 13.1-13

Love bears all things, believes all things, hopes all things, endures all things.   1 Corinthians 13.7

We should slant all our laws in such a way that they always bring out the necessity of love. When they are of service and useful to our neighbour, we must keep them; when they are harmful we are to let them go.

Take a rather crude example! Supposing a housefather had the rule that in his house fish, meat, wine and beer must be eaten and drunk as it is available and procurable. And supposing that one of his servants became sick and could no longer drink beer or wine, or eat meat or fish, but that the housefather was not prepared to allow him any change of diet, saying, "You know what the rule is! It's that or nothing else!" What would you think of such a housefather? He should be put on a permanent diet of hellebore to purge his brains!

If he had any sense at all he would simply say, "It is quite true that today, according to my rule or ordinance, we should be eating meat or fish. But because this food does not agree with you, eat what you like!"

David illustrates this point when he ate the bread of the Presence which it was not lawful for him to eat nor for those who were with him, but only for the priests (Matthew 12.3). Neither David nor his servants were consecrated. Did he and his servants sin, then, in eating the consecrated bread which only the priests were permitted to eat (1 Samuel 21.1-6)? God's command was quite clear. David did not sin here. Why? Because the higher law, the law of love, compelled him to act in this way.

In a Christian context, all laws must be slanted or bent according to the love of one's neighbour. Where necessity demands it, love knows no laws.

SL.XI.1678,10,13

PRAYER: O God, our heavenly Father, pour out your love into our hearts in such a manner that it always flows over into our lives in fervent love for one another, in and through your beloved Son, Jesus Christ. Amen.

THURSDAY

LESSON: 1 PETER 4.7-10

Which of you, having an ass or an ox that has fallen into a well, will not immediately pull him out on a sabbath day?
Luke 14.5

He means to say here, "You fools! Are you not quite mad and foolish? You do this for an ox or an ass worth, perhaps, a few florins; much more should you be prepared to do it for your neighbour when he has need of your help, regardless of whether it happens to be a sabbath day." For the sabbath as He points out elsewhere was made for man and not man for the sabbath. Hence, the Son of Man is lord also of the sabbath (Mark 2.27,28).

Laws like the sabbath laws received great emphasis among the Jews; their kings also laid great stress on them. They had to be strictly kept. When the prophets appeared and tried to interpret the Law in accordance with love, insisting that this is also how Moses meant the Law to be understood, there were false prophets at the royal courts who stuck fast to the text, claiming, "There it stands written; it is God's Word and it dare not be interpreted otherwise". No matter how loudly the prophets insisted on the correct understanding, they encountered nothing but deafened ears. Not only this, but the kings, poor blind men that they were, started up and killed one prophet after the other.

Ecclesiastical authorities follow much the same procedure even today. If one tells such people that we are not obliged to obey all their laws but only those slanted towards love, they immediately cry out, "Heretic, heretic!" And if they can do so, they put such a heretic to death, as they have already done quite extensively.

SL.XI.1680,15-16

PRAYER: Lord God, heavenly Father, you have shown us extensively in your Word, but more especially in your Gospel of salvation, that with you love is always everything. Implant your love in our hearts that we may live by it in our lives, through Jesus Christ our Lord. Amen.

FRIDAY

LESSON: PSALM 138.1-6

When you are invited by any one to a marriage feast, do not sit down in a place of honour, lest a more eminent man than you be invited by him; and he who invited you both will come, and say to you, "Give place to this man", and then you will begin with shame to take the lowest place. But when you are invited, go and sit in the lowest place, so that when your host comes he may say to you, "Friend, go up higher"; then you will be honoured in the presence of all who sit at table with you.   Luke 14.8-10

This is an illustration for all of us; we must all heed the instruction given here whether we are high or lowly. Jesus reproaches the Pharisees and the bigwigs who want to sit at the top and are prepared to trample over others to get there. Such people are always looking for places of honour. When such a place is offered us by someone with authority to offer it to us, we can accept it. Even so, there is never any excuse for trampling over others to get there.

There are those, however, who think it possible to combine the spiritual and earthly realms and that therefore it is enough to be humble in heart and still make for the place of honour. True humility of heart must express itself in outward works, otherwise it is a feigned humility. Each of us should always go and sit in the lowest place. We should throw ourselves at the feet of others rather than try to force our way to the top, unless we are forced by circumstances beyond our control to accept such a seat of honour. If we follow this course, all will be well with us. If we do not learn this lesson, we shall ultimately be put to shame.

SL. XI.1684,25-26

PRAYER: Lord Jesus Christ, by precept and example you have taught us that in your kingdom the greatest of all is always the servant of all, and that the humble shall be exalted. Make us content to take with gladness the lowest place and, if it pleases you to call us higher, preserve within us a simple and humble heart, to your glory and honour. Amen.

SATURDAY

LESSON: MATTHEW 20.20-28

The tax collector, standing far off, would not even lift up his eyes to heaven, but beat his breast, saying, "God, be merciful to me a sinner!" I tell you, this man went down to his house justified rather than the other; for every one who exalts himself will be humbled, but he who humbles himself will be exalted. **Luke 18.13, 14**

St. Augustine adds a gloss at this point. I wish he had left it somewhere on the way because it smells of Adam's cask. He says, "A ruler should not push the matter of humility too far lest the prestige of his government may be weakened thereby". That is speaking like a heathen and worldling and not as a Christian. But we can forgive him this mistake; not even in the saints is everything perfect.

The sum and substance of this Gospel, then, is: Love and necessity are above all laws, and there is no law which should not be slanted and bent according to love. If this cannot be done with any particular law it should be abolished, even if it has been set up by an angel from heaven. All this should be of great service in strengthening our hearts and conscience. On this basis the Lord teaches us here how to humble ourselves and subject ourselves to others.

SL.XI.1685,27-28

PRAYER: Lord God, always look upon us in your mercy and grace and empty us of the false pride that so easily clings to us as children of Adam. Grant that we may walk in the paths of true humility, in and through our Saviour Jesus Christ. Amen.

SUNDAY

LESSON: MATTHEW 22.34-46

Open my eyes, that I may behold wondrous things out of thy law.   Psalm 119.18

Today's Gospel supplies answers to two questions. The first is the one which the lawyer puts to Jesus on behalf of the Pharisees, **"Teacher, which is the great commandment in the law?"** The second is the question which the Lord Himself puts to the Pharisees and scribes, **"What do you think of the Christ? Whose son is he?"**

These two questions also concern us Christians. For anyone who wants to be a Christian must be well-informed in these two respects: first, what the Law is and what is its function; secondly, who Christ is and what he should expect from Him.

Christ here interprets the Law for the Pharisees and points out to them what is its sum. He answers in such a way that they are effectively silenced by His replies, and finish up knowing quite precisely what the Law is and what Christ is.

From this it follows that where unbelief is, although it has the appearance of wisdom and holiness before the world, it nevertheless remains folly and unrighteousness before God, especially where there is no knowledge of the two questions being discussed here. For he who does not know what the function of the Law really is, and what he should expect from Christ, certainly knows nothing of the true wisdom of God, no matter how wise or clever he may be.

SL.XI.1686,1-2

PRAYER: O God, our heavenly Father, make your holy will known to us with such clarity on the basis of your holy Law that we may cling ever more firmly to our Saviour, who has fulfilled this law for us. We ask this in the name and for the sake of Jesus our Saviour. Amen.

MONDAY

LESSON: 1 SAMUEL 16.1-7

You shall love the Lord your God with all your heart, and with all your soul, and with all your mind. This is the great and first commandment. And a second is like it, You shall love your neighbour as yourself. On these two commandments depend all the law and the prophets.

Matthew 22.37-40

Jesus means to say here: He who has kept these two commandments dealing with the love of God and the love of one's neighbour, has everthing, and he has also fulfilled the Law. For the whole Law and the prophets concentrate on these two issues, namely, how one should love God and how one should love one's neighbour.

There may be those who feel inclined to wonder how everything depends on these two commandments when people like the Jews were given circumcision and many other laws which cannot so easily be related to these two chief commandments. In replying, we should note first of all how Christ explains obedience to the Law. He says that we must obey it from the heart.

For Christ, obedience to the Law is something spiritual. He who does not obey the Law from his heart and tackle it with his spirit, will never fulfil it. Hence the Lord here sets before the lawyers the basis and kernel of the Law, saying that the chief commandment of the Law is to love God from the heart and one's neighbour as oneself.

It follows from this that anyone who does not keep the Law from the heart is not really circumcized, does not fast and does not pray, even if he does perform such acts externally. External performances without obedience of the heart are nothing before God. God looks at the heart and not merely at the external work or appearance. It does not help a man to perform any number of works if his heart is not engaged thereby.

SL.XI.1687,4-5

PRAYER: Lord God, heavenly Father, grant your people grace to serve you with pure hearts and minds in obedience to your holy Law, and with firm confidence in your Gospel, through Jesus Christ our Lord. Amen.

344

TUESDAY

LESSON: PSALM 40.1-8

Blessed are those who keep his [the Lord's] testimonies, who seek him with their whole heart.   Psalm 119.2

Man's unbelief has invented and set up countless substitutes for the two main commandments of the Law, resulting in forms of ungodliness which Scripture describes as **"grieving"** God and the Holy Spirit (Ephesians 4.30; Isaiah 63.10). Should not God be angry with me when He commands me to show love to my neighbour and I proceed to follow my own dreams and those of other men? It is just as if a housefather orders his servant to do some ploughing and the servant goes off and washes dishes. Would not a housefather be justified in becoming angry with such a servant?

This is also the case with God. He wants us to obey His commandments. We should regard them more highly than the commandments of men. He wants all commandments to relate to love so that they may all be comprised in the two commandments of which Jesus speaks in the Gospel, **"You shall love the Lord your God with all your heart, and with all your soul, and with all your mind . . . and your neighbour as yourself"**. If you want to do something that pleases God, do it in such a way that it flows from a heart of love.

On the other hand, it is easy to conclude that all works are nothing which do not flow from love, or which are against love. No commandments or laws should ever be given any validity excepting such as put the law of love into practice.

SL.XI.1692,16-17

PRAYER: Give us grace, heavenly Father, to keep the greatest of all the commandments by loving you with our whole heart, and soul, and mind, and the second commandment which is like it, by loving one another for your sake, in the name of Jesus our Lord. Amen.

WEDNESDAY

LESSON: GALATIANS 2.15-16

It is not the hearers of the law who are righteous before God, but the doers of the law who will be justified.

Romans 2.13

How many are there who really understand the commandment, "**You shall love the Lord your God with all your heart, and with all your soul, and with all your mind**"? Few, indeed; and there are fewer still who actually keep and observe this commandment. How are they to keep what they do not know? We are blind and our nature is also completely blinded. Human reason hardly knows less about anything than it knows about what God wants in His Law.

Christ confers a benefit upon the Pharisees and lawyers in two respects. First, He removes their blindness and teaches them what the Law is. Secondly, He teaches them how impossible it is for them to fulfil the commandments. He removes their blindness and teaches them what the Law is by showing them that the Law is basically love.

Reason cannot understand this today, even as the Jews also failed in this respect. For if reason had been able to grasp this, then, to be sure, the Pharisees and the lawyers would have grasped it, for they were the best and cleverest men among the Jews of that time. They thought that the fulfilment of the Law depended solely upon the performance of the external works of the Law, whether they were performed willingly or unwillingly. They never really faced up to their inner blindness, greed and wicked hardness of heart. They imagined themselves to be fully conversant with all the reqirements of the Law and regarded themselves as very fine fellows, holy and godly. As Jesus says, "**If then the light in you is darkness, how great is the darkness!**" **Matthew 6.23.** No one can fulfil the Law unless he has been completely renewed.

SL.XI.1693,19-20

PRAYER: O God, our transgressions of your holy Law are many and grievous. Eternal praise and thanks be to you for the obedience our Saviour rendered to your Law on our behalf and in our stead, an obedience now reckoned to us for His sake and in His name. Amen.

THURSDAY

LESSON: ROMANS 7.7-17

I delight in the law of God, in my inmost self, but I see in my members another law at war with the law of my mind and making me captive to the law of sin which dwells in my members.   Romans 7.22,23

Be quite sure of this, that reason can never understand the Law or fulfil it, even though it may actually know what the Law requires of man. When do you do to someone else what you would like him to do to you? Who really loves his enemy in his heart? Who is glad to die? Who suffers disgrace and shame gladly? Show me a man who would prefer to hear an evil report about himself or to live in poverty?

Nature and human reason avoid such misfortunes as much as possible. They shun them and are alarmed and dismayed by them. Human nature, moreover, will never be able to accomplish what God requires of us in this Law, namely, that we resign our will to God's will, that we renounce our own understanding of matters, our own will, might and powers, and say with all our heart, "Your will be done!"

You will certainly never find a single individual who loves God with his whole heart and his neighbour as himself. It may well happen that two people who are bosom friends manage to get along in a friendly manner. But there can also be hypocrisy in such relationships. They often last only as long as no injury intervenes to break up the relationship. Then you will see soon enough how much you love that special friend and whether you are flesh or spirit. The Law requires of us that we should always be really friendly towards someone who has injured us — but who keeps the Law to this extent?

SL.XI.1694,21

PRAYER: Lord God, heavenly Father, forgive us our many sins against your holy Law, in Christ's name and for His sake. Amen.

347

FRIDAY

LESSON: ROMANS 8.1-11

There is therefore now no condemnation for those who are in Christ Jesus. For the law of the Spirit of life in Christ Jesus has set me free from the law of sin and death.
Romans 8.1-2

Christ wants to show us in this week's Gospel (Matthew 22.34-36) that the Law is preached correctly only when we learn from it that we cannot fulfil it, and that on the basis of the Law we are really the devil's own children. Experience teaches us this and it is also indicated in various parts of Holy Scripture, especially in the epistles of Paul. Paul says in Romans, **"The mind that is set on the flesh is hostile to God; it does not submit to God's law, indeed it cannot; and those who are in the flesh cannot please God". Romans 8.7,8.**

So consider this commandment in the Gospel very carefully, **"You shall love the Lord your God with all your heart"**. Concentrate on this commandment and really make a serious effort to keep it. Do some searching here! Study the nature of the commandment! You will find, of course, that you are far from fulfilling it, that is, from accepting with your whole heart what God wants from you on the basis of this commandment.

It is sheer hypocrisy for anyone to crawl away into some corner and think, "I will love God", or "O how I love God, my Father! How well disposed I am to Him!" and similar self-congratulations. It is not difficult for us to fulfil the law on our own terms, especially if we can persuade ourselves that we enjoy His favour. But when misfortune intervenes and opposition is encountered, it can be a very different story. Then we soon lose sight of God as our loving Father.

SL.XI.1694,22

PRAYER: We thank and praise you, heavenly Father, for the victory over all sin, including all our sins against your holy Law, which you have provided for us in and through our Saviour Jesus Christ, in whose name we pray. Amen.

SATURDAY

LESSON: ROMANS 5.18-21

Now we are discharged from the law, dead to that which held us captive, so that we serve not under the old written code but in the new life of the Spirit.   Romans 7.6

Where true, genuine love of God flows from a man's heart, there is also true resignation to God's holy will. Such a heart should readily declare, "Lord God, I am your creature; do with me as you will. I know that all is for the best, because I am yours. This much I know. And if it is your will that I should die forthwith, or suffer some great misfortune, I will accept whatever is your will with my whole heart. I will never regard my life, honour, welfare or whatever I own, as higher and greater than your will. For my whole life I shall be pleased to do your will."

You will never find anyone who can make such a declaration, one who has given full obedience to God's commandment, in this Gospel (Matthew 22.34-46). For, in accordance with the requirements of this commandment, the whole of the life which you live in this body in your five senses, and whatever you do in this body, must all be done to the greater honour and praise of God who says, "**You shall love the Lord your God with all your heart, and with all your soul, and with all your mind**". Where is there a single man who can make such a claim?

But thanks be to God! Christ is set before us and given to us by His Father to free us from our sins, death, an evil conscience, and especially also from all the accusations of the Law. If we cling to Christ we are acquitted and free from the Law and all its demands.

SL.XI.1695,24,28,30

PRAYER: Thanks and praise, heavenly Father, for your mercy and grace in the gift of your Son, who by His suffering and death has freed us from sin, death, and the condemnation of your holy Law, for the glory of your mercy and grace, in and through Jesus Christ. Amen.

SUNDAY

LESSON: MATTHEW 9.1-8

When Jesus saw their faith he said to the paralytic, "Take heart, my son; your sins are forgiven".   Matthew 9.2

These words in a brief summary tell us what the kingdom of Christ really is. It is the kingdom in which our hearts are touched by a sweet voice bringing us maternal and paternal words, **"Your sins are forgiven"**. For a correct understanding we must not regard the kingdom of Christ otherwise than the way in which we should live in relation to God. In this connection, you in your love will know that the most important thing is to be able to quieten the troubled conscience so that we know how we stand with God and our neighbour.

The kingdom of Christ, then, is a kingdom in which there is consolation pure and simple, and the forgiveness of sins. It is not just a matter of words proclaimed to us setting forth future blessings, but of realized facts, as we see from the example set before us in this Gospel. Jesus did not merely speak these words into the paralytic's ears. He actually forgave this man his sins and conferred real consolation upon him.

I have often stated, and I say it here again, that you should make a serious effort to understand the nature and the peculiar character of Christ's kingdom correctly. We know only too well how reason in all respects is inclined to fall away from faith and the correct knowledge of Christ's kingdom to reliance on works. But in this Gospel you see no works at all, no merit. There is no question here of any commandment or law. There is nothing else here than the offer of Christ's help, His consolation and grace. The paralytic experiences nothing but Christ's sheer friendship.

SL.XI.1712,2-3

PRAYER: Gracious and merciful Father, you have given us many comforting and assuring consolations in your Gospel, and none more comforting than the assurance of the forgiveness of our sins. May we never reject these assurances or belittle them in any way, but ever cling to them, in and through our Saviour Jesus Christ. Amen.

MONDAY

LESSON: COLOSSIANS 2.13-19

It is the God who said, "Let light shine out of darkness", who has shone in our hearts to give the light of the knowledge of the glory of God in the face of Christ.

2 Corinthians 4.6

If the kingdom of Christ is to be extended, you must not bring the Law into your calculations or have any truck with works. It is quite out of character to say to men, "Go out and run here and there to atone for your sins; you must hold this and do that if you want to get rid of your sins". In diametrical opposition to anything in the shape of law and all works, we must assure men that their sins are forgiven by pure grace alone. To try to force them into the kingdom of Christ by the Law is putting yourself outside of this kingdom.

It is true that this truth may reach our ears and even roll off our tongues, but only too often it has not really penetrated our hearts. Sin always clings to us very closely (Hebrews 12.1) so that we are compelled to confess with Paul, **"I know that nothing good dwells within me, that is, in my flesh. I can will what is right, but I cannot do it. For I do not do the good I want, but the evil I do not want is what I do." Romans 7.18,19.** This is how it will be until at death we pass into life eternal.

Because there is always so much weakness, failure and sin among Christians, it is often claimed by radicals and enthusiasts that faith and love are not enough. They insist on more radical procedures and decisions, and often claim the special patronage of the Holy Spirit in this connection. The devil's weeds always accompany any planting of the Gospel. See to it that you always retain and maintain a healthy understanding of Christ's kingdom and its teachings.

SL.XI.1712,4-5

PRAYER: We are deeply conscious, heavenly Father, of our sinfulness and unworthiness, and in this respect must ever stand as beggars before you. But we have been emboldened by the assurances of your Gospel of salvation to approach your throne of grace in all confidence and assurance. This we do in the name and for the sake of Jesus our Saviour. Amen.

TUESDAY

LESSON: LUKE 12.32-34

To them /his saints/ God chose to make known how great among the Gentiles are the riches of the glory of this mystery, which is Christ in you, the hope of glory.
Colossians 1.27

The kingdom of Christ is of such a kind that we waive all our glorying and boldness in our dependence on God's grace. All other works are free. We must never make them matters of any compulsion. Nor must we imagine that we can become Christians from our works, but with our works we reach down and serve the interests of our neighbour. Hence we should listen carefully to what this week's Gospel (Matthew 9.1-8) has to tell us, and take a firm grasp of its statements and impress them on our hearts so that this light, these words and this lamp, may shine forth brightly in us that thereby we may instruct others.

Jesus says to the paralytic, "**Your sins are forgiven**". We should take hold of these and similar words and grasp them with our hearts, because they are words of pure grace alone. There is nothing of any work here, suggesting that a conscience should be forced to attempt to do something meritorious. And so you must fortify yourself with these words against false prophets.

We have planted the Word to a certain extent. This the devil cannot abide. He never sleeps. The caterpillars and the beetles will come to defile what we have planted. And so it must be. For Christ wants to prove His Word, to carry out a test to see who has grasped it or not. Let us, then, remain on the correct path which leads to the kingdom of Christ, not operating with works and legal pressures and compulsion, but with the words of the Gospel alone, "Be joyful, take heart, your sins are forgiven".

SL.XI.1714,9-10

PRAYER: Heavenly Father, we poor sinners are blessed, indeed, in the assurance of the forgiveness of sins which you have emphasized so much for us in your Gospel of salvation. Give us a faith which always clings wholly and solely to the forgiveness of sins where you have provided it for us, in and through Jesus Christ. Amen.

WEDNESDAY

LESSON: PSALM 103.1-13

I, I am he who blots out your transgressions for my own sake, and I will not remember your sins.   Isaiah 43.25

The forgiveness of sins is a very short phrase but it comprises the whole kingdom of Christ. Men always have sins, but they must be recognized and acknowledged. When I have recognized them, forgiveness and grace are readily available. Before forgiveness enters the picture, there is absolutely nothing but sin. I am compelled to acknowledge this. I feel and know that all that is in me is blindness. Without this acknowledgement, the forgiveness of sins will not hold its ground. We never fall short in the matter of sins, but we do fall short in our acknowledgement of sins. The forgiveness of sins follows the acknowledgement of sins.

There is, however, quite a difference between God's forgiveness of our sins and our forgiveness of our neighbour's sins. When we forgive our neighbour, we may recall that sin again subsequently and throw it in our neighbour's face. When God forgives us our sin it is something much higher. God no longer condemns us; He abandons all His wrath. Indeed, He never thinks of our sins again as He reminds us in the texts from Isaiah.

And having abandoned His wrath, He also removes hell, the devil, death and every misfortune which the devil may bring along. Instead of wrath He gives us grace, consolation, salvation and every good thing that He Himself is.

SL.XI.1715,12

PRAYER: There is always forgiveness with you, O God, as you assure us times without number in your holy Word. Implant this wonderful truth in our hearts in such a manner that we trust in it and believe in it implicitly, in and through our Saviour Jesus Christ. Amen.

THURSDAY

LESSON: MARK 9.38-41

Whoever gives to one of these little ones even a cup of cold water because he is a disciple, truly, I say to you, he shall not lose his reward.   Matthew 10.42

We must spread the Word very diligently and energetically among our fellowmen. I must eat and drink, adorn and clothe myself, not merely to preserve my life but to spread the Word. Wherever the best interests of God's Word are not the determining factor in a Christian's life, that life is not as it should be. I must help men in regard to their conscience according to the Word. I must provide my neighbour with food and drink and do all I can for him to assist him in the most important matter of all, the settlement of his conscience.

This is the service that his friends render to the paralytic in this week's Gospel. They certainly render him a bodily service or work, but they are also at the same time instrumental in the settlement of his soul. Hence, if I feed a hungry man, give a thirsty man a drink, clothe a naked man and so forth, I do it not only to give him this bodily help, but in the hope that by these works I may also influence him to turn to Christ and to win him for Christ.

These works are performed outside of the kingdom, for those not in the kingdom, in the hope of bringing them into the kingdom. Whether you are man, woman or child, you should know that Christ gives you His Gospel and brings you into His kingdom so that you should make it the one aim of your whole life to help others, the sick and the needy, in the hope of bringing them also into Christ's kingdom or confirming them in their Christian faith.

SL.XI.1719,22-23

PRAYER: Lord God, heavenly Father, it is your will that we should readily help our fellowmen in every need and wherever possible make your wonderful goodness known to them through us. Enable us at all times to let our light shine so that men may glorify you, through Jesus Christ our Lord. Amen.

FRIDAY

LESSON: PSALM 130

And when he had said this, he breathed on them, and said to them, "Receive the Holy Spirit. If you forgive the sins of any, they are forgiven; if you retain the sins of any, they are retained."   John 20.22,23

The Pharisees knew quite well that it was God's work alone to forgive sins. They regarded Christ as a blasphemer because He whom they regarded as nothing more than a man presumed to forgive sins.

Sin is forgiven in two ways. First, sin is driven out of the heart and grace is poured in. This God alone can do. Secondly, the forgiveness of sins is proclaimed; this one man can do for another man.

Christ here does both. He gives the paralytic the forgiveness of sins inwardly in his heart, and He proclaims the forgiveness of his sins outwardly to him by means of His Word. This is the forgiveness of sins by means of the Word and the proclamation and public preaching of this internal forgiveness.

This power belongs to all who are baptized Christians. Hereby they praise Christ and carry the Word of the forgiveness of sins in their mouth so that they can and may say whenever they so desire and as often as it is necessary, "Take heart; your sins are forgiven! Believe it; be quite sure of it!" and whatever other words they choose to use.

This proclamation will not cease among Christians until the last day: "Your sins are forgiven you; take heart and be assured!" These words a Christian always has in his mouth and he openly proclaims the Word in which sins are forgiven. In this way, every Christian has power and authority to forgive sins.

SL.XI.1722,28-29

PRAYER: We bless and praise you, O Lord, for the wonderful privilege you have conferred on us as your children, to announce the full and free forgiveness of sins to sinners. May we ever remain conscious of this privilege and practise it in love towards our neighbour, in and through Christ our Saviour. Amen.

SATURDAY

LESSON: PSALM 32.1-5

"Why do you think evil in your hearts? For which is easier, to say, 'Your sins are forgiven', or to say, 'Rise and walk'? But that you may know that the Son of man has authority on earth to forgive sins" — he then said to the paralytic — "Rise, take up your bed and go home". And he rose and went home. When the crowds saw it, they were afraid, and they glorified God, who had given such authority to men.

Matthew 9.4-8

If there were no human being on earth who could forgive us our sins, and there were only laws and works, what a feeble, wretched thing our poor, afflicted conscience would be! But now that God has filled every mouth so that it can say to its neighbour, "Your sins are forgiven you, no matter where you may be", a real jubilee year has dawned for all men.

As a result of this we should adopt a bold stance over against sin. When we encounter a brother who is in fear and trembling because of his sins, we should tell the poor man quite confidently: "Be joyful and assured, my brother, your sins are forgiven you! Although I cannot give you the Holy Spirit and faith, I can nevertheless proclaim them to you. If you believe you will receive." And those to whom Christ gives the Holy Spirit and faith, thank and praise God as the people did in the Gospel (Matthew 9.1-8).

This also means that God has given man the power and authority to forgive sins. This is extending the kingdom of Christ, healing and establishing a troubled conscience. We do this through the Word. God grant that we may grasp it in this way.

SL.XI.1723,31

PRAYER: Blessed indeed are we, heavenly Father, in the knowledge and assurance of the forgiveness of sins. Let us never underrate this glorious message, even when it is proclaimed to us by one of our brethren, in and through Christ our Saviour. Amen.

SUNDAY

LESSON: MATTHEW 22.1-14

The kingdom of God does not mean food and drink but righteousness and peace and joy in the Holy Spirit.
Romans 14.17

Christ forms the Christianity which He has brought into being in such a way that He calls it, and all that has reference to its sway here on earth, the kingdom of heaven. He does this to indicate that through the Gospel He has called a people for Himself on earth and separated them from the rest of the world. He does not call it a kingdom because He wants it to be fashioned and ordered just like any other external, secular regime, with wordly dominion, authority, goods and the maintenance of external, secular righteousness, discipline, defence and peace. There has been plenty of this set up from time immemorial and this secular rule has been entrusted to man and left to the best of his abilities. Through sin, however, secular authority has been weakened and corrupted so that conditions are never quite as they should be, and a poor, wretched and weak earthly regime is as weak and transient as this body of ours, this maggot-sack, and never continues any longer, even under the best of conditions, than bodily needs and conditions allow.

Over and above all this, God has ordered and set up His own heavenly regime for Himself, after making Himself known in His unfathomable grace and giving us His Word in addition. In this way He has prepared and gathered together a people for Himself and saved them from His wrath, eternal death and sin. They had fallen into this wretched condition through sin and were altogether unable to help themselves out of their troubles by any human wisdom, counsel or might. In His grace, however, God leads them to a true knowledge of Himself, whereby they praise and glorify Him for ever.

This is what Christ calls the kingdom of heaven.

SL.XI.1747,2-3

PRAYER: Give us at all times a true and correct understanding of the nature and purpose of your Church, heavenly Father, in which you bestow heavenly blessings upon us through your Holy Spirit, given us in and through our Saviour Jesus Christ. Amen.

357

MONDAY

The kingdom of heaven may be compared to a king who gave a marriage feast for his son, and sent his servants to call those who were invited to the marriage feast.

Matthew 22.2,3

The Lord Jesus Christ portrays the kingdom of heaven for us in this parable in a most loving and comforting manner. He tells us that in some respects there is a resemblance between what happens in the kingdom of heaven and at a royal marriage feast. At such a marriage feast, the king's son is given a bride and it is a scene of the highest joy and splendour with many being invited to share in the joy.

Among all the parables by which God illustrates Christ's kingdom for us, this is a choice and lovely picture. Christianity or the Christian estate is called a marriage, or a marriage union, in which God Himself chooses a Church here on earth for His Son which He, on His part, receives to Himself as His own bride.

Here, by means of our own life and experience, God wants to explain and indicate, as in a mirror, what we Christians have in Christ. Through the most common estate on this earth, that estate in which we were begotten, brought up and have lived ourselves, he preaches a daily sermon and exhorts us to remember and to think of this great mystery, as St. Paul calls it in Ephesians 5.32.

St. Paul tells us that the union of a man and his wife in marriage, as ordained by God, should be for us an important, beautiful and wonderful sign and a comprehensible, though spiritual, picture which demonstrates and indicates something special, outstanding and important, something hidden and incomprehensible to human reason, namely, Christ and His Church.

SL.XI.1748,5

PRAYER: Lord Jesus, our beloved Saviour, you have assured us in so many ways of your unceasing love for us, and have proved it in your suffering and death on the cross. Abide with us with all your love, now and for evermore. Amen.

TUESDAY

LESSON: 1 TIMOTHY 4.1-5

He who finds a wife finds a good thing, and obtains favour from the Lord.   Proverbs 18.22

Wherever the estate of marriage lives up to its name and you have what may be called a proper marriage with man and wife getting on well with each other, there is, first of all, true mutual trust and confidence on both sides.

Among other praise which Solomon bestows on a pious wife, he notes it as something especially praiseworthy that **"the heart of her husband trusts in her". Proverbs 31.11.** He can rely on her, entrust his body and life, property and honour to her.

On the other hand, the wife's heart is also attached to her husband; he is her greatest and most precious treasure on this earth. She knows that she can rely on him for honour, protection and help in all her needs.

Such a united, perfectly mutual and constant trust of the heart is not to be found among other persons and estates as between a master and servant, a woman and her maid, not even between parents and children. For in all these cases love is not equal in strength, not as completely mutual, and does not remain such a constant bond as it does in the estate of marriage ordained by God.

This has been God's intention from the beginning, for He said after the creation of Eve, **"Therefore a man leaves his father and his mother and cleaves to his wife, and they become one flesh". Genesis 2.24.**

SL.XI.1749,6

PRAYER: Heavenly Father, already at the creation of the world you ordained the estate of marriage for man as one of his choicest and richest blessings. May all who are your children and members of your kingdom always regard this estate as something very precious and experience in it the true joy that you intended men to find in it, for Christ's sake. Amen.

WEDNESDAY

LESSON: MATTHEW 19.1-6

Husbands should love their wives as their own bodies. He who loves his wife loves himself. For no man ever hates his own flesh, but nourishes and cherishes it, as Christ does the church, because we are members of his body.

Ephesians 5.28-30

The love of a man and woman in marriage is a parable or a picture of the great, hidden, but wonderful union of Christ with His Church. All believers are members of that Church, and, as St. Paul says, they are members of Christ's body (Ephesians 5.30), of His flesh and bones, as in the beginning, at the creation, the woman was taken from the man.

What a great, unfathomable and unspeakable love God must have for us for the divine nature thus to become united with us and merged with our flesh and blood, for God's Son truly to become one flesh and one body with us and to receive us into such a lofty status! He is not merely content to become our brother, He also becomes our bridegroom, turns to us and gives us as our very own possession all His divine blessings, wisdom, righteousness, life, strength and power. Yes, we are even destined to become "**partakers of the divine nature**", as St. Peter declares, **2 Peter 1.4.** All this He wants us to believe.

We have had this great honour and many blessings conferred upon us so that we should joyfully and in all confidence take comfort in this Lord like a bride in her bridegroom's property and honour. Christ's Christendom is, therefore, wife and queen in heaven and on earth; for she is called the bride of God who is Lord of all the creatures. In the highest manner possible, He gives authority and power over sin, death, the devil and hell.

SL.XI.1750,8

PRAYER: Thanks and praise be yours, O Lord, for the wonderful love you have shown to us and bestowed upon us in the gift of your Son. May we ever maintain the tie of love which unites us with Him, and experience all the joys of full and free salvation in His name. Amen.

THURSDAY

LESSON: PHILIPPIANS 4.4-7

Your hearts will rejoice, and no one will take your joy from you.   John 16.22

We must learn to accept and to believe the Word. Christ Himself proclaims this Word to us and God has commanded us to believe it as the truth. To reject this Word is tantamount to calling Christ a liar. We must learn to believe and trust the Word despite what our feelings may be inclined to suggest to us.

If you are to believe the Word, you cannot cling to what your own thoughts or feelings may suggest. You must cling to God's Word, no matter how little you actually feel or experience it. If you are a person who realizes his need and wretchedness, and have a hearty desire to participate in the consolation and love of Christ, give your ears and heart to Christ. Take hold of the comforting picture presented in the Gospel (Matthew 22.1-14), in which He shows that He wants you to acknowledge Him and believe in Him. You can be sure, He has an even deeper love and concern for you than any earthly bridegroom has for his beloved bride. On the other hand, He expects such a heartfelt confidence and joy from you towards Himself that it exceeds that of any bride for her bridegroom.

We could all probably find any amount of cause here to reprehend our unbelief and declare, "If such warm, heartfelt confidence and joy can be found between a bride and bridegroom, after all a rather insignificant and transient matter, why do I not find greater joy in my godly and faithful Saviour Christ, who gave Himself for me as my very own possession? What a wretched thing this unbelief is! It keeps my heart from being full of laughter and eternal joy."

SL.XI.1752,13

PRAYER: Lord, remove from us all diffidence, lukewarmness and unbelief, and confirm us in the full joy of salvation, which is always ours in and through our Saviour Jesus Christ. Amen.

FRIDAY

LESSON: 1 CORINTHIANS 2.6-13

This is a great mystery, and I take it to mean Christ and the church.   Ephesians 5.32

It is always our own old Adam, the corrupted nature of man, which prevents our heart from fully recognizing the joy and consolation which should be ours as members of Christ's kingdom. It is, and in some respects remains, a mystery, a secret, hidden, deep, concealed and incomprehensible. That is also why Paul calls all this **"a great mystery"**, **Ephesians 5.32**. But it is nevertheless something great, excellent and wonderful.

It is something mysterious not only to the blind, foolish world which never even thinks of these high spiritual matters and does not understand them, but also to the beloved apostles and outstanding Christians who find that there is quite enough to learn and to believe. No matter how long they concern themselves with these matters, preach about them and search them out, they are compelled to confess that there is a mystery in these matters for them in this life. Even St. Paul speaks quite freely about the limitations imposed on his understanding by the weakness of his flesh. He says, **"I am carnal, sold under sin. I do not understand my own actions." Romans 7.14,15**. David, too, raises complaints in many of his psalms. But there will be no mysteries in the future life, where we shall see without any coverings or darkness, and live in eternal joy.

In this present life it can still remain in some respects a hidden, concealed spiritual marriage which one cannot see with one's eyes or grasp with one's reason. Only faith can grasp these matters, faith which clings to the Word alone which tells us about these things and which we may be able to grasp only weakly here because of the perversity of our flesh.

SL.XI.1753,14

PRAYER: There are many things in your Word, especially in your Gospel of salvation, heavenly Father, which are mysteries and beyond our understanding. Give us at all times the faith to accept your Word and to believe it with our whole heart, for Christ's sake. Amen.

SATURDAY

LESSON: ACTS 5.1-11

Everything is ready; come to the marriage feast.
Matthew 22.4

Friend, how did you get in here without a wedding garment? Matthew 22.12

In order to provide guests for the marriage feast the king's servants must never cease to continue with their proclamation, inviting all whom they meet to come to the marriage feast. The king wants a full table at this feast. The most important, holy and mighty people who were invited first would not come. As Luke tells the parable, the king then sent out his servants to invite **"the poor and maimed and blind and lame"**. Luke 14.21. These are the heathen, who were not numbered among God's chosen people, had nothing about which to become presumptuous, and were quite glad to accept the invitation extended to them.

On inspecting the guests, the king found a scoundrel amongst the crowd sitting at the table whom he quickly recognized and condemned. He did not have a wedding garment. He had not come to this marriage out of any feeling of respect, but to disgrace the bridegroom and the king who had invited him. By this man is indicated those who are numbered among true Christians, who hear the Gospel and are to be found in the external fellowship of the Church but who merely make a pretence of accepting the Gospel in hypocrisy.

Here we see that the Church on earth, considered according to its external fellowship, is a congregation of such as hear the true teaching of the Gospel from Christ, and believe and confess it. They also have the Holy Spirit who sanctifies them and works in them through the Word and Sacrament. Among these, however, there are still to be found some false Christians and hypocrites.

SL.XI.1759,29-30

PRAYER: Lord God, you have told us very clearly in your Word that only the pure in heart will see you. Give us such singleness of heart and mind that we may always serve you in spirit and truth, without any hypocrisy, in and through Christ our Saviour. Amen.

SUNDAY

LESSON: JOHN 4.47-54

**One Lord, one faith, one baptism.   Ephesians 4.5
You are all one in Christ Jesus.   Galatians 3.28**

This Gospel sets before us an example of faith. St. John reminds us in no less than three places that this official believed in Jesus. We can easily understand, therefore, how someone might feel inclined to ask what kind of faith this man had, seeing that the evangelist seems to make so much of it. We have said so much about faith and the Gospel in our sermons, that I think we should understand it very well. But because it tends to crop up again and again, we must look at it quite frequently.

In the first place, as I have frequently stated, faith, through the Gospel, brings the whole of the Lord Jesus Christ to men with all His blessings. One Christian has just as much as any other Christian. A child baptized today has no less than St. Peter and all the saints in heaven. We are all alike in faith. One man has the treasure as fully and completely as another man.

This Gospel also speaks of the increase of faith. This, it would seem, introduces differences in faith. Although faith enjoys Christ and all His blessings fully, it must always be cultivated and practised so that a man becomes quite sure of it and holds fast to his treasure. Here there is a difference between two positions, between the man who has something and the man who takes a good hold of it, that is, between a strong faith and a weak faith.

A treasure as great as the one offered to us in the Gospel must be grasped firmly and kept so that it is not lost carelessly or taken away from us. The treasure is certainly mine even if it is wrapped up in a poppy-leaf; but it is not as well kept as when it is locked in an iron chest.

SL.XI.1762,1-3

PRAYER: We thank and praise you, heavenly Father, for the mercy and grace you have shown us in bestowing upon us all the blessings of your kingdom. Keep us ever mindful of the treasures that we enjoy in your kingdom and grant that we ever cling to them with all our heart, in and through Christ our Saviour. Amen.

MONDAY

LESSON: ROMANS 4.13-25

At Capernaum there was an official whose son was ill. When he heard that Jesus had come from Judea to Galilee, he went and begged him to come down and heal his son, for he was at the point of death.   John 4.46,47

Scripture teaches that there must be increase and progress in faith. It is quite true that you have Christ by faith, even if your treasure is wrapped only in a poor piece of cloth. But you must still make an effort to retain it and not lose it.

This royal official, whoever he was — I think he was a servant of King Herod — had advanced so far in his faith that he believed that if only he could persuade Jesus to come to his house, his son would certainly receive all the help he needed. He had heard the Gospel concerning Christ, namely, that he was ready to help everyone who was brought to Him and refused His goodness to no one. This good news his faith grasped; it compelled him to go to Jesus. If he had felt in his heart that no one could really be certain that Jesus would help him, he would not have come to Him. It is quite certain that prior to this he had made up his mind and firmly believed that Jesus would help him.

It is the nature and character of faith to build up a picture in a man's heart which reflects the goodness of Christ. The writer of Hebrews says that **"faith is the assurance of things hoped for"**, **Hebrews 11.1**, that is, of good things hoped for from God. The faith of this man is of such a kind that if he had continued in it he would certainly have been saved thereby. The Lord was certainly pleased with this man's faith.

SL.XI.1764,6-7

PRAYER: Heavenly Father, you have given us countless examples of the riches of your goodness toward us in your holy Word and especially in your Gospel. Grant us at all times steadfastness of faith and trust, that we may always believe your promises and assurances with our whole hearts, in and through our Saviour Jesus Christ. Amen.

TUESDAY

LESSON: JOHN 20.26-29

Jesus therefore said to him, "Unless you see signs and wonders you will not believe". John 4.48

We have mentioned the outstanding faith of this royal official and pointed out that Jesus was pleased with his faith. How does this agree with what we read here? If his faith and confidence brought this official to Jesus, why does Jesus now say to him, **"Unless you see signs and wonders you will not believe"**? He wants to show this man that his faith is not yet strong enough; he still wants to see and experience the presence of Christ.

Christ also reprimanded the disciples in the ship when the storm came upon them, saying, **"Why are you afraid, O men of little faith?" Matthew 8.26**. It is as though He meant to say to them, "Where is your faith now?" Therefore, no matter how good and upright faith is, it is bound to fall short in a moment of crisis if it is not exercised and developed.

You must never think that it is enough to begin to believe. You must always exercise a very watchful care to remain established in faith, otherwise it will decline. You must take precautions to retain the treasure which you have obtained. The devil is always using his cunning and power to tear this treasure from your heart.

The increase of faith is as strong as its beginning, and probably even stronger. But it is all God's work. Like infant milk, faith at first is sweet and small. When some real blasts arise and assail faith, God must strengthen it, otherwise it will not stand up to the blows. It is Christ's intention here to strengthen this official's faith with the remark, **"Unless you see signs and wonders you will not believe"**.

SL.XI.1764,8-9

PRAYER: Strengthen our faith, O Lord, so that with our whole hearts we trust in the promises and assurances of your Word and saving Gospel, in and through our Saviour Jesus Christ. Amen.

WEDNESDAY

LESSON: ROMANS 10.14-17

Jesus said to him, "Go; your son will live". The man believed the word that Jesus spoke to him and went his way.
John 4.50

If Jesus had told this man previously that his son was living he could not have believed it. But now he does believe it. The Word bursts into his heart and stirs up a different faith in him so that he becomes another man. To meet the greater shock which he received, the Lord gave him greater strength. Now he must cling to what he does not see. Previously he did not believe that Christ had the power to help his son without seeing him or going to him.

It requires quite a strong faith for a man to believe in his heart what he does not see or comprehend, something that is contrary to his understanding and reason, and to cling to the Word alone. Nothing shows its face here. He has recourse to nothing at all but to believe.

In faith one must put everything out of one's sight except the Word of God. Anyone who lets his eyes stray anywhere else is already lost. Faith clings alone to the pure and simple Word; it will not take its eyes off the Word. It sees nothing else but the Word and knows nothing at all of its own works and merits. If the heart is not bared to faith in this way, all is lost.

Faith clings to the Word of God alone and so remains a living reality, for the Word is always a living reality. Hence, he who clings to the Word, lives and abides for ever, because the Word lives and abides for ever.

SL.XI.1766,12-13

PRAYER: Lord, you want our faith at all times to be simple and pure. Grant us your Holy Spirit to bring us to such a pure and simple faith, in and through our Saviour Jesus Christ. Amen.

THURSDAY

LESSON: LUKE 11.5-13

Go; your son will live. John 4.50

In the matter of faith one must let everything go and cling to the Word alone. When we have gripped that, let the world, death, sin, hell and every misfortune storm and rage. But if you let go of the Word, you will be doomed.

We can see this in people whose stability depends on their earthly livelihood. When there is enough in the house and the barns are full, they trust in God all right and even speak of having a gracious God. But when they have nothing left they begin to doubt. Soon it is all over with their faith. They trust only what they actually see before their eyes. When they can see nothing there, they do not know where to look for succour. Worry and care about earthly, bodily needs drive out faith. If they had really taken hold of the Word in true faith they would have declared, "My God lives. He has promised to care for me and nourish me. I will set to work and trust God to bring to pass what Christ has said: '**Seek first his kingdom and his righteousness, and all these things shall be yours as well**'." Matthew 6.33.

Clinging to the Word and dispelling worry about earthly needs is the Christian way. As long as you keep your eyes fixed on your poverty, you cannot believe. This royal official also had probably formed such a view of things that he may have thought, "He will not listen to me. He has given me a rather sour reply. He does not want to come along with me; He is putting me off." Had he viewed the matter like this, his mission would have been an utter failure. But when he refuses to entertain such a view, he hears words of real consolation from Christ, "**Go; your son will live**".

SL.XI.1767,15

PRAYER: God our Father, you ask nothing of us but faith alone and give us the assurance that you will provide us with all our needs. Keep us always strong in an unwavering faith, fixed on your mercy and grace in Jesus Christ our Saviour. Amen.

FRIDAY

LESSON: COLOSSIANS 1.9-14

The man believed the word that Jesus spoke to him and went his way . . . He himself believed and all his household.
John 4.50,53

We must always keep ourselves in trim so that we do not just remain at the one fixed level but continually increase. Hence there must be a cross, temptation and tribulation in which faith can grow and become strong. Even as clarity of faith increases, so also there is progress in the disciplining of the body. The stronger faith becomes, the weaker the flesh becomes. The smaller our faith, the stronger our flesh becomes, and the less success we have in putting it off.

We are inclined to think; "If I am to be always helping my neighbour, what is going to become of me? I shall be going to him for something in the end." If we had a correct faith, one which reflects Christ in us, we would not be doubtful about having enough, but would declare in all confidence, "God will provide for us in every need". If we give up at every little puff, how shall we face up to something really big?

Faith must be practised to increase. Simply to go on and always remain every day what we were yesterday, and tomorrow what we are today, is not a Christian life. In this Gospel John takes special care to point out how this royal official increased in faith.

What did he believe after he came to his house? Not that his son had recovered and been restored to him. He could see his living son before his eyes. From the way in which he had experienced Christ's help, he now also believed that Christ would help him in any other troubles that would cross his path.

SL.XI.1768,17,19

PRAYER: Increase our faith, Lord Jesus, by removing all doubt and uncertainty from our hearts, filling them with the certainty and confidence of faith, for your name's sake. Amen.

SATURDAY

LESSON: PSALM 103.13-22

We rejoice in our sufferings, knowing that suffering produces endurance, and endurance produces character, and character produces hope, and hope does not disappoint us, because God's love has been poured into our hearts through the Holy Spirit which has been given to us.   Romans 5.3-5

Faith exercises itself in trials and temptations and every day brings new trials. Experience does not repeat itself so often, as we see also in this Gospel (John 4.47-54). The way in which this official set his faith working is past. These particular circumstances will not crop up again, but there will be other trials. If the same temptations present themselves, it should, of course, be easier to cope with them. The more victories one has, the more firmly one takes hold of Christ and becomes skilled in bearing everything that Christ chooses to lay upon one.

In this Gospel you have received an example of an increasing faith. It is clear enough; take it to heart! Each Christian will always be given opportunities to practise his faith. He can also trust that God will always help him. In this way he will have the experience of God's help to lead him on to greater faith.

There is always something new cropping up so that we may see and grasp that our Lord God is true. If we have the trust and confidence that He will nourish and preserve our body, we can also believe that He will save our souls.

SL.XI.1770,20-22

PRAYER: You are our loving heavenly Father, O God. As such, you can never forget the needs of your children. Grant us ever stronger faith, tested and proved in trials and temptations, for the sake of our Lord and Saviour Jesus Christ. Amen.

THE WEEK OF TRINITY XXII

SUNDAY

LESSON: MATTHEW 18.23-35

Rulers are not a terror to good conduct, but to bad.

Romans 13.3

The Gospel or the kingdom of God is nothing else but the estate or regime in which there is nothing but the forgiveness of sins. Where there is a regime in which sins are not forgiven, there is no Gospel or kingdom of God. Therefore the two kingdoms must be kept clearly apart: the one in which sin is punished, the other in which sin is forgiven; the one in which rights are demanded, the other in which rights are given up. In God's kingdom where He rules through the Gospel, no rights are demanded, nor does one operate with rights. In God's kingdom there is nothing but forgiveness, remitting and donating, no wrath or punishment, nothing but brotherly service and benevolence.

This does not, however, abolish secular law and justice. This parable teaches us nothing about the secular realm; it teaches us only about the kingdom of God. When a secular prince rules his people in such a way that he allows no one to perpetrate an injustice and punishes evildoers, he does well and deserves praise.

We need such a regime but we cannot get into heaven thereby. The world cannot be saved by its secular government. But secular government is necessary to prevent the world from becoming worse than it is, and to ward off and hinder evil. If there were no secular government, one man would simply swallow up the other man and no one in the end would be able to retain life, property, wife or child. To prevent universal destruction and ruin, God has set up the authority of the sword so that evil might be in part restrained, and that the secular authority might establish peace and prevent men from doing each other injustice and wrong. This order of things the Christian must also accept.

SL.XI.1788,4

PRAYER: We thank and praise you, heavenly Father, for all the blessings which we have been privileged to enjoy in our earthly lives through good government and good rulers. Keep us ever mindful of our duties in the secular realm, for Christ's sake. Amen.

MONDAY

LESSON: MATTHEW 18.18-22

Out of pity for him the lord of that servant released him and forgave him the debt.   Matthew 18.27

Then his lord summoned him and said to him, "You wicked servant! I forgave you all that debt because you besought me; and should not you have had mercy on your fellow servant, as I had mercy on you?"   Matthew 18.32,33

In the Gospel there is nothing but sheer forgiveness. The lord of the servant forgave him his whole debt and the lord expected that servant to forgive his fellow servant and release him from his debt. This is how God wants matters to stand in His kingdom. No one should ever be so displeased with his neighbour or angry with him that he cannot forgive his neighbour.

As Christ points out in the context immediately preceding, even if your neighbour incurs your anger not just seven times **"but seventy times seven"**, Matthew 18.22, that is, as often as it would be possible to do so, you should drop your rights and freely remit him everything. Why? Because Christ has also done this for you.

He has initiated and set up a kingdom in which there is nothing but pure grace, a kingdom which will never end, in which everything will be forgiven you as often as you have sinned. He has sent out His Gospel which proclaims not punishment but pure grace alone. As long as this regime stands, you can always rise again, no matter how deeply and how often you have fallen away from it.

One thing Christ expects of you, that you forgive your neighbour the sins he has committed against you. Otherwise you cannot hold your place in His kingdom of grace or enjoy the good news that your sins are forgiven you. This, in brief, is the gist and meaning of this Gospel.

SL.XI.1789,6

PRAYER: We thank you from the bottom of our hearts, O God, for the full and often repeated forgiveness of our sins which we enjoy in your kingdom of grace. May we always be found ready, in the enjoyment of your forgiveness, to forgive our neighbour his sins, through Jesus Christ our Saviour. Amen.

TUESDAY

LESSON: 1 JOHN 2.1-6

The kingdom of heaven may be compared to a king who wished to settle accounts with his servants. When he began the reckoning, one was brought to him who owed him ten thousand talents; and as he could not pay, his lord ordered him to be sold, with his wife and children and all that he had, and payment to be made. So the servant fell on his knees, imploring him, "Lord, have patience with me, and I will pay you everything".   Matthew 18.23-26

The message which this servant heard from his lord and master was anything but joyful. In all seriousness and deadly earnest the master delivered a most startling and shocking judgement. The servant becomes so distressed that he falls down and begs for patience. He makes a promise exceeding all his power of fulfilment, saying, **"Lord, have patience with me, and I will pay you everything"**. Here we have a picture, a portrait of those for whom the Gospel really has a message.

This is also how matters stand between us and God. When God wants to settle accounts He sees to it that His Law is preached through which we learn to know our indebtedness. For example, He tells our conscience, "You shall have no other god but regard Me alone as your God, love Me with your whole heart and place all your trust and reliance on Me alone". This is the account, the register, in which what we owe Him is written down.

What does the servant do? He makes an offer, fool that he is, to pay his debt. He falls down and asks his lord to have patience with him. Nothing can save this man but the lord's mercy and forgiveness.

SL.XI.1791,8-11

PRAYER: Lord God, when we look at our lives in the light of your holy Law, we see nothing but sin and condemnation. Our sins are truly many and great. Our one and only consolation is that as our loving heavenly Father you do not look at our sins according to your Law but that you regard us in accordance with the righteousness offered us in your Gospel, in and through Christ our Saviour. Amen.

WEDNESDAY

LESSON: HEBREWS 9.11-14

Out of pity for him the lord of that servant released him and forgave him the debt.   Matthew 18.27

The lord has pity on this servant in his wretched condition. The servant is securely caught and entangled in his sins and foolish enough to suppose that he can help himself out of his hopeless plight. He does not look for mercy. He knows nothing about grace. He feels nothing but his sins which oppress him sorely. There is no one to whom he can turn for help. Even while he is in this wretched plight, the lord turned to him in pity and released him.

In this action of the lord there is portrayed to us what the Gospel in its nature really is, and how God deals with us. If you are entangled in your sins and are afraid that you can find no help to rescue you from your sad plight, the Gospel comes to you and says, "No, not so, my dear friend, it does not help you to martyr yourself to the point of distraction and to become alarmed. It is not your works but God's mercy alone which moves Him to have pity on you in your wretched situation. He sees that you are in the grip of fear, that you are throttling yourself in the mire of your sins, that you cannot extricate yourself from your plight. He can see that you cannot pay your debt. In pity and mercy He forgives you your whole debt. Therefore, it is a case of pure mercy. He forgives you your debt not because of your works or any merits. He has pity on your cries, entreaties and the requests you have made on your knees."

This means that God regards a humble heart, as David declares, **"The sacrifice acceptable to God is a broken spirit; a broken and contrite heart, O God, thou wilt not despise".** **Psalm 51.17**. A heart that is broken, he says, and contrite, that cannot help itself and is quite content to have God reach out a helping hand to it, is the most acceptable sacrifice before God and the right way to heaven.

SL.XI.1793,14-15

PRAYER: Eternal praise and thanks be yours, heavenly Father, for your mercy and grace and the rescue from all sins available to us in your Gospel of salvation, as revealed to us in and through our Lord Jesus Christ. Amen.

THURSDAY

LESSON: ROMANS 4.9-12

If it is by grace, it is no longer on the basis of works; otherwise grace would no longer be grace.   Romans 11.6

In his mercy the lord in the parable of Matthew 18.23-35 pities the wretched situation of the servant before him. He sets aside and gives up his rights and says no more about selling his servant "**with his wife and children and all that he had**". He could certainly have insisted on his rights, declaring, "You have to pay up; I have my rights and have no intention of giving them up for your sake". No one could have found fault with him on this score.

But he does not want to deal with his servant on the basis of rights. He exchanges rights for grace and has pity on his servant. He sets him free, together with his wife and children and all that he has, and forgives him his whole debt. This is also what God proclaims through the Gospel, saying to us, "He who believes shall not only have his debt forgiven but also the punishment he has merited".

Works must never come into consideration here. Anyone who suggests that one can get rid of the guilt and punishment for sin through works has denied the Gospel. That God should have pity on you and that you should earn or merit His favour cannot be harmonized in any way. Paul's argument is unanswerable, "**If it is by grace, it is no longer on the basis of works; otherwise grace would no longer be grace**". **Romans 11.6.** If you pay what you owe, there is no need for His mercy. If you are the recipient of His mercy, you are not paying for it. Hence we must allow Him to initiate His dealings with us and to act quite alone; we must receive from Him and believe in Him. That is what the Gospel is all about, as we see also from this parable.

SL.XI.1794,16

PRAYER: As lost and condemned sinners, without any righteousness or merits of our own, O God, we have no other recourse but to throw ourselves on your mercy and love. It is the glory of your Gospel that it assures us that your grace alone is our effective means of salvation, in and through Christ our Saviour. Amen.

FRIDAY

LESSON: PSALM 119.33-40

With the Lord on my side I do not fear. What can man do to me? The Lord is on my side to help me; I shall look in triumph on those who hate me. It is better to take refuge in the Lord than to put confidence in man.   Psalm 118.6-8

Because this servant (Matthew 18.23-35) is humbled by the knowledge of his sins, the Word becomes a source of mighty consolation to him. The lord absolves him and forgives him his debt and punishment. Hereby we should note that the Gospel does not touch profligate hearts, nor those who are openly insolent in their wickedness, but only those whose conscience is terrified, whose sins oppress them, who would gladly get rid of them if they could. On such God has mercy. He grants them full remission.

In accepting the Word, this servant became God's friend. If he had not accepted the Word, it would not have helped him; there would have been no remission. Hence, it is not enough for God to offer us the forgiveness of sins and to proclaim a jubilee year of grace; the Word must be accepted and believed.

If you believe the Word you are free from your sins and all is simple. This is the first part of a Christian life which this Gospel and all others teach us. It consists basically in faith, by which alone we have dealings with God. In addition, however, we are shown here that the Gospel cannot be grasped unless conscience has been previously afflicted and is in distress.

SL.XI.1794,17

PRAYER: Heavenly Father, your assurance to us is that we have the full forgiveness of all our sins by your grace alone through faith alone. Keep from us all trust in our own works and merits as we cling to your grace alone, for Christ's sake. Amen.

SATURDAY

LESSON: PSALM 119.57-64

God is able to provide you with every blessing in abundance, so that you may always have enough of everything and may provide in abundance for every good work. 2 Corinthians 9.8

When we believe that we have a gracious God and that we need nothing further, it would, presumably, be time for us to die as soon as possible. But if we are to continue our life here on earth it must not be directed towards gaining God's favour by our works.

Anyone who holds such a view makes a mockery of God and blasphemes God. Yet this is what was taught for such a long time in the Church. We were informed that we must keep on pestering God with our good works, prayers, fasts and the like, until we obtained His grace. We did obtain grace, not by our works, but from God's mercy.

In your life of faith you certainly have to get busy and do something, but, as Christ informs us, everything we do must be done for the interests of our neighbour. The servant in the parable, we are told, "**went out**". He "**went out**" in love. Faith leads men from people to God. Love leads them out to people. Our faith must break out and prove itself in action before our fellowmen. God does not need your works; He has enough in your faith. But He wants you to do works as fruits of faith, to demonstrate the reality of your faith before the whole world in works.

This servant (Matthew 18.23-35) is an example or a picture of all who should serve their neighbour in faith. But what does he do? He does what most of us do. We imagine that we have faith and in part this is true. We rejoice at having heard the Gospel and we may even be able to talk a great deal about it. But only too few really live in accordance with the Gospel. There are even those in our midst who seem to become worse after hearing the Gospel.   SL.XI.1796,21-24

PRAYER: Heavenly Father, give us at all times a true and genuine faith which proves itself in works of love to our neighbour, and becomes ever stronger and more willing to walk the paths of your choosing, in and through Christ our Saviour. Amen.

SUNDAY

LESSON: MATTHEW 22.15-22

When they heard it, they marvelled; and they left him and went away.   Matthew 22.22

This is written for our consolation so that those of us who believe in Christ should know that we Christians are in possession of a wisdom that outranks all other wisdom, and that we have a strength and righteousness with which no human strength or righteousness can stand comparison. Against the Holy Spirit no human counsel is of any avail. Through Christ we have the power to tread sin underfoot and to trample upon death, and a wisdom that exceeds the wisdom of the whole world. If Christ dwells in us by faith, He is ours and will attend to all this in us. But in the hour of trial and temptation we do not always feel this. Therefore, when I need it, He comes to me and enables me to make my way through my difficulties with renewed strength.

We should never be apprehensive that our doctrine will go under and be disgraced. No matter whether all the learned and wise men of this world rise up against God's Word and make a merry sport of their opposition to the Word, they are doomed to ultimate failure. It can happen that they bark against the Word and bite it to such an extent that people think that the Gospel will be overwhelmed. But when they set themselves to overthrow the Gospel it is quite certain that they will fail in a disgraceful manner, and they themselves will be caught in the trap by which they hoped to overthrow the Gospel. This is what happened here in this Gospel to the men who tried to trip up Jesus. They thought themselves smart enough to outwit Christ in every way, but their wisdom and smartness let them down.

SL.XI.1806,8-9

PRAYER: Grant us a full measure of your Holy Spirit, O God, the Spirit of truth and understanding, that we may always cling in firm faith to the teaching of your Word, for Christ's sake. Amen.

MONDAY

LESSON: PSALM 118.1-9

If God is for us, who is against us? He who did not spare his own Son but gave him up for us all, will he not also give us all things with him?   Romans 8.31,32

All who set themselves against the divine wisdom and Word of God must bring discredit on themselves or suffer disgrace. Let no one therefore be afraid, even if all the cleverness and might of the world range themselves against the Gospel, and even if efforts are made to subdue it with bloodshed. The more blood that is shed, the more Christians will increase. Tertullian well observed that the blood of the Christians is the seed from which Christians grow. The devil is drowned in Christian blood. Hence it is not a very smart thing to try to suppress the Gospel by force.

In a certain respect the Gospel resembles the palm tree. It is the nature and character of this tree to lie on top, no matter how much loading one puts on to it. If a beam is made of it, it does not yield to any load but actually raises itself against the load. That is also how the Gospel is. The more opposition it encounters, the greater pressure it exerts, and the more men try to quench it, the more and more it grows.

We should never be afraid of might and force; what we should really fear is success and good days. These are quite likely to do us more harm than anxiety and persecution.

We should also not be afraid of the wisdom and cleverness of the world. This can do us no harm. The more the wisdom of the world opposes the truth of the Gospel, the purer and clearer the truth becomes.

SL.XI.1807,10-11

PRAYER: Be the defender and protector of your Word and Gospel, O God, in all attacks made on it by its enemies. May your Word and Gospel continue to go from strength to strength, in and through our Saviour Jesus Christ. Amen.

TUESDAY

LESSON: 2 CORINTHIANS 12.7-10

We put no obstacle in any one's way, so that no fault may be found with our ministry, but as servants of God we commend ourselves in every way: through great endurance, in afflictions, hardships, calamities, beatings, imprisonments, tumults, labours, watching, hunger; by purity, knowledge, forbearance, kindness, the Holy Spirit, genuine love, truthful speech, and the power of God; with the weapons of righteousness for the right hand and for the left; in honour and dishonour, in ill repute and good repute. We are treated as impostors, and yet are true; as unknown, and yet well known; as dying, and behold we live; as punished, and yet not killed; as sorrowful, yet always rejoicing; as poor, yet making many rich; as having nothing, and yet possessing everything.   2 Corinthians 6.3-10

Nothing better can happen for the Gospel than for the world to oppose it with might and cunning. The more that sin and the devil assail my conscience, the stronger becomes the justice of my cause. For the sins that press upon me hurt me; this makes me all the more persistent in my prayer and cries to God; hence my faith and confidence in my cause become stronger and stronger continually. This is also what St. Paul means when he states, "My power is made perfect in weakness". 2 Corinthians 12.9.

Inasmuch, then, as we have a treasure which becomes stronger through temptation and adversity, we should never become afraid, but be of good courage and even rejoice in tribulation as Paul also observes.

If the devil were clever enough to keep quiet and simply allow the Gospel to be preached without trying to hinder it, he would certainly have less trouble on his hands. For if the Gospel is not attacked, it grows rusty and has no particular reason for manifesting its power and might.   SL.XI.1807,11

PRAYER: Lord God, heavenly Father, we are by nature weak and beggarly, having nothing in us with which to oppose our enemies — the devil, the world, and our own sinful flesh. Make us strong, especially in the blessings of the Gospel available to us in rich measure, in and through Christ our beloved Saviour. Amen.

WEDNESDAY

LESSON: 1 CORINTHIANS 3.18-23

Jesus did not trust himself to them, because he knew all men and needed no one to bear witness of man; for he himself knew what was in man.   John 2.24,25

Whenever we are assailed by the enemies of our faith, we always have the strong consolation that Christ is in us and will carry off the victory through us. Christ is so close to us that we always conquer through Him because we are in Christ. When we are not beset by any adversity we do not feel the need of His presence. But when we are under attack and are being crushed, He makes His presence felt and puts our enemies to shame.

Here, too, we should note that those who are a cut above others, cleverer, more powerful, with special gifts of understanding, nature and fortune; those who are more artistic, more learned and wiser than their fellows, who can speak well and who are equipped to exercise leadership over others, who can rule and regulate everything in the best possible manner, these people, for the greater part are opposed to God and faith, and tend to rely more on the powers of their own reason than on God. Poisoned nature prevents them from being prepared to employ their gifts to the best advantage, for the use and benefit of their neighbour. Relying on their own gifts, they simply set their minds on this or that and hold the view that they do not need help or strength in any way.

They resemble the Pharisees of the Gospel (Matthew 22.15-22). They were quite confident that they would get the upper hand over Jesus by setting Him a trick question. They felt that He could not possibly escape from their clutches because He would be in serious trouble if He answered either "Yes" or "No".

SL.XI.1808,13

PRAYER: The wisdom of this world is folly with you, O God, and your wisdom is foolishness with the world. Be pleased to open our hearts to receive the foolishness of the Gospel, through Jesus Christ our Lord and Saviour. Amen.

THURSDAY

LESSON: PSALM 106.6-8

For consider your call, brethren; not many of you were wise according to worldly standards, not many were powerful, not many were of noble birth; but God chose what is foolish in the world to shame the wise, God chose what is weak in the world to shame the strong, God chose what is low and despised in the world, even things that are not, to bring to nothing things that are, so that no human being might boast in the presence of God. 1 Corinthians 1.26-29

In this week's Gospel (Matthew 22.15-22) we have a very good portrayal of the cunning and perversity of human nature. There is nothing in men by nature but evil, lies, deceit, cunning and all that is vicious. By nature man is nothing else but a liar, as the psalmist declares. You cannot trust a single person. Don't think for a moment that you will ever hear a word of truth from anyone; man is a liar whenever he opens his mouth. How so? The spring is evil, that is, the heart is no good. Therefore the streams are no good either.

This is why the Lord at times described men as a **"brood of vipers"**, **Matthew 12.34**, and **"serpents"**, **Matthew 23.33**. Is not this an apt title for these people? Let anyone come forward here to boast about his piety and the powers of his own free will! Before the world it is possible to put on a fine exterior, and to be pious and holy, with much outward glitter. But there is really nothing else there than a brood of vipers and serpents, especially in the most valued, excellent, wise and clever men. When you read the histories of the Greeks, Romans and Jews, you will find that the best and cleverest princes, those who ruled well by human standards, were not conscious of receiving anything from God but relied on themselves alone, ascribing nothing at all to the power of God.

SL.XI.1809,15

PRAYER: Dear Lord, heavenly Father, in your mercy and grace you bestow upon us everything in our lives that deserves to be called good. May we ever cling to you in firm faith, the giver of all good gifts, in Christ our Lord. Amen.

FRIDAY

LESSON: PSALM 40.1-5

Thus says the Lord: "Cursed is the man who trusts in man and makes flesh his arm, whose heart turns away from the Lord". Jeremiah 17.5

The less a man is trained in the ways of the world, the less he is opposed to God. Those who have made progress and gained recognition before the world, deceive and lie more than the others. They think that in the deceitfulness and cunning procedures of their actions, their deceit and vice are covered up. It is true, that they are masters at covering up and hiding their activities! But the Holy Spirit is very keen-sighted and He knows them very well. Holy Scripture calls such fellows lions, wolves, bears, swine and wild animals. They are always raging, and they devour and consume everything with their treachery.

In the Old Testament the Jews were forbidden to eat certain animals because they were to regard them as unclean. They included those we have just mentioned, as well as others. A possible reason for this was that they were a figure and indication of certain people who are strong, powerful, rich, gifted, learned, prudent and wise, who are to be strictly avoided as something unclean, namely, as people who mislead and deceive others with their outward brilliance, power and cleverness. They are people of such a kind, that one would never suspect them of any evil intentions. Hence, we must never put any confidence and trust in any man as such.

Do not believe anyone. If a man can do so, he will surely mislead you. If you trust him, you will find yourself in opposition to God so that you do not trust God. This is what Jeremiah wants to teach us in the passage cited above.

SL.XI.1809,16

PRAYER: As your children, heavenly Father, we owe all our faith and trust to you alone and not to men, through Jesus Christ our Lord. Amen.

SATURDAY

LESSON: 1 JOHN 5.6-12

Let God be true, but every man a liar.   Romans 3.4 A.V.

Someone may ask: What will happen if we cannot trust anyone? We must have some involvement and dealings with others; how otherwise could human society continue? We must buy and sell and distribute our wares among others. If no one believed or trusted anyone else, all human transactions would come to an end.

It is true, of course, that we must have dealings with each other and one needs the other's help. But the point I am trying to make is this: your dealings with any man, whether it be buying or selling, must be regarded as a matter of uncertainty on which you cannot rest your faith or build anything with absolute certainty.

This much is sure: if you trust anyone, you are already deceived. Human nature, to the best of its ability, can do nothing but lie and deceive. Everything, accordingly, which depends on man must always retain an element of uncertainty; man's works and words are subject to constant change and instability. Be quite sure of that!

We must trust God alone and say, "O Lord, you are my life, my soul and body, my property and goods, and all that is mine: direct and order it all in accordance with your will. You I believe. You I trust. You will never forsake me in any dangerous situation with this man or that man. I cannot trust man. If you know that it will be good for me, bring it to pass that he keeps faith with me. If you know that it will not benefit me, let him break faith with me. I am well content to let your will be done."

SL.XI.1810,17

PRAYER: O God, we pray that your good and gracious will should always prevail in all our relationships with you and our fellowmen, for Christ's sake. Amen.

SUNDAY

LESSON: MATTHEW 9.18-26

The gospel of God which he promised beforehand through his prophets in the holy scriptures, the gospel concerning his Son.   Romans 1.1-3

You know that the Gospel is nothing else but the proclamation of the one single person who is called Christ. Although at various times many other books have been written and many sermons have been preached on many different people, both heathen and Christians, and, indeed, even on the mother of God, St. Peter, the angels and many other saints, they are not Gospels. That only is the true Gospel which holds up Christ before us and teaches us what good we are to expect from Him.

At times the Gospel makes mention of John the Baptist, Mary and the apostles. But this is not the Gospel in the strict sense. Mention is made of these people to point out more fully whence Christ came and what His office is. What we read of John the Baptist and the Virgin Mary in Luke's Gospel is not written for their sakes, but solely for the sake of the person of Christ. Everything that is found in the Gospel is related to this person only.

In St. Paul's epistles nothing is written about the saints; everything concerns Christ alone. The evangelists describe the miracles and wondrous signs that Christ performed. They do not describe a single work of John the Baptist or Mary. They are interested only in what Christ Himself achieved, how He helped people in body and soul, and how people became attached to Him as a result.

SL.XI.1834,1-2

PRAYER: We praise and thank you, heavenly Father, for the wonderful gift of your Gospel of salvation with its revelation of salvation in Christ alone. Implant your Gospel in our hearts in such a way that we really find Christ there, and cling to Him with all our hearts now and always, for His name's sake. Amen.

MONDAY

LESSON: 2 CORINTHIANS 4.1-6

We preach Christ crucified, a stumbling block to Jews and folly to Gentiles, but to those who are called, both Jews and Greeks, Christ the power of God and the wisdom of God.
1 Corinthians 1.23,24

God has determined it as His will that all men should adhere to the one man Christ, hope in Him, and take hold of Him, if they are really concerned about their salvation. They should know nothing about anyone else except Christ crucified, who alone is the mercy-seat put forward for us by God, as Paul says (Romans 3.25).

Up till now one man has clung to this saint, another to that one; one man has been attached to Mary, another to St. Barbara and there have been any number of sects and orders. But no regard at all was paid to Christ; only His name was retained. We have had many intercessors, all of whom we should have abandoned and clung to Christ alone.

St. Paul declares that the Gospel concerning God's Son was promised through His prophets (Romans 1.2). He sets up very tight and narrow limits to make it clear that in the Gospel there is only one matter of real significance, namely, this one person, Jesus Christ. He who knows this can be thankful to God that he knows where to look for consolation and help, and where to place his confidence. Such a man will also despise and reject all contrary proclamation.

SL.XI.1836,3

PRAYER: Lord God, you have not left us any room at all to doubt what you offer us in the salvation provided for us in the Gospel. You have made it quite clear that all this is available to us by faith alone. Make us strong in faith that we may always cling firmly to our only Saviour, in whose name we also ask this. Amen.

TUESDAY

LESSON: PSALM 145.8-13

When he saw the crowds, he had compassion for them.
Matthew 9.36

In this Gospel (Matthew 9.18-26) Christ is pictured to us as mingling with the people and drawing all men to Himself by His sweet doctrine. They could really have clung to Him with their whole hearts and entrusted themselves to His goodness with high hopes of receiving both spiritual and bodily blessings from Him. You do not see Him taking anything from those whom He has benefited. To be sure, He gets nothing but mockery and scorn. Blessings go out from Him; He receives mockery and scorn in return.

This is now preached and reported to the whole world so that men may learn to know this man aright, that we may know how to become Christians, not how to become pious and godly. Others, who teach outside the Gospel, bring men under various pressures to inculcate piety in them, such as the books of the heathen masters and the secular law books. The legends of the saints also urge men to live as the saints lived.

It is not the business of the Gospel to make men pious, but to make Christians of them. Being a Christian is far more than being pious. A man can be pious without being a Christian. A Christian has nothing to say about his piety; he finds in himself nothing good or pious. If he is to be pious he must look elsewhere than in himself for true piety.

SL.XI.1837,4-5

PRAYER: Dear Lord Jesus, as our helper, friend, Redeemer and Saviour you are for us the treasure beyond all compare. The message in your good news is altogether sweet and lovely. Abide with us so that we may enjoy you and your blessings now and for evermore. Amen.

WEDNESDAY

LESSON: EPHESIANS 4.11-16

Abide in me, and I in you. As a branch cannot bear fruit by itself, unless it abides in the vine, neither can you, unless you abide in me. I am the vine, you are the branches. He who abides in me, and I in him, he it is that bears much fruit, for apart from me you can do nothing.   John 15.4,5

Christ is set before us in this Gospel (Matthew 9.18-26) as an inexhaustible fountain at all times running over with pure goodness and grace. And for such goodness and kindness He takes nothing at all. The godly who recognize such goodness and grace thank Him for it and praise and love Him. The others may even load Him with mockery. That is how they repay His goodness and grace.

A man cannot be called a Christian simply because he does much; he is a Christian because he receives from Christ and draws on Him, and suffers Christ to bestow His blessings upon him. When anyone has ceased receiving from Christ, he is no longer a Christian, so that the term Christian has relevance only in receiving and not in giving and doing.

A Christian is one who has received nothing from anyone else but Christ. If you have regard for what you are doing, you have already lost the Christian name. It is true, of course, that one must do good works, helping others with counsel and gifts. But no one can be called a Christian from such works. Thereby no one becomes a Christian.

SL.XI.1837,6

PRAYER: Lord Jesus, give us ever of your fullness and thus equip us as your children to always bring forth much fruit, for your name's sake. Amen.

THURSDAY

LESSON: GALATIANS 3.23-29

To all who received him, who believed in his name, he gave power to become children of God.   John 1.12

If one takes the word in its strict meaning, we should always recognize a Christian from the fact that he receives from Christ alone and has Christ in him, for that is what the term Christian basically means. Just as one calls someone "white" from his whiteness or "black" from his blackness or "big" from his bigness, so also a Christian is named from Christ whom he has in himself and from whom he receives good. If, then, a Christian receives the name "Christian" from Christ, he can never be called a Christian from his works. Similarly, it follows from this that no one ever becomes a Christian from his works.

Therefore those who ply our congregations with their commandments, works and statutes are seducers who cannot possibly make Christians out of men. Although they profess the Christian name, they still want to load us down under the dead weight of the commandments and works which they set forth. According to works I can be called a faster, a prayer-maker, a pilgrim, but not necessarily a Christian.

Even if you wove all your works together and added the works of all others to them, it would not necessarily mean that you have Christ and were entitled to be called a Christian. Christ is completely separated from and higher than any law or human commandment. He is God's Son, prepared only to give and not to receive.

SL.XI.1837,7-8

PRAYER: You are our all, Lord Jesus, and in us all. Without you we are nothing. Grant that we may ever abide in you and you in us in the tie of faith and love, for your name's sake. Amen.

FRIDAY

LESSON: GALATIANS 1.6-9

"I am the Alpha and the Omega", says the Lord God, who is and who was and who is to come, the Almighty.

Revelation 1.8

This week's Gospel (Matthew 9.18-26) teaches us that Christ is elevated as the greatest and highest person in the whole world, not to terrify men but that He may be able to bestow all earthly and heavenly blessings upon them so that all men should rely on Him, trust Him, and always look to Him as the source of all blessings. When a certain sin is terrifying my conscience and the preachers of the Law come forward and want to help me with works, they accomplish nothing at all. Christ is the only one who can help me here and no one else. The others only make matters worse, even if it were St. Peter or St. Paul, or even Mary, the mother of God. Christ alone is successful here because He has been ordained by God to make proclamation that my sins are freely forgiven me, without any works or merit, out of pure grace, through faith in this Saviour, Jesus Christ.

If I accept this proclamation I have the consolation that my sins are forgiven me before God and the world. If I cling to this proclamation with my whole heart, I am a Christian. I give thanks to God through Christ who keeps on giving me the Holy Spirit and His grace so that sin does me no harm either in this life or before God's judgement-seat on the last day.

SL.XI.1838,9

PRAYER: We thank and praise you, heavenly Father, for the wonderful gift of full and free salvation in Christ. May we never turn from this one sure source of salvation to any man-made plans of salvation which are always full of uncertainties. In Jesus' name. Amen.

THE WEEK OF TRINITY XXIV

SATURDAY

LESSON: TITUS 2.11-14

He saved us, not because of deeds done by us in righteousness, but in virtue of his own mercy . . . through Jesus Christ our Saviour. Titus 3.5,6

He who wants to have a cheerful conscience which does not fear sin, death, hell or God's wrath, must not push this Mediator, Christ, out of the way. He is the fountain overflowing with grace who imparts temporal and eternal life. Open your heart and accept Him as your Mediator and you will have all you need. He gushes and flows forth and can do nothing else but give, flow forth and gush, if only you can believe it. You have the right to the name Christian only when you are a Christian in receiving; otherwise, if you want to give much, you are no Christian. This is the rich, precious Word which Paul praises so highly and can never praise enough, that God intermingles His Son so graciously among us that He pours out His grace over all who accept it.

From all this it follows that if a Christian does good works and manifests love to his neighbour he does not become a Christian or acquire a godly status thereby, but he must first be a Christian and have acquired a godly status and then good works result. He certainly does good works, but his good works do not make him a Christian. The tree brings forth or produces good fruits; the fruits do not make the tree. So here also, no one becomes a Christian by good works, but through Christ alone.

From all this you should understand what kind of people Christians are, and what their kingdom is. As a group, they cling to Christ and with Him they all have the one spirit and like gifts. On this basis Christians are all equal; the one does not have more in Christ than the other.

SL.XI.1839,11-12

PRAYER: Lord God, our heavenly Father, give us a faith that is ever active in works of love to our neighbour, in and through Christ our Saviour. Amen.

SUNDAY

LESSON: MATTHEW 24.15-28

When you see the desolating sacrilege spoken of by the prophet Daniel, standing in the holy place (let the reader understand), then let those who are in Judea flee to the mountains; let him who is on the housetop not go down to take what is in his house; and let him who is in the field not turn back to take his mantle. Matthew 24.15-18

In this chapter we have a description of the conclusion and end of two kingdoms, the kingdom of the Jews as well as the end of the whole world. These two the evangelists Matthew and Mark toss together without observing any due order as the Gospel of Luke does. All that these evangelists want to do is to give and to relate the words of Christ; they do not trouble themselves with what He spoke first or subsequently. But Luke takes special care to write more clearly and with more order, and reports this whole discussion twice. First, briefly in chapter nineteen he speaks of the destruction of the Jews at Jerusalem and then in chapter twenty-one he reports these two matters in succession.

You must know, then, that Matthew here wraps together and takes up at the same time the end of both the Jewish people and the end of the world, and cooks this up into one broth. If you want to understand it, you have to separate and draw out each part to its end, that which is spoken of the Jews and that which is spoken of the whole world.

SL.XI.1870,1-2

PRAYER: Lord Jesus, guide and direct us by your Holy Spirit so that we may always accept your Word given us through men and in human form as the Word of truth and salvation, for your name's sake. Amen.

MONDAY

LESSON: LUKE 19.41-44

Do you not know that you are God's temple and that God's Spirit dwells in you? If any one destroys God's temple, God will destroy him. For God's temple is holy, and that temple you are.   1 Corinthians 3.16,17

When Christ ascended into heaven He did not lock up His kingdom in the land of the Jews; He spread it out into the whole world through the Gospel which was preached and heard everywhere. But, like the Jews, we deny and persecute God's Word and put to death the Christians who confess and preach it. The Romans were the first to do this but their example has been continued by the pope, the bishops, princes, monks and priests right up to our day. For five hundred years or more no one was permitted to preach God's Word without, at least for appearance sake, reciting the text of the Gospel from the pulpit. But these preachers mostly extracted the doctrine of men from these texts or dragged it into these texts. Whenever anyone raised objections to this he was silenced with fire and sword.

Daniel's word about the "desolating sacrilege" is certainly important also for us. This "desolating sacrilege" is the false doctrine current in the Church that men must save themselves by performing all the works imposed on them by the Church and its hierarchy, and by falling in line with all the machinery that has been set up in the Church to force men into obedience to this "desolating sacrilege".

The pure doctrine of the Word is the doctrine which we proclaim that we are saved from sin, death, the devil and all misfortune through Christ and established in God's kingdom through the Word and faith.

Where this is preached and believed, Christ dwells and reigns in the hearts spiritually without means. There the Holy Spirit also dwells with all the blessings and fullness of God's riches.   SL.XI.1875,17-19

PRAYER: O Lord our God, you have warned us in no uncertain manner that false doctrine can be sacrilege. May we never fall into the sacrilege which sets aside the clear truth of your Word and substitutes for it the doctrine of men ending in spiritual sin. In Jesus' name. Amen.

TUESDAY

LESSON: GALATIANS 3.10-14

If any one says to you, "Lo, here is the Christ!" or "There he is!" do not believe it.   Matthew 24.23

We should know and understand this passage and similar ones very well. There have always been those who have tried to gain currency for their ideas of the kingdom of Christ by attaching the Christian Church to external, visible features and circumstances, or even by identifying it with certain prominent leaders, claiming that the kingdom of Christ is wherever a certain leader is to be found. Their chief objective is that we should find them and be influenced by personal relationships and particular styles in our religious persuasions. In other words, everything is decided by external factors. Monasteries and ecclesiastical institutions have often been influenced in this way. "If you accept our way of life", they say, "eat as we do, dress according to our direction, pray and fast as we do, you will atone for your sins and be saved".

Christ gives us a good description of this kind of thing here. He is aiming His remarks especially at all the monasteries, religious ranks and all the special works with which they try to help the souls of men. He warns us to be on our guard and not to allow ourselves to be torn from the foundation on which we stand, namely, that we do not become Christians by any of these institutions, ranks or works, but are saved from all evil and brought into His kingdom through His blood alone, if we believe in Him.

He removes from our sight everything temporal and external, and with one word strikes down all doctrine which does not preach faith purely, and all living which is not governed by the correct doctrine of faith. He says here in brief, **"If any one says to you, 'Lo, here is the Christ!' or 'There he is!' do not believe it"**. He means to say, "Be on your guard against everything that leads you to works; for it will deceive you and tear you away from Me". SL.XI.1879,25

PRAYER: Lord Jesus, protect us at all times against all false doctrine and misunderstandings which would modify our faith and trust in you alone and direct us to our own vain works and merits, for your mercy and truth's sake. Amen.

WEDNESDAY

LESSON: MARK 13.14-23

False Christs and false prophets will arise and show great signs and wonders, so as to lead astray, if possible, even the elect. Matthew 24.24

These are choice, earnest but also terrible words that these preachers of works will push such teaching into the people with such outward glitter and emphasis that even the saints who stand fast in the faith will not be able to guard themselves against it but will join in error with the rest. This is indeed what happened. The dear fathers, Augustine, Jerome, together with St. Bernard, Gregory, Francis, Dominic and many others, although they were holy, nevertheless all fell at times into error as I have often demonstrated elsewhere.

Their error was the error of their time. Together with their contemporaries, they tied Christianity to certain external practices and they pushed matters so far that they adopted such practices outwardly in their lives. We see this in the books of St. Bernard. He writes very poorly in reply to questions on the monastic vocation. But when he writes freely out of his inner Christian spirit, he is a fine preacher whom it is a pleasure to hear. This is also the case with Augustine, Jerome and Cyprian, the fine Christian martyrs. When they were asked a question about the Law or external ordinances, whether one should observe them this way or that, they flopped right into things so that they came very close to being misled.

This is still one of the chief objections we hear from our opponents. "Could so many holy men and teachers have erred, and could God have forsaken the world to such an extent?" they ask us. They do not see how this passage really turns them topsy-turvy.

SL.XI.1880,26

PRAYER: We know how easy it is, heavenly Father, for even outstanding believers and teachers to fall into error. Guide us by your Holy Spirit into the truth and keep us in it, through Jesus Christ our Saviour. Amen.

THURSDAY

Jesus spoke to them, saying, "I am the light of the world; he who follows me will not walk in darkness, but will have the light of life".   John 8.12

Christ's words lie before us plain and clear. We must believe them and let them stand. We cannot get over them, even though the holy angels in heaven opposed them. Is not Christ holier than they are, and should not His Word have as much authority as theirs? He does not speak of many, nor of the large body who always make up the majority, but of the smallest group made up from the elect. These are going to stumble to such an extent that there is every likelihood that they could be misled. He warns us not to cling to them when we see them clinging to mere externals. If they never err, then Christ cannot be quite truthful in making this announcement. Hence, even if all the saints were to come forward and tell me to believe in the pope, I will still not do so, saying, "Even though you are the elect, Christ has said that there will be such terrible and dangerous times that even you will err".

We must cling alone to Scripture and God's Word which declares that He is not here or there. I must be where He is. He is not necessarily where my work or particular rank is. Anyone who teaches me otherwise, deceives me. Hence, I repeat, there is no point in raising the objection that the holy fathers and teachers held such and such a view, and lived such and such a life, and therefore we must hold the same views and live the same lives.

The only argument we admit runs as follows: "Christ taught and held such and such views and therefore we must also hold these views". Christ has more authority for us than all the saints.

SL.XI.1881,27

PRAYER: As your beloved children, heavenly Father, we must always believe and obey you rather than men. Fill our hearts with such trust and confidence that we always obey your Word, in and through our Saviour Jesus Christ. Amen.

FRIDAY

LESSON: LUKE 17.22-37

If they say to you, "Lo, he is in the wilderness", do not go out; if they say, "Lo, he is in the inner rooms", do not believe it.   Matthew 24.26

At the time of the holy fathers, like Anthony and others, shortly after the time of the apostles, the error of which Christ spoke here had already arisen, although strongly opposed by Anthony. Everybody became interested in the wilderness and many thousands of saints made their homes there. This kind of devotion soon gained such repute and publicity that Jerome and Augustine became its adoring devotees and could not praise it highly enough.

If we look at this business without blinkers on, however, we see that Christ's words here in the text are absolutely opposed to it, and that among all these thousands there were many heretics who must have been damned. Although there were also holy people in the deserts who escaped being seduced, the example they set was certainly dangerous and not to be held up for emulation.

The Christian life must not simply be linked with the desert but must be allowed freedom to develop everywhere. Christ lived His life here on earth in the midst of the world and so also did His apostles. It is Christ's will that we should step out into the world even today to preach publicly and exhort men to come to Christ.

Those who went out into the wilderness simply forsook their fellowmen and refused to stay in the world because they thought that they were being called upon to suffer too much in this world. They chose their own ascetic way of life because they wanted to be higher-ranking Christians than the others who remained in the world.

SL.XI.1882,28

PRAYER: Lord God, heavenly Father, it is your will that we should spend our lives in the midst of our fellowmen here in this world. Give us at all times the insights and the love to really serve our fellowmen in a way that will bring them, together with us, to the enjoyment of the blessings you have prepared for us, through Christ our Saviour. Amen.

SATURDAY

LESSON: MATTHEW 24.36-44

For as the lightning comes from the east and shines as far as the west, so will be the coming of the Son of man.
Matthew 24.27

Christ means to say here: "Do not believe it if some attempt is made to make you believe that Christ is limited to this place or that place and someone tries to lead you from faith to works. I warn you not to fall away from pure faith. You do not know at what hour I will come again. When no one is really expecting it, I will suddenly be here again as quickly as a flash of lightning lights up the heavens. Those who have not kept the faith will then be lost. See to it that the day does not come upon you unawares. Be strong in faith so that you do not become lazy and sleepy and the devil tears you away from faith."

These words are simply written down here one after the other, without order. Matthew heaps up everything here without order. So the following words do not really fit in very well here: **"Wherever the body is, there the eagles will be gathered together"**. **Matthew 24.28**.

What He means is that we should not ask for the exact place where Christ will come again. "No matter where I am, we shall probably find each other, as we say, 'Wherever there is a body there the eagles will gather together'. Eagles do not fly to some particular spot that they have selected for themselves; but wherever there is a body they gather together. Hence those who are Mine will doubtless find Me. Where I am, My chosen ones will also be."

This text speaks of the end of the Jews and of the world. Matthew mingles this with the signs of the last day. Luke writes of these matters quite clearly.

SL.XI.1883,29-30

PRAYER: Heavenly Father, you have taught us clearly in your Word that this world will end, and that your Son Jesus Christ is coming again to judge the living and the dead. Keep us strong in faith so that we are always prepared to meet Christ when He comes again, trusting in His merits and clothed in His righteousness, for your mercy and truth's sake. Amen.

SUNDAY

LESSON: MATTHEW 25.31-42

Men will come from east and west, and from north and south, and sit at table in the kingdom of God. And behold, some are last who will be first, and some are first who will be last.   Luke 13.29,30

In this Gospel great prominence is given to good works as proof of the possession or absence of true faith. Those on Christ's right hand at the judgement, the sheep, have proved the genuineness of their faith in works of love to needy brethren. Those on His left hand, the goats, who have been rejected for eternal punishment in hell have proved that they really had no saving faith at all by the absence of such works of love to their brethren. Here Christ also indicates that there are many among those regarded as Christians who actually become worse than heathen after hearing the preaching of the Gospel of the forgiveness of sins and of God's grace through Christ. Christ Himself declared, **"Many that are first will be last and the last first".** Matthew 19.30.

At the final judgement it will become quite evident that many of those who should have proved themselves to be true Christians because they heard the Gospel, actually became worse and more unmerciful than they were before. One sees clear evidence of this on all sides today. Previously, when good works were enjoined under papal perversions and false acts of worship, everyone was ready and willing to do good works. A single prince or one city was able to provide greater and richer endowments and alms than can be provided today by the joint efforts of all kings and the Emperor.

Today the whole world has learnt nothing else but to lay others under contribution, to practise oppression, open robbery and stealth by means of lies, deceit, usury, overcharging and other pressures. Every man tries to gain an advantage over his neighbour, as though he regarded him not as a friend and even much less as a brother in Christ.

SL.XI.1888,9-12

PRAYER: Never let our faith die as a result of greed and selfishness, O God, but let it always be in us a real power unto salvation, productive of many good works, in and through our Saviour Jesus Christ. Amen.

MONDAY

LESSON: LUKE 19.11-26

As you did it not to one of the least of these, you did it not to me.   Matthew 25.45

What do you think that Christ on His judgement-seat will say in all brevity to such an unchristian lack of mercy? This is what He will say: "You want to be called a Christian and you make your boast of the Gospel. Did you never hear this sermon which I Myself preached warning you what My judgement and final sentence would be? **'Depart from me, you cursed, into the eternal fire prepared for the devil and his angels; for I was hungry and you gave me no food, I was thirsty and you gave me no drink, I was a stranger and you did not welcome me, naked and you did not clothe me, sick and in prison and you did not visit me.' Matthew 25.41-43.** Why have you disregarded all this and acted more disgracefully and more unmercifully against your own brethren than a Turk or a heathen? Are you thinking of making matters right for yourself by offering the excuse, 'When did I see my brother in any of these situations or conditions?' Here your own conscience will remind you that there were those of your acquaintance who preached to you, or poor scholars who should have been taught and trained in the Word of God, as well as persecuted, poor and needy Christians, who should have been given food, drink, and clothing, and also visited."

Surely we should hang our heads in shame over against our parents and forefathers, the lords and kings, princes and others, who so richly and benevolently gave gifts even to a point of excess to churches, parishes, schools, institutions, hospitals and the like, as a result of which neither they nor their descendants became any poorer. What would they have done if they had had the light of the Gospel which we have received?   SL.XI.1890,14-15

PRAYER: Lord our God, in your Gospel of salvation you have supplied us richly with the most precious gifts and blessings that we can ever enjoy. Strengthen us at all times with your grace that we may make full use of all these blessings in love towards our brethren and fellowmen, for Jesus' sake. Amen.

TUESDAY

LESSON: MATTHEW 10.40-42

Then he will say to those at his left hand, "Depart from me, you cursed, into the eternal fire prepared for the devil and his angels . . ." And the King will answer them, "Truly, I say to you, as you did it to one of the least of these my brethren, you did it to me."   Matthew 25.41,40

If such a terrible and drastic condemnation awaits those who have neglected works of love towards their brethren, what is to become of those who have not only neglected such opportunities, have given Christ nothing, have rendered Him no service at all in His poor ones, but have even robbed them of what they had and forced them into hunger, thirst and need and, in addition, have even persecuted, hounded, captured and murdered them?

Such men are so incontrovertibly wicked and damned into such depths of hell with the devil and his angels that He no longer thinks of them here or speaks of them in particular. But it can be regarded as quite certain that He will not forget such robbers, tyrants and bloodhounds just as certainly as He will not forget or leave unrequited those who have suffered hunger, thirst, destitution and persecution, more particularly for the sake of Christ and His Word.

Even here he does not actually forget the latter although He is speaking in particular to those who have had mercy on those in need and have helped them. On these He bestows high and glorious praise when He says, **"Truly, I say to you, as you did it to one of the least of these my brethren, you did it to me".** Matthew 25.40.

SL.XI.1891,17

PRAYER: Lord God, we thank and praise you for the clear warnings of your Word in which you urge upon us an earnest and consistent profession of our faith. In your mercy and grace grant us also such obedience of faith that we may always be certain of receiving our Lord's approval when He comes to judge the living and the dead. In Jesus' name. Amen.

WEDNESDAY

LESSON: PSALM 143.7-12

Then the King will say to those at his right hand, "Come, O blessed of my Father, inherit the kingdom prepared for you from the foundation of the world".   Matthew 25.34

Why does Jesus use the fifth commandment to assess our works of mercy and to point out how men have failed in this respect?

Those of us who have been called as Christians have obtained mercy through our Lord and have been rescued from God's wrath and eternal death, receiving in place of all this a gracious God who bestows all that is good upon us in time and eternity. He wants to remind us that we have received all this from God, not only for our salvation, but that we should also regard it as an example to be followed in our own conduct. Because God has shown us mercy that we are not lost in body and soul, we should always act in such a way towards our neighbour that we never come into conflict with the fifth commandment, which basically demands love and mercy.

We should do this not merely for the sake of the commandment, or any threat of judgement, but because of the example we have received in the exceptionally high and rich goodness that God has manifested to us. This example should not remain without fruit, just as God's work of redemption is not without power and fruit.

Although the majority of the hearers may become worse after hearing the Gospel, there must always be some who grasp it correctly and abide by it. For He tells us that He will separate them into two distinct groups. Some of the hearers will prove themselves to have been devout and godly hearers who obey this commandment.

SL.XI.1893,21

PRAYER: Bestow such a measure of grace upon us, O Lord, that our faith overflows in love and goodness towards our fellowmen, for Christ's sake. Amen.

THURSDAY

LESSON: 1 THESSALONIANS 2.11-13

You are not lacking in any spiritual gift, as you wait for the revealing of our Lord Jesus Christ.   1 Corinthians 1.7

Our Lord, come!   1 Corinthians 16.22

See to it that you are always numbered among those who are good and merciful for Christ's sake, or suffering for His sake. Then you can await the last day with joy and not be afraid of the judgement. For He has already drawn you out and set you up among those on His right hand.

We who are Christians should have the earnest desire and hope that the judgement would come, as we also pray in the words, "**Thy kingdom come**" and "**Thy will be done**" and "**Deliver us from evil**". Matthew 6.10,13. Hence we shall also rejoice to hear the words, "**Come, O blessed of my Father, inherit the kingdom prepared for you from the foundation of the world**". Matthew 25.34. For this judgement we are waiting. This is one of our chief concerns as Christians. For the sake of this hope, we suffer oppression both from the devil and our own flesh, who try to upset our faith and joy in this regard. Then, too, we have to endure the tyranny and enmity of the world.

On all sides we are forced to see and to hear the wanton malice which the devil and the world continually stir up against the Gospel, and so much wretchedness here on earth, that we should become thoroughly fed up with this life and cry, "Come, dear Lord, come and redeem us!"

SL.XI.1893,22-23

PRAYER: Lord Jesus, as your disciples we look forward with joyful anticipation to your coming to carry out your work of judgement and to receive us to yourself. Of your mercy and grace, keep us ever steadfast in the faith so that your glorious coming may be for us the consummation of all our hopes and joy, for your love's sake. Amen.

FRIDAY

LESSON: MATTHEW 10.32,33

We must all appear before the judgement-seat of Christ, so that each one may receive good or evil, according to what he has done in the body.   2 Corinthians 5.10

Those hearts are established and sure which await Christ's judgement-seat joyfully and with a good conscience. For they belong to the group and fellowship of those who believe in Christ, and demonstrate the fruits of their faith in the love and goodness they bestow on the poor, or in the patience with which they suffer with them. He who does not have this faith will not practise these works of mercy on his fellow Christians. But he who does these works, and does them because he believes that he has a faithful Saviour and Redeemer in Christ who has reconciled him to God, must also have a good and friendly heart towards his neighbour and even towards his enemies helping them whenever he sees them in need. To be sure, he also has his own sufferings in the opposition his faith encounters from the devil and the world.

He who is thus minded, I say, should be joyful and in good spirits. He may well already apply to himself the blessed and joyful judgement, **"Come, O blessed of my Father, inherit the kingdom prepared for you from the foundation of the world"**. Matthew 25.34. He may well regard himself as **"one of the least"** of Christ's brethren, one who has himself suffered hunger and thirst or has served the hungry and the thirsty and shown them mercy, as Christ has shown him mercy.

SL.XI.1894,24

PRAYER: Of your mercy and grace, Lord Jesus, give us at all times a loving heart like your own heart so that we abound in fruits of faith to our brethren and fellowmen, for your name's sake. Amen.

SATURDAY

LESSON: REVELATION 7.9-12

Whatever is born of God overcomes the world; and this is the victory that overcomes the world, our faith. 1 John 5.4

You cannot train the youth in particular for God's kingdom without proper schools nor uphold the Word of God without preaching it from the pulpit. If one allows schools and the pulpit to decline and disappear, one can only expect a Sodom and Gomorrah to eventuate. One must expect also results like those which fell upon Sodom and Gomorrah when these cities cast off the restraints of God's Word and no longer listened to pious Lot or tolerated him.

The prophet Ezekiel faced a similar situation when he prophesied concerning Jerusalem, **"As I live, says the Lord God, your sister Sodom and her daughters have not done as you and your daughters have done. Behold, this was the guilt of your sister Sodom: she and her daughters had pride, surfeit of food, and prosperous ease, but did not aid the poor and needy. They were haughty, and did abominable things before me; therefore I removed them, when I saw it."** Ezekiel 16.48-50.

This is how matters stand on all sides today. Every man, the peasant, the burgher (citizen), the nobleman, gathers together nothing but money; he keeps on scraping in his greed, gluttonizes and imbibes and carries on just as if God were nothing at all. No one takes up the beggar's staff of the poor Christ, but rather tramples it underfoot. As in the case of Sodom and Gomorrah all obedience, discipline and respect will go by the board. No amount of admonition and preaching seems to have any results, and evils seem only to increase so that it does not appear that we can continue like this much longer.

SL.XI.1898,32-33

PRAYER: Give us courage and strength at all times, O God, to carry on bravely in the midst of pressing difficulties and even indifference and opposition. Prove yourself to be God for us by giving us a faith that really overcomes the world, for Christ the Saviour's sake. Amen.

REFORMATION DAY

LESSON: ROMANS 3.19-26

I am not ashamed of the gospel: it is the power of God for salvation to every one who has faith, to the Jew first and also to the Greek. For in it the righteousness of God is revealed through faith for faith; as it is written, "He who through faith is righteous shall live".   Romans 1.16,17

When Scripture speaks of Christ's work of salvation, the word "righteous" must not be referred to the righteousness by which God pronounces judgement, which is called the strict righteousness of God. For if Christ came to us with this, who could stand before Him? Who could receive Him? Not even the saints could pass such a test. God's righteousness in Christ which brings unspeakable joy is the grace whereby God justifies us. I wish the terms, *iustus, iustitia* (righteous, righteousness), as used in the Vulgate, had never gained currency in the sense of "righteous" and "righteousness", because their real meaning is "pious" and "piety". When we say, "He is a pious man", Scripture says, "He is *iustus* (just and righteous)".

Scripture calls the strict righteousness of God "earnestness, judgement, rightness". When the prophet says, **"Your king is coming to you, just", Zechariah 9.9 A.V.**, it means that He makes you just or pious through His grace. He knows very well that you are not pious. Your piety is not to be your doing but His grace and gift; you are to become righteous and pious through Him. St. Paul also speaks in this manner saying, He alone is **"just and righteous".** **Romans 3.26.** This means that Christ alone is pious before God and He alone makes men pious. Similarly, in **Romans 1.17: "The righteousness of God is revealed"** in the Gospel means, the piousness of God, namely, His grace and mercy whereby He makes us pious, is proclaimed in the Gospel as you see from this prophecy (Zechariah 9.9). Christ is preached for our piety; He comes to us pious and just and in faith we are to become pious and just through Him.

Mark this passage carefully. Where you find the term, "God's righteousness", in Scripture, you must not understand it to refer to the essential, inner righteousness of God as the papists understand it, and as many holy fathers have also mistakenly understood it, otherwise you will be terrified by it. According to Scriptural usage, it means the grace and mercy of God poured into us through Christ, whereby we are accounted pious and righteous before Him. For this reason it is called God's righteousness or piety because God gives it to us by grace; it is not of our doing.

In a similar way, mention is made of God's work, God's wisdom, God's strength, God's word, God's mouth — what He works and speaks in us. All this St. Paul clearly attests in **Romans 1.16,17** when he says: **"I am not ashamed of the Gospel: it is the power of God"** (understand: which He works in us and thereby strengthens us) **"for salvation to every one who has faith. . . . For in it the righteousness of God is revealed through faith for faith; as it is written, 'He who through faith is righteous shall live'."**

Here you see that he is speaking of the righteousness of faith. He calls it **"the righteousness of God revealed"** in the Gospel, for the Gospel teaches nothing else but this: He who believes has grace, is righteous before God and is saved. This is also how you should understand the word of the Psalmist: **"In thy righteousness deliver me"**, **Psalm 31.1**, that is, with thy grace, which makes me pious and righteous.

SL.XI.14,36-37

PRAYER: Thanks and praise be to you, heavenly Father, for the wonderful revelation of your mercy and grace made known to us in the Gospel, God's power unto salvation, that in Christ our Saviour we have God's own righteousness, by which our sins are fully and freely forgiven and we stand justified before you. Amen.

Wartburg Castle entrance and watch-tower.

Main entrance to Luther House, Eisenach.

Luther Street, Eisenach, with Luther House on the right.

Castle and Castle Church, Wittenberg.

Lecture room, Luther House, Wittenberg.

Facade of Luther House, Wittenberg.

Luther's grave in the Castle Church at Wittenberg.

Melanchthon and Luther statues, central square, Wittenberg.

Luther monument in Worms, the town in which Luther defended his teachings before the Parliament in April, 1521. Top: Martin Luther; at the base, left: Jerome Savonarola [with hood]; right: Johan Hus [with cross] and Philip Melanchthon [standing], Luther's chief assistant; extreme left with raised sword: Prince Frederick the Wise, of Saxony, Luther's sponsor.